D1299923

The American Flag,
1777–1924

Socialized in home, church, and school, generations of Americans have grown up revering the flag as the most sacred symbol of their nation. (Photo courtesy of the Library of Congress.)

The American Flag, 1777–1924

Cultural Shifts from Creation to Codification

Scot M. Guenter

Rutherford • Madison • Teaneck
Fairleigh Dickinson University Press
London and Toronto: Associated University Presses

Associated University Presses
440 Forsgate Drive
Cranbury, NJ 08512

Associated University Presses
25 Sicilian Avenue
London WC1A 2QH, England

Associated University Presses
P.O. Box 39, Clarkson Pstl. Stn.
Mississauga, Ontario
Canada L5J 3X9

The paper used in this publication meets the requirements of the American National Standard for Permanence of Paper for Printed Library Materials Z39.48-1984.

Library of Congress Cataloging-in-Publication Data

Guenter, Scot M., 1956–
    The American flag, 1777–1924 : cultural shifts from creation to codification / Scot M. Guenter.
        p.   cm.
    Includes bibliographical references.
    ISBN 0-8386-3384-6 (alk. paper)
    1. Flags—United States—History.   I. Title.
CR113.G83   1990
929.9′2′0973—dc20   89-45578
                                                                          CIP

To the memory of Gene Wise,
who urged me to develop
a "connecting mind."

Contents

Preface

As the last decade of the twentieth century begins, it is evident that American society will continue to debate and redefine the acceptable boundaries for use and respect of the national banner. Those boundaries have received much media attention in recent years.

Controversy over the Pledge of Allegiance, alleged flag burning, and the use of the American flag in campaigning emerged as significant elements in the Bush-Dukakis race for the presidency. On 21 June 1989 (one week after Flag Day) the Supreme Court ruled Gregory Lee Johnson exercised freedom of speech when he torched the flag of the United States outside the 1984 Republican National Convention in Dallas. This ruling provoked an emotional response, with many, including the president, calling for a constitutional amendment to protect and honor the flag.

Congress put off the amendment argument by enacting new federal legislation against flag desecration. Nevertheless, it is probable that eventually this new legislation will be challenged in the courts, and through the process of appeals the highest court in the land will take up the question again. The 1990s may prove to be a decade in which not only the perimeters of flag usage but of first amendment rights are legally readjusted.

However our personal opinions might vary in the debate on flag desecration, it behooves all interested in the political and cultural history of the United States to understand the powerful and evolving relationship between the symbol of the American flag and the development of the nation. Loving the flag is a patriot's prerogative. Comprehending the historical, sociological, and cultural reasons why people behave in such a fashion is a scholar's challenge. Understanding the difference between the two is an intellectual liberation. May the following study provide you such liberation, allowing you the opportunity to question and/ or strengthen your own beliefs as you interpret the "text" of the flag of the United States, allowing you to embark on a philosophical journey of cultural and crosscultural inquiry.

9

Acknowledgments

I am indebted for guidance and assistance to the History, English, and American Studies faculties at the University of Maryland, and to the following individuals and organizations: Whitney Smith, director of the Flag Research Center; Grace Rogers Cooper, former president of the North American Vexillological Association; William G. Crampton, director of the Flag Institute; George F. Cahill, president of the National Flag Foundation; Harold D. Langley, associate curator, Naval History Division, Smithsonian Institution; the staff of the Art and Reference Library in the Office of the Architect of the United States Capitol; and the staff of the Library of Congress. I have been given direction in database management by Mark Pelletier, and sage suggestions and peer support by Patrice McDermott Secrist and Kathy Vandell. Neal Porter demonstrated his talents as an illustrator. Jim Thomas, Hans Galinsky, and Danny Watkins offered pragmatic counsel on manuscript preparation and refinement. Lauren Lepow helped me understand the book publication process, and Jenna Dolan and Michael Koy, both at Associated University Presses, aided this work's progression through that process. My greatest debt is to R. Gordon Kelly, whose sound advice and excellent editorial suggestions guided the project from the outset. I salute all of the above, and thank them sincerely for their help and inspiration.

A portion of chapter 2 appeared in an earlier form in *John and Mary's Journal,* a portion of chapter 3 in *The Flag Bulletin.*

The American Flag,
1777–1924

1

Assessing the Symbol

On Flag Day 1914, Secretary of the Interior Franklin K. Lane delivered an address before the Washington, D.C., employees of the Department of the Interior. In this speech, "Makers of the Flag," Lane told the story of a government clerk who, on his way to work, heard the flag call out to him, saying that by living and working in an honorable, industrious, patriotic fashion, the clerk and all Americans endow the flag with meaning everyday. Lane wished to encourage such behavior; in so doing, he revealed an important theoretical basis to his philosophy: the meaning, significance, and use of the flag of the United States are culturally determined. "Then came a great shout from The Flag: . . . I am whatever you make me, nothing more. I am your belief in yourself, your dream of what a People may become. . . . I am the clutch of an idea, and the reasoned purpose of resolution. I am no more than what you believe me to be and I am all that you believe I can be. I am what you make me, nothing more."[1]

Americans have chosen to make much of the flag of the United States. A ubiquitous feature of our symbolic environment, it flutters in the breeze over our schools, our government buildings, our parks, and our homes. We acknowledge it ritually before or during a wide range of athletic, cultural, and social events—at baseball games, school band concerts, scout meetings, and community festivals. At a very early age we learn to equate it with "the republic for which it stands." Repetition of the image in a variety of media contexts constantly reinforces our socialized response to the flag. As typical citizens, we come not only to recognize its representation of the political configuration known as the United States of America, but to identify ourselves as citizens of the nation that flag represents. Emotionally responding with varying degrees of loyalty, patriotism, and nationalism, we make a moral commitment to it, conforming to value systems well established in our society.

Commitment to the flag is culturally determined. The many uses of the flag in American customs, rituals, and legends have

15

sociohistorical origins and have been modified and transformed as the American cultural system has developed and changed. To understand better the uses of the flag in contemporary society, we must understand the changing uses of the flag in the past. This requires a bit of effort, for we must not jump to the conclusion that our interpretations and applications of the symbol transcend all time and space. The importance of the flag of the United States and the different uses considered appropriate for it have shifted over the years since the colonies first declared their independence. Taking the time to examine those shifts carefully can help us begin to appreciate the cultural history of the flag both in terms used in those earlier cultural contexts and as a repository for the heritage the banner can signify today.

This is a rich, untapped area of cultural analysis. To begin to understand it, the following study explores changing uses of the national banner of the United States in presentation, legend, and ritual from 1777, when the Continental Congress passed the first Flag Resolution creating a national banner, to 1924, when the Second National Flag Conference finalized a formal code of flag etiquette for citizens of the United States. Because this is an exploration of cultural history, it examines not only the changes that have occurred, but also *who* introduced these changes and *why* these changes were enacted. Emphasis, then, is placed on analyzing usage. How have presentations of the flag changed? Who brought about these changes? What have been the roles of social groups and institutions in promoting these changes?

Although any public library will contain at least a few books or pamphlets devoted to the flag of the United States, few studies of the flag have moved beyond documentations of design or historical alteration. Most books on the flag tend toward patriotic praise, becoming flag-waving examples of the very cultural phenomenon this study intends to examine.

Some flag historians have recognized the impact of culture on the shifting significance and usage of the national banner, although none have ventured a full-scale probe of the subject. For example, when Milo Quaife published *The Flag of the United States* in 1942, at a time when war quite naturally aroused a heightened sense of nationalism among the public, he claimed that few knew the true history of the American flag: "In its stead, a volume of myth and tradition has developed, which by force of frequent repetition has impressed itself upon the public mind as actual history."[2] To a certain extent he was taking up the charge of William Elliot Griffis, who suggested in 1929 that many common misconceptions concerning the flag needed to be corrected, such as the belief that the Stars and Stripes was carried as a battle flag in the American Revolution. It is evident in our society today that these misconceptions have not been corrected; in some cases, they have been even more strongly reinforced.[3] This indicates the need to identify and analyze how individuals, groups, and institutions have participated in the ongoing cultural rituals, legends, and presentations of the flag.

There have been some seminal works of scholarship on the history of the American flag, most notably George Henry Preble's *History of the Flag of the United States of America*, published in various editions from 1872 through 1917; Boleslaw and Marie-Louise D'Otrange Mastais' *The Stars and the Stripes*, a study of the American flag in art and history published in 1973; Whitney Smith's *The Flag Book of the United States*, first published in 1970 and revised in 1975; and, most recently, *So Proudly We Hail*, published by the Smithsonian Institution in 1981. Twenty years in preparation, this last work was written by two navy men, Rear Admiral William Rea Furlong and Commodore Byron McCandless, with editorial assistance from Harold D. Langley, the Smithsonian's associate curator in the Division of Naval History.

None of these earlier studies, however, focuses on the flag as a symbol employed by specific individuals, groups, and institutions in the process of socialization. Preble acknowledged that his concern was to "revive and preserve . . . a patriotic sentiment for our starry banner."[4] Quaife, while pointing the way to an analysis of changes in perception based on growth of legends or evolution of rituals, maintained that the flag "is instinctively identified in our thoughts with all that is highest and holiest."[5] The Mastais emphasized design rather than history; and in championing the variety of designs of the flag produced before an executive order required one standardized version (which, incidentally, did not occur until 1912),[6] they saw the flag as a vibrant entity with a "multifaceted personality."[7] Furlong and McCandless "wished particularly to avoid confusing fact with legend,"[8] and although neither lived to see their study completed, Langley did a thorough job in distinguishing between fact and legend in the published edition. Nevertheless, even this most recent, precise account of the flag does not squarely address the issue of cultural determinants in shifting uses of the banner.

Probably Smith's brief discussions of flag use come closest to this issue. He points the way for more scholarship to analyze the data already accumulated and, although his emphasis is on historical design and alterations, he recognizes the flag as a cultural artifact with meaning, significance, and usage determined by the particular system employing it.

Although covering different territory than a cultural history of the flag from 1777 to 1924, some scholarship in sociology and psychology has broached the subject of flag use as a cultural activity worthy of analysis.[9] More significant is the work of William G. Crampton in political science. Crampton is writing a doctoral thesis at Manchester University, focusing on the internalization and promotion of a new series of national symbols in Germany during the Weimar Republic. Also concerned with the advent of new symbols are historical studies on the adoptions of the flags of Canada and South Africa: J. R. Matheson's *Canada's Flag, A Search for a Country* (1980) and Harry Saker's *The South African Flag Controversy 1925–28* (1980). Significant in that they consider techniques employed for promoting new flags, these works do not, however, trace historically the cultural transmission and dissemination of new uses of these flags.

All these scholarly works on national flags, in history and the social sciences, recognize the power of a flag as a symbol. Dan Sperber, a French anthropologist, offers an approach to symbolism that has implications for a sociohistorical analysis of flag use. Appropriating Sperber's definition of a symbol can pave the way for a discussion of how the symbol of the flag might be interpreted as part of a larger constellation of symbols and values known as "civil religion." Approaching these points in this order can build a framework that permits a workable historical analysis of important cultural determinants in the shifting uses of the American flag. This analysis can lead, in turn, to insights into our historical past, our sense of national identity as a people, and on a more private level, to the origins of our personal attitudes toward the American flag.

The definition of symbolism continues to be controversial depending on one's discipline of study, philosophical beliefs, perception of the world—in short, on one's cultural conditioning. However, almost all definitions of symbolism acknowledge that an explicit form, such as the flag of the United States of America, is unintelligible except in a context of culturally constituted meaning in and through which that form takes on meaning. Among other aspects, the flag comes to represent "America." Semiologists equate this relationship to that between sound and meaning in language; the flag is a *signifier*, "America" is *signified*. Sperber, however, claims that the mechanism involved in symbolic representation deals with complex responses that language cannot. "A representation is symbolic," he writes, "precisely to the extent that it is not entirely explicable (that is to say—expressible by semantic means)."[10]

For Sperber, the process of interpretation of a symbol has two essential aspects: (1) a displacement of attention, which he calls focalization; (2) a search in the memory, which he calls evocation.[11] "When Westerners speak in a vague way of meaning they are really talking about evocation,"[12] he concludes, and he stresses that, although the ability to symbolize is a distinctively human capability, the manner of symbolization can be highly culturally determined: "the more numerous are the beliefs, rituals, etc. which are taken into account, the more the evocational field is determinate, the more restricted is the range of possible evocations, and the more the members of a single culture are led to similar evocations."[13]

This is a persuasive hypothesis, and the emphasis on the complex power of evocation is compelling when applied to a study of the American flag. Although each person's evocation in response to the flag as a symbol will be a personal construct—a complexly interwoven, densely compacted assortment of memories and impressions, images and associations—many Americans will share communally in various memories or associations that are evoked, as a result of shared experiences in the socialization process of members of our culture or the identification process of maintaining a sense of national identity. In both of these instances the flag is a vital symbol. Its use in evoking these responses comes about because of its eminent position and power in American civil religion. It has achieved this rank through the historical contributions of specific individuals, groups, and institutions. As the representations of the flag proliferated and rituals developed and spread between 1777 and 1924, those who worked to ensure that the use of the flag would evoke feelings of nationalism, patriotism, and loyalty sought to restrict and specify the determinate field of evocations it engendered.

Although it would be extremely difficult to probe the entire personal store of accumulated cultural knowledge of even one individual in an attempt to present a detailed reconstruction of what the American flag evokes, (and although it would be even harder to examine larger groups or make claims for the American society as a whole,) there remains a logical alternative to such reconstructions. We can shift from an emphasis on individual meaning to an emphasis on usage, to a careful consideration of who have been involved in changes in flag presentation, ritual, and legend, to an analysis of which institutions and communication systems have been involved in the mediation of these changes, and to a study of the reactions, if they are discernable, made by the public in response to these changes. What the flag symbolizes is at once a private, personal commitment for each American (in varying degrees) to what he or she considers "America" to be and a loosely defined national consensus drawn from overlappings of memories and associations in all our particular accumulations of cultural knowledge.

One useful concept for the study of the cultural transmission of patriotic responses was begun in the sociology of religion in 1967 and has since spread to the fields of church history, intellectual history, and comparative religion. As it diffused, the concept of "civil religion" took on a variety of applications, some arousing controversy. For example, in 1985, Keith B. Richburg invoked the term to castigate Secretary of Education William Bennett's call for more religion in the public schools.[14] Others who have attacked the use of the term, such as John F. Wilson and Michael W. Hughey, have noted that some of those who employ it move from scholarly analysis of a cultural phenomenon to criticism of their own society, advocating social change to restore a decayed social order.[15] Nevertheless, a brief reexamination of the concept reveals potential for its use in grounding a study of the cultural determinants in the shifting uses of the American flag from 1777 to 1924.

Rousseau first used the phrase "civil religion" in *Social Contract* to refer to a transcendental quality that supported a political state. Robert N. Bellah created something of an academic sensation in 1967 when he appropriated the phrase as a basis for a discussion of shared values that he felt transcended our history—an "abstract faith" illustrated in specific symbols and rituals.[16] In his essay "Civil Religion in America" he championed traditional middle-class Protestant values, and called for "a rebirth of imaginative vision," reapplying those traditional values to the unique, modern American historical situation.[17] His purpose was not to establish the grounds for an unbiased, sociological analysis of a cultural phenomenon, but rather to diagnose a cultural condition and call for a change.

That purpose, however, does not negate the usefulness of the concept of civil religion. An early astute reply to Bellah's use of the concept came from Phillip E. Hammond, who noted that Bellah was right in his cultural analysis—he had correctly identified the existence of a set of ideas, but others should now move beyond that identification to analyze "the social structures through which this 'culture' lives."[18] Essentially, Hammond called for an examination of the specific roles played by individuals, organizations, and institutions in the historical evolution of a civil religion.

This suggestion has gone largely unanswered. Responses to Bellah have emphasized the religious aspect of the concept rather than a grounding in the use of symbols in the processes of socialization or cultural reinforcement. Moreover, the phrase *civil religion* has been used widely and indiscriminately.

In 1980, Ellis M. West suggested a neutral definition that would reduce scholarly bickering and promote historical knowledge:

> A civil religion is a set of beliefs and attitudes that explain the meaning and purpose of any given political society in terms of its relationship to a transcendent, spiritual reality that are held by the people of that society, and that are expressed in public rituals, myths, and symbols.[19]

This definition offers a useful foundation, but as Michael W. Hughey has warned in *Civil Religion and Moral Order,* there is a danger of reification. "Values, even orthodox values, are not transcendent. . . . That is, values always express the needs, aspirations, and ideal and material interests of particular groups of people existing in particular times, places, and institutional contexts."[20] Hughey's warning is important to remember in a consideration of the flag as a focal element in the production, propagation, and dissemination of American civil religion. Using West's definition and Hughey's caveat as guides, the following chapters will trace the cultural determinants in the shifting uses of the American flag as a symbol representing "America" from 1777 to 1924. During this period the flag of the United States served as one of a constellation of symbols used to represent the country and to invoke nationalism. When these symbols coalesced into a recognizable civil religion is debatable; evidence in the following chapters indicates emergent strands—what Raymond Williams would call "structures of feeling"—of such a system in the antebellum period. The Civil War stimulated a recognizable civil religion in the North, and that system evolved throughout the rest of the historical period of this study.

The following chapters will thus be an historical overview of cultural shifts in the presentation, reproduction, and use of the flag of the United States in art, music, legend, custom, and ritual, from the time of its creation to the codification of flag etiquette, paying careful attention to the contributions of individuals and groups. A wide and varied range of sources have influenced these shifts, among them churches, public schools, the American legal system, the communications industry, sports culture, voluntary societies and lodges, the military, scouting organizations, and nativist movements.

Such an analytic study contributes not only to cultural history, but to the field of vexillology. Vexillology, a term derived from the Latin word for flag, *vexillum,* is defined as "the scientific and scholarly study of flag history and symbolism."[21] As a discipline it is "still very much in its infancy,"[22] according to Whitney Smith (Executive Director of the Flag Research Center), who holds the assorted titles of past president of the North American Vexillological Association, former Secretary General of the International Federation of Vexillological Associations, and Editor in Chief of the *Flag Bulletin,* a bimonthly journal first published in October, 1961. The growth of that journal, from a mimeographed newsletter to an international periodical coordinating a world flag project slated for the year 2011, is indicative of the growth of vexillology.

Although there are some professional flag historians, Smith acknowledges that almost all vexillologists are amateurs, interested in flags as a hobby.[23] Many, too, are imprecise in drawing the line between patriotism and vexillology. In 1982, Smith published an article calling for more social scientific analyses of the flag, moving beyond the traditional histories and explanations of symbolism and design that still accounted for practically all flag scholarship.[24] This book is in part a response to that plea, approaching the consideration of flag use from an interdisciplinary perspective.

Although vexillologists might display more interest in the details of flag design than other citizens, almost all Americans, admittedly in varying degrees, have been culturally conditioned to respond to the symbol of the flag as a representation of a spiritual reality in which we all share. Many would agree that the flag is the most significant symbol of our civil religion; it certainly is the most ubiquitous. We can better appreciate its significance today if we understand changes in its use from 1777 to 1924.

The American flag rose to prominence in the United States in a manner quite distinct from national banners in other western nations. Many do not realize that the United States was the first country to have a Flag Day, a Pledge of Allegiance to the flag, and a flag etiquette code[25]—all later copied and modified by a variety of nations. Few studies have been done on the role of foreign flags in civil religion. G. L. Mosse traces the developments of "secular religion" in France and Germany before focusing on the Nazi phenomenon in *The Nationalization of the Masses* (1975), but considers flags peripherally within his discussion of "national liturgy."[26] Articles on the role of flags in Great Britain and France both indicate that their American counterpart is much more crucial to a respective national sense of civil religion.[27] These beginnings suggest cross-cultural comparative analyses that might be done once the historical use of the symbol in our own society is more clearly understood.

The chapters that follow trace chronologically the shifting uses of the flag of the United States in American culture from 1777 to 1924. Chapter 2, "A New Constellation," places the creation of the first flag of the new nation in its vexillological context, while distinguishing the standard uses of the flag during the early years of the republic. Chapter 3, "Flag Culture in the Antebellum Period," evaluates the expanding uses of the national banner in poetry, fine art, patriotic campaigns, and nativist demonstrations. Chapter 4, "Symbol of the Union: Flag Use during the Civil War," demonstrates how, as a result of the Confederate firing on Fort Sumter, the flag was elevated by patriotic Yankees to the prominent position in civil religion that it still maintains. Chapter 5, "The Cult of the Flag Develops," recognizes the impact of the Centennial and the influence of veterans' and hereditary societies in establishing a cult of devotion to the Stars and Stripes in the 1880s and 1890s. Chapter 6, "Flag Ritual Comes to the Public Schools: Development and Dissemination of the Pledge of Allegiance," recounts the work of George T. Balch and, subsequently, the staff of *The Youth's Companion,* to give young people an enduring ritual intended to instill patriotic respect for the flag. Chapter 7, "The Emergence of Legislation against Flag Desecration," analyzes how, once supporters of the cult of the flag had succeeded in placing flags in schools and popularizing a pledge of allegiance, they turned their attention to outlawing flag uses they considered inappropriate. Chapter 8, "A Civilian Code of Flag Etiquette," reviews early twentieth-century transformations and modifications of flag culture as well as the impact of World War I flag legislation, before culminating in consideration of the American Legion-sponsored National Flag Conferences of 1923 and 1924. "Some Concluding Thoughts" summarizes the study, also offering speculations for further cultural analysis in this vein. The appendix contains some relevant poetry, lyrics, and prose discussed in the text, much of it inaccessible in most libraries, providing a handy reference guide for readers.

A cultural history of the varied uses of the American flag from 1777 to 1924 need not be an act of iconoclasm; neither should it be an exercise in propaganda. By probing the changes in custom, legend, and law, we can arrive at a new awareness of our history and our heritage, still saluting the Grand Old Flag, but with a more thorough understanding of how it came to represent "America."

2

The Uses of a New Constellation

The first flag of the United States of America, created by an act of Congress on 14 June 1777, answered a need for the identification of naval and governmental possessions. Without fanfare, it quietly joined a small cluster of symbols that served as the prototype for an emerging American civil religion. To appreciate its creation and original uses, we need to understand something about its predecessors. What were the flags of the colonial period, and how did colonists use them? Once the Continental Congress resolved to establish this new flag, what were its uses, and how widespread was its dissemination? And after the Treaty of Paris, how did the American flag come to represent not only military or naval identification, but also the expanding commercial shipping of the United States? During the War of 1812, Francis Scott Key's poetic tribute to the flag, "The Star-Spangled Banner," offered the first enduring hymn to the symbol, a hymn that would grow in popularity as the larger society came to emphasize the symbol more and elevate it to greater prominence in the civil religion of American culture.

National flags enjoy a wide variety of uses today—in education, sports, advertising, and government—but originally flags had but one significant function: to serve as totemistic devices in early religious activities. Whitney Smith speculates that carved figures carried about on poles during religious ceremonies quite possibly could have evolved into pieces of cloth emblematic of the idol represented.[1] As cultural systems became more complex and the need arose for distinctions between different groups in the activities of commerce and war, leaders adapted flags as standards of military units on land and as identification markers for seafaring vessels. These practices can be traced back to examples in ancient Phoenicia, Egypt, and India, to references in the Pentateuch or the historical writings of Pliny.[2] On land, flags not only designated the allegiance of a military installation, they also served as means of battlefield identification for soldiers in combat—the terms *colors* was applied to a flag used in this manner as early as the reign of Elizabeth I. The rank of Ensign was assigned to the officer who carried the colors into battle, and from this came the later adaption of the term *ensign* to mean the flag itself.[3] These traditional categories of flag use continued in the seventeenth- and eighteenth-century European cultures that shaped the American colonists. To better understand the historical context in which the flag of the United States of America was created, one must be aware of what was considered appropriate flag use in the colonial period in these three areas of religious, military, and naval application.

Although influential forces in American society would later elevate the flag to a focal position in rites of civil religion, Puritan leaders conscientiously altered colonial flags in New England to avoid any connection to idolatrous practices. John Endicott, who succeeded John Winthrop as chief magistrate of the Massachusetts Bay Colony, ordered the Cross of St. George, "a badge of superstition," to be removed from a flag in Salem in 1634, and even though this act was censured by the General Court, the Court subsequently allowed the military commissioners to remove the cross from the local regimental colors in 1636. For the next half century, flags representing government and military forces would vary in New England—sometimes including the cross, sometimes excluding it—depending on the religious interpretations of those in power.[4]

In seventeenth-century America the British Union Jack flew over Crown property, principally government buildings and forts. Colonists do not seem to have strictly observed this custom, however, since the need arose for a law to mandate the behavior in 1707.[5] The passing of such a law indicates that social practice had not yet conformed to such symbolic recognition of authority. Perhaps this was due to a lack of respect, but it is also possible that the military and government authorities responsible for such flag flying did not consider the use of the flag an important issue, only a compliance to government directive. Aside from the use of regimental colors, both by local militia and forces sent from Great Britain, flags do not appear to have been a factor in the everyday life of colonists, with the exception of those whose livelihood was connected with maritime pursuits.

The regimental colors carried by militiamen varied widely, in shape, size, and design.[6] We should keep in mind that eighteenth-century colonists did not have a well-established sense of unified national identity, and if a militiaman of this period identified strongly with a flag, it probably would be the flag of his particular regiment. As the colonists moved toward confederation in political rebellion against the British government, however, regional symbols began to spread in popularity. Erratically, a prototype of American civil religion began to emerge, containing a cluster of symbols representing not a separate nation but a group of Englishmen caught between their loyalty to the Crown and their sense of inherited political rights. Some of these symbols appeared on a variety of colonial flags; most important among them were the snake, the liberty pole, the pine tree, and the stripes of rebellion.

The snake symbol first gained attention when Benjamin Franklin drew a cartoon of a dissected snake to symbolize the disparate colonies. He published this in the *Pennsylvania Gazette* prior to the Albany Congress of 1754, at which representatives first discussed the possibility of unifying the colonies. The cartoon enjoyed a resurgence of notoriety in 1764, and in the period 1774–76 reappeared on flags in the form of a coiled rattlesnake, ready to strike. These flags bore the motto "Don't Tread on Me."

The liberty pole evolved from the liberty tree, and served the same purpose of providing a central location at which the dissidents could meet. Both were most prominent in New England, especially after the Sons of Liberty began rallying around such a tree in Boston. Another New England symbol was the pine tree, a representation of which became the official flag of the Massachusetts Navy in April 1776. Earlier, Colonel Joseph Reed, Washington's military secretary, in a letter dated 20 October 1775, had written to the army contractors outfitting the fledgling Continental Navy asking them "Please to fix upon some particular Colour for a flag—& a Signal, by which our Vessels may know one another," including his suggestion for the Green Tree flag, which featured a pine tree and the motto "An Appeal to Heaven."[7] Two days later the contractors, Colonel John Glover and Stephen Moylan, responded that schooners commanded by Captain Broughton and Captain Selman had set sail, and "as they had none but their old Colours, we appointed them a signal, that they may know each other by, & be known to their friends."[8]

Such a decision, seemingly of some importance to us, was rather casually left up to the contractors. And although they complied, they only informed Reed that they had designated a flag—they did not even describe the flag to him, or mention if his suggestion had been followed. Their concern was for a signal flag for that particular situation with those two ships—the future significance of one flag serving the Continental Navy and the entire nation did not occur to them.

The stripes of rebellion were first used in America on banners of the Sons of Liberty, a group of revolutionary radicals that assembled beneath the Boston Liberty Tree. These colonists, prepared to take up arms to protect their rights, flew a flag of nine alternate red and white stripes. These red and white stripes reappeared on the Continental Colors.

The Continental Colors, also known as the Great Union or Grand Union Flag to later students of history, was the first flag in general use throughout all the colonies, serving this function from 1775 to 1777. The first verified use of this flag occurred on Prospect Hill in Charleston (now Somerville), Massachusetts outside Boston, when General Washington, to mark the birth of the Continental Army on 1 January 1776, had the red flag of the Charleston liberty pole replaced with the Continental Colors, a flag bearing thirteen alternating red and white stripes to symbolize unity in rebellion yet retaining in its canton (the upper inner quarter of a flag's field) the Crosses of St. George and St. Andrew. The liberty pole was seventy-six feet high, enabling a viewer in Boston to see the change in flags.

The retention of the British crosses in the flag could lead to varying interpretations of its symbolic meaning. Did it symbolize a revolt against the Crown, and if so, why did it retain the Cross of St. George, representing the King of England, and the Cross of St. Andrew, representing the King of Scotland? Indeed, Washington noted in a letter to his military secretary, Colonel Reed, dated 4 January 1776: "It was received in Boston as . . . a signal of Submission—we learn by a person out of Boston last night—by this time I presume they begin to think it strange that we have not made a formal Surrender of our Lines."[9]

It is evident from a reference in Washington's letter that Colonel Reed knew the Continental Colors as "the Flag of the United Colonies." This flag was used on land at various forts, on sea as the ensign of American ships, and even on the currency of North Carolina.[10] Why did it not continue as the flag of the United States? The answer lies in two facts: symbolically, the Continental Colors was ambiguous; practically, its use was limited enough so that no well-established, widespread support group developed to lobby for its recognition and ensure its continued use. It was not meant to be a battle flag. Different military units had their own regimental colors which distinguished them; the Continental Colors served predominately as a banner for naval identification, and here its ambiguity presented the possibility of problems.[11]

For one thing, as Washington himself discovered, some interpreted the retention of the British symbol in the canton as hope for reconciliation under the Crown. Once the Declaration of Independence was announced, such a position could no longer be supported by the members of Congress or the citizens in rebellion. Being in rebellion, however, the members of the Continental Congress were concerned with the very survival of the newborn republic, and the design of a few flags on the small navy did not appear to be a pressing issue. The birth of a new state in the eighteenth century did not immediately require the recognition of a new state flag; this was an innovation of the nineteenth century and continued in the twentieth, as flag use grew in cultural significance.

Congress took no action upon the design of the flag when independence was declared on 4 July 1776. However, on that auspicious day a committee was established to design an appropriate seal for the new republic. The members of the Continental Congress shared a culture that included familiarity with British heraldry and the use of an official seal of state in validating government documents; almost immediately upon declaring themselves independent they appointed the prestigious committee of John Adams, Ben Franklin, and Thomas Jefferson to devise a suitable seal. Since the use of an official flag would at this time have been limited to state buildings, forts, and the limited number of American ships at sea, perhaps no one considered it a crucial point worth troubling over immediately; clearly, the question of an appropriate flag did not rate the attention that the question of a seal did.

In a letter written in July 1776, John Jay noted that Congress as yet had made no order "concerning continental colors, and that captains of the armed vessels had followed their own fancies."[12] Requests to official government bodies to set a standard eventually came from two quite different sources: a Philadelphia merchant who handled naval supplies and an American Indian.

William Richards, the merchant, wrote to the Pennsylvania Committee on Safety in August 1776 and again in October 1776 requesting a standard marine flag be officially designated for the new republic. There is no record of any reply, but the following May the State Naval Board made payment "to Elizabeth Ross for fourteen pounds, twelve shillings, and two pence, for making ship's colours."[13] Betsy Ross did indeed make flags for the young navy, but the design she followed cannot now be ascertained, and there is no evidence of a flag with a "star-spangled" canton in official (or unofficial) use prior to the Flag Resolution of 14 June 1777.

An American Indian requesting a flag in 1777 might at first surprise a modern reader, but Indians had recognized the colorful European banners as part of the white man's regalia since the arrival of the first explorers and colonists. During the colonial period, the English government presented flags to Indians at council meetings and treaty signings, with a twofold purpose of insuring the peace and encouraging support. Just as we must remember that the meaning of the flag can differ over time in one culture, so should we keep in mind that the meaning of the flag will differ between cultures. In general, American Indians often believed that a warrior transferred some of his own power into the war symbols he carried. Thus, the physical flag itself could be seen as a source of power.[14]

On 3 June 1777, the President of the Continental Congress presented that body with a request from Thomas Green, an Indian, for an American flag to take to "the chiefs of the nation" for their protection should they travel to meet with the Congress. Included were "three strings of wampum to cover cost."[15] Such a request no doubt led to the revelation that, as yet, the Congress recognized no official flag. The Marine Committee might have been informed of Richards's earlier query on the subject, for some Congressmen, such as Colonel Joseph Reed, served on the Pennsylvania Committee on Safety and in the Continental Congress at the same time.[16] Eleven days after the communique from the Indians, tucked away in the middle of a series of resolutions dealing with naval activity, came the following resolution: "RESOLVED: that the flag of the United States be made of thirteen stripes, alternate red and white; that the union be thirteen stars, white in a blue field, representing a new constellation."

According to inherited British custom, this flag would serve ships at sea and forts on land; thus it would be appropriate to the needs of both Richards and Green. The fact that the resolution appears on the agenda between a discussion of what the Delaware fleet should do in case of British attack and a call for the replacement of Navy Captain John Roach indicates it is a naval matter; the fact that is one brief sentence indicates it is a bit of work the Marine Committee considered relatively routine and unmomentous.

For many years flag historians have argued over the design of the stars in this flag. Were the thirteen stars arranged in a circle? Such a format has come to be known as the Betsy Ross flag, based on the popular legend of her involvement in the creation of the flag—a legend, it should be noted, that first surfaced in 1870 and is full of historical inaccuracies. The tenacity of the legend, evidenced by such paeans as Robert Morris's 1982 study, *The Truth about the Betsy Ross Story*, is itself an interesting component of American civil religion that deserves analysis as this legend disseminated and evolved in nineteenth- and twentieth-century America. However, for speculation on the design and use of this first Stars and Stripes, we must look not to the legend that developed later but to what can be construed from recorded data.

Historians have maintained that the "Betsy Ross" arrangement was just one variant of the first Stars and Stripes, that since the specifications are so vague, any design that met the basic requirements was legitimate, and among these alternatives, the circle of stars was an infrequent choice.[17] The Mastais' *The Stars and the Stripes* amply illustrates the great variety of designs in use down through the War of 1812, based on the whims of the flagmakers. Still, the phrasing "a new constellation" to this reader suggests a design the congressmen had probably seen—constellations, after all, are not amorphous, nor are they given to rearrangement in the evening sky. Arnold Rabbow has made a convincing argument that the particular design indicated here actually was the Betsy Ross variant, only it was the work of Francis Hopkinson, either with a committee or alone.[18]

Even during the cultivated spirit of the Age of the Enlightenment, Hopkinson stands out as an exemplary Renaissance man. The first graduate of the College of Philadelphia in 1757, he achieved recognition as an accomplished poet, essayist, harpsichordist, lawyer, and politician. His interest in heraldry led him to participate in the design of the Great Seal of New Jersey in 1776, as well as the design of seals, currency, and various heraldic ornamentations for the Board of Treasury, the Board of Admiralty, and the University of Pennsylvania. As a delegate from New Jersey, he signed the Declaration of Independence.[19]

Evidence points to Hopkinson as creator—or, at the least, as a contributor to a group effort in the creation—of the national banner of the United States. In May 1780 Hopkinson requested a quarter cask of public wine from the Continental Congress for eight items of "fancy work" that included a design of the flag of the United States. The following month he sent Congress a bill showing he felt the flag design was worth twenty-four dollars in cash. Eventually the Board of Treasury rejected the account for two reasons: (1) "Hopkinson had not been the only person consulted on those exhibitions of Fancy" and (2) Individuals already receiving a salary from Congress should not try to charge the public more for "these little assistances."[20]

Although he was never paid by the young government for designing its new naval flag, Hopkinson's claim to the distinction has never been repudiated. A reference to "the ensign of the United States proper" by the Third Committee on the Greal Seal in 1782 clearly designates the circle of stars in an accompanying design and by so doing acknowledges that, although variants were in use, this configuration was the "constellation" that the Congress approved.[21]

Whether the "new constellation" implied a circle of stars, as this committee indicated, or the more popular arrangement of stars in a series of three or five staggered rows, or any of the many other variants possible, public recognition and acknowledgment of the resolution came slowly. No notice of the action can be found in the press in the months of June and July 1777. Finally, on 30 August 1777 the *Pennsylvania Evening Post* carried information on the flag resolution, and this was picked up by Dunlap's *Pennsylvania Packet, or the General Advertiser* on 2 September 1777. In a few weeks the information had begun to spread to other colonies, appearing in the *Boston Gazette,* 15 September 1777 and the *Massachusetts Spy,* 18 September 1777.[22] Another possible reason for the delay in dissemination of this information could be the lack of a problem: perhaps the information was only considered newsworthy when a disagreement or dispute arose between flagmakers and naval captains. This, however, is only speculation, and no primary sources as yet have been found that offer more insight into this lag in communication announcing the first official Stars and Stripes.

Reference to this flag as the first Stars and Stripes follows a contemporary usage. This is in compliance with the hierarchical designations of heraldry, which traditionally call for a discussion of the components of the canton before describing the general field. However, in the early years of the republic emphasis was placed first on the stripes of rebellion, then on the stars of the canton. In the Flag Resolution quoted above, and in subsequent legislation in 1795 and 1818, it is the stripes that are first considered, and references to the "stripes and stars" are common in patriotic poems and songs before the Civil War.[23]

A bit of correspondence transmitted the year after the Flag Resolution was passed reveals the limited attention that the new ensign received. While commissioners in Paris, Benjamin Franklin and John Adams received a query from the King of the Two Sicilies about the flag of the young republic. How would one recognize an American vessel during this time of war? On 9 October 1778 they replied: "It is with pleasure we acquaint Your Excellency that the flag of the United States of America consists of thirteen stripes alternately red, white and blue; a small square in the upper angle, next the staff, is a blue field, with thirteen white stars, denoting a new constellation."[24] They obviously knew of the Flag Resolution but they lacked the details, and had never ascertained what was by then the official design.

John Paul Jones flew a flag with tricolored stripes in his celebrated capture of the British frigate *Serapis* in September 1779, and similar designs turn up on European flag charts of the period and in a German flag manual published in Berlin in 1784,[25] indicating that this alternative continued in use well after the Flag Resolution was passed. Vexillologists have documented many other variations in color, in number of stripes, and in arrangement of stars.[26] On a practical level, the basic availability of materials could be a determining factor. To replace all the flags in use with uniformly similar ones would have required centralized organization and funding beyond the capabilities of the American Navy, which was more concerned with fighting for its very existence.

During the Revolution, whatever variant was used, the flag of the United States represented American naval forces. Militiamen do not appear regularly to have carried it into battle on land as the "colors" that the soldiers used for identification. Nor did the Continental Army carry the Stars and Stripes as a national battle flag. The confederation of states lacked the strong federal cohesiveness so often taken for granted today (and reinforced by the ubiquitousness of the flag); even if a military order had been passed for uniform flag use on land, it would doubtlessly have achieved the same level of success—mixed—as the Flag Resolution did for ships at sea.

The assumption that the same flag should serve both army and navy is more modern, in any case. On 10 May 1779, almost two years after the Flag Resolution had been approved, the Secretary of the Board of War wrote to George Washington: "The Baron Steuben mentioned when he was here that he would settle with your Excellency some plan as to the Colours. It was intended that every Regiment should have two Colours—one the Standard of the United States, which should be the same throughout the

Army, and the other a Regimental Colour which should vary according to the facings [uniform fabric] of the Regiment. But it is not yet settled what is the standard of the U. States."[27]

What we think of as the first Stars and Stripes was originally conceived and thought of as a symbolic designation primarily for the navy. From 1779 until 1783, at which time Washington received officially the Military Standards, his Board of War urged "that the Standard of the United States should be a variant of the Marine Flag."[28] This "Marine Flag" refers to the flag described in the Flag Resolution, and the call for a variant supports the position that there was in fact one quasi-officially recognized interpretation of the constellation's design. Because the Flag Resolution came from the Marine Committee and the flag it described became known as the "Marine Flag," to Washington and his Board, any usage of it by the army would be "personal and unofficial from the standpoint of the Board of War."[29] Maintaining proper etiquette as well as they could, colonists followed British customs for carrying flags into battle. A British army regulation in 1751 ruled that there would be two "colors" in each regiment: the national standard and the regimental flag; these were carried by men designated as "Ensigns." Eventually the Board of War adopted a standard for the United States: a blue silk banner embroidered with the national arms (the eagle bearing a shield on his breast and an olive branch and arrows in his talons). It was not until 1813, in the midst of another conflict with Great Britain, that the duty of flagbearer was taken from Ensigns and given to Color Sergeants. Perhaps this minor yet conscious break from British tradition contributed to a sense of American distinctiveness for soldiers fighting the Second War of Independence.

It may surprise some readers to learn that the army carried the coat of arms as the "national colors" for three generations, until just prior to the Civil War. At that time the military switched the coat of arms flag to the designation of "organizational color" of the army, and the Stars and Stripes to the role of "national color." As we shall see, its use in battle intensified the process of flag consecration in the value system of the American people. As technology and military strategy changed, so did the significance of this national symbol, and old traditions made way for new. The practice of carrying colors into battle only persisted through the Civil War for Americans, and was last used by the British at the Battle of Laings Nek in 1881, in the first Boer War. The ritual of carrying colors lingers on today, albeit transformed, in the pageantry of military ceremonies.[30]

Artists employed the flag as a minor element in portraits and historical paintings during the Revolution and the early federal period. In this respect it served its traditional function as a symbol of military or naval identification. Still, it must be remembered that the Marine Flag was one of several different types of flags that designated different military statuses in this period. Other flags designated particular regiments, state property, and high-ranking officials. For instance, in many of Charles Willson Peale's portraits of Washington (Peale turned the portraiture of Washington into a thriving family industry), when a flag is used as a secondary element, it is usually Washington's headquarters flag. This flag displayed thirteen stars on a field of blue and also appeared at different times with the stars arranged in varying designs.

Before the American Revolution, flags were already necessary elements in historical paintings dealing with war scenes, as exemplified in Benjamin West's *The Death of Wolfe* (1770), which used classic style but transferred its focus to a contemporary event. John Trumbull was the American artist who assumed responsibility for capturing the major battles of the Revolution on canvas and in so doing promoted the genre of historical painting in the United States. Some claim that he shows the Stars and Stripes in recording the Battle of Princeton (26 December 1776) and the Battle of Trenton (3 January 1777). Others maintain that closer examination reveals he had in fact painted Washington's personal command flag, the headquarter's flag mentioned above.[31]

If an artist does include the Stars and Stripes in his rendering of a historical scene, this does not automatically indicate that that particular flag was actually at the original event. Trumbull's attention to vexillological detail has been questioned; his rendering of the British flag, for instance, is incorrect in *The Death of General Warren.*[32] Since Trumbull generally pays close attention to detail in his historical paintings, his inexactness about flags may tell us something about the general concern for flags in this era. With many variants in use, specificity in flag design was probably not important. An artist would no doubt be influenced by the variants to which he was exposed, and by the variants in current use at the later date when he set out to paint his re-creation of a historical event. These factors, as we shall see, became crucial in artistic depictions of the flag in the second half of the nineteenth century. Overall, Trumbull tended to favor a canton with twelve stars in a rectangle and a thirteenth star in the middle. His *The Surrender of Lord Cornwallis at Yorktown,* painted 1787–94, uses this design;

while a study, now owned by Yale, has fourteen stripes, a large version, on permanent display in the Capitol rotunda, has thirteen stripes.[33]

Commenting on the popularity of the canton design Trumbull used in *The Surrender of Lord Cornwallis at Yorktown*, Smithsonian textiles expert Grace Rogers Cooper says "the design, which seems to have been forgotten in the annals of history, may well have been a common one. Twelve stars in a square would certainly be a logical arrangement and would have been easy for the seamstress to plan and execute." Cooper also presents as evidence *American War Horse,* an anonymous folk art painting from the first quarter of the nineteenth century, which employs this particular flag design.[34]

All in all, the American flag as painted during the early years of the republic mirrors its function in the larger society. It might serve to identify a government installation, such as the tent in Trumbull's *The Surrender at Saratoga 1781* or the fort in Jonathan Budington's *View of the Cannon House and Wharf* (ca. 1812). It is interesting to speculate whether the comparatively gigantic size of the flag (it is as large as the three-story buildings in the painting) in the latter is due to the need to leave room to paint the design in the canton, the naive style of the artist, or a pervading sense of heightened nationalism as the country moves toward war. Most likely, the answer can be found in some combination of these theories. Flags certainly designated American naval vessels in art, although sometimes the variance would be extreme, such as in Jonathan Phippen's 1793 watercolor of the frigate *South Carolina,* which sports an American flag with green and red stripes and a yellow canton filled with thirteen crosses.[35]

Although the use of variants seems to have continued in the 1790s, it is the Marine Flag that came to symbolize America to European navies and commerce, and as early as 1784, to our new trading partners in China. Service at sea was thus the flag's primary role until the outbreak of the Second War of Independence. It is worth noting that the first American flag "flown" in England was on a merchant ship—and in a painting. John Singleton Copley, whose family was comprised of Tory émigrés to England from Massachusetts in 1774, nevertheless had some sensitivity for his countrymen's cause by the end of the war. On 5 December 1782, present at court when King George III recognized American independence, Copley immediately went to his studio and painted an American flag on the mast of a ship in the background of a portrait he was painting for Elkanah Watson, a Rhode Island merchant. He then displayed the unfinished portrait in his studio.[36]

American flags also appeared on other artistic renderings of the nation's commercial ships, most notably on British china produced cheaply for colonial exportation. Taking advantage of new technology and methods of mass production, Josiah Wedgwood pioneered a new era of decorated ceramic pottery. Large quantities of identical dinnerware could be manufactured, although the decoration would continue to be applied by hand. Wedgwood's firm, founded in 1759, found a ready market in America for cheap goods and seconds, and quite practically discovered, in decorating the dinnerware, that sympathy for the American cause was also profitable. After King George's recognition of American independence, many Liverpool manufacturers portrayed naval battles, prominent Americans, military events, tributes to particular localities, or tributes to American trade and industry on jugs, mugs, and punchbowls made exclusively for export to America. Flags appeared in designs depicting merchant ships traveling or navy ships battling vessels of the Royal Navy. Much china manufactured in Liverpool for the American market during the War of 1812 could be considered forms of treason, as it celebrated the exploits and successes of the enemy, yet the economic demand insured a constant supply.[37]

After direct trade was established with China, beginning in 1784, Americans could order specific patterns of china delivered from that far-off country, and some patriotic themes emerged. Plates enameled with pictures of clippers flying the American flag or the image of the American eagle became popular imports from China. In many instances floral borders in the British style were retained.[38]

When the flag appeared on the ceramics from China or England, it most often flew from the mast of a sailing ship. Although the images of sailing ships were not as popular as portraits of patriots, figures of Justice and Liberty, or representations of the American eagle, they were still common in the collection of motifs gracing ceramicware imported from the late eighteenth century on. Here, as in other artwork, great care was not always paid to flag design. One Liverpool jug, for example, displays a ship flying an American flag with yellow and blue stripes. Apparently whatever color was available was used. True seamen might also find amusement in depictions of ships being driven by forceful winds in billowing sails; in these the flag would often inexplicably be blowing in the opposite direction.[39] But for settlers who moved westward across the Alleghenies, away from the ocean, the flags on the clipper ships painted on the ceramicware they carried with them could well have been the most regular, realistic image of the flag seen, and a subtle suggestion of pride in identifying with the exploits of a young nation's maritime expansion.

There is also evidence that flag motifs were incorporated into wallpaper at the end of the eighteenth century.[40] An example from the mid-Atlantic states, dated ca. 1790, has vertical rows of two designs: (1) American flags braided into a winding vine and (2) a display of five flags dominant behind a small tristarred shield bearing seven white stripes and six red, in keeping with heraldic mandates for color arrangement.[41] Eagles running vertically balance displays of the five-flag motif, but the flag—which has the stars arranged in rows that fill the canton—is clearly the dominant symbol on the wallpaper, not a secondary element as is almost always the case during this time period.

Creators of textile products that depict the American flag in the federal period use it in ways similar to its use in paintings or on ceramicware: it is usually a secondary symbol denoting military or naval identification. In reviewing Herbert Ridgeway Collins's massive catalog *Threads of History: Americana Recorded on Cloth 1775 to the Present,* published by the Smithsonian Institution in 1979, one scholar has recently commented on the apparent lack of flags up until depictions of the Battle of New Orleans on an 1816 bandana;[42] actually, careful analysis reveals the American flag and some of its predecessor variants are included in artwork on kerchiefs, bandanas, and yard goods produced for American use during the early years of the young republic.

The stripes of rebellion are worked into the border of a kerchief honoring George Washington made in 1775; they reappear, carried before Washington by an Indian, in an English-made yard good ca. 1785. A red on white handkerchief done in England at the close of the war symbolically depicts Washington's involvement in achieving American independence; it includes Continental troops amassed behind two banners, one of which appears to be the Stars and Stripes. A blue on white kerchief, now owned by the Winterthur Museum, done by Henry Gardiner of Surrey in the early 1790s, bears an unmistakeably large Stars and Stripes flying from a merchant vessel pulled up on shore behind a toga-bedecked Benjamin Franklin and the figure of Commerce. And a Scotch yard good dated 1814 includes several American flags flying from battleships in ten different naval scenes from the War of 1812.[43]

In these early years of American nationalism, the beginnings of a civil religion, explaining the purpose of the United States in terms of a society destined for greatness, focused not on the flag, but on other more anthropomorphic symbols. Although there was a clear and decisive rejection of the monarchy, some considered making Washington a king, and even during the Revolution he had already become a larger-than-life figure, receiving the highest award his countrymen could bestow, the Congressional Medal, on 25 March 1776. Alive, he represented the values and virtues of the United States of America; dead, he became the foremost sacred figure of the developing civil religion. A vast iconography and mythology quickly grew up around his memory. Not only was he celebrated in sculpture and oil paintings, but in smaller paintings, miniatures, and engravings. His likeness adorned glass, china, clocks, mirrors, wall hangings, figurines, and the aforementioned textile products.[44]

Along with Washington, other symbols represented America in this period, although not as strongly as "The Father of Our Country" but clearly more regularly than the Stars and Stripes. Often these symbols were drawn from European symbolic conventions. America was sometimes depicted as one of the Four Continents, four women in Roman dress symbolically representing Asia, Africa, Europe, and America. In such a situation, America often carried a shield emblazoned with an eagle, and was attended by an American Indian.

Comparable to the personification of America were personifications of Liberty and Columbia; eventually they would all merge into one persona most notable today in the Statue of Liberty, which received national attention as it underwent restoration and celebrated a centennial.

Beside these human figures, one other symbol tended to overshadow the flag in these early years: the eagle, which embodied strength, independence, and majesty. As a national symbol it had a long tradition that stretched back to imperial Rome and included historic associations in many European countries, among them Austria, Russia, and Poland. In graphic, artistic, or literary contributions to civil religion before the War of 1812, the figures of Washington, Columbia, and the eagle were much more prominent than the flag. However, during the War of 1812 a significant event occurred that would gradually, over time, influence the rise to preeminence of the American flag in civil religion: while watching the Battle for Fort McHenry rage through the night of 13 September 1814, Francis Scott Key, an attorney from Georgetown, wrote "The Star-Spangled Banner."

Key was certainly not the first American patriot to take pen in hand and compose a tribute to the United States. He was, however, the first to write a noteworthy piece focusing on the flag as the vital symbol of the country. Since one of the flag's key functions was to designate control of a military installation such as Fort McHenry, the increased nationalistic fervor aroused by defense of one's homeland coupled with this to strengthen patriotic sensitivity to the flag during this war. Key experienced this as he watched the battle continue through the night from a British ship in the harbor; the following morning, assured that the fort had not fallen by his sighting of the Star-Spangled Banner, he scribbled down some inspired lines on the back of a letter he had in his pocket, and completed the poem that night in his hotel room in Baltimore.[45]

The particular flag that moved Key to creative response quite naturally became known as the Star-Spangled Banner. Because of what came to be seen as its pivotal role in an historic episode, it attained an individual degree of sacredness as American civil religion came to focus increasingly on the flag later in the century. Today that flag is preserved on permanent display for public veneration in the Smithsonian Institution in the nation's capital. It was made by Mary Pickersgill, whose mother, Rebecca Young, made flags for the Continental Army during the American Revolution. After the Battle of Fort McHenry, Lieutenant Colonel George Armistead, who had commanded the fort during the battle, took possession of the flag, and passed it down in his family. His grandson, Eben Appleton, donated it to the Smithsonian in 1912.

A visitor to the Smithsonian examining this flag will note the use of not only fifteen stars but of fifteen stripes. In 1793 the Senate acknowledged the admission of the states of Vermont and Kentucky by introducing a motion to add these two symbolic stars and stripes. The motion passed the Senate, as it eventually did the House, but there it met some interesting opposition that confirms earlier observations of eighteenth-century American attitudes toward flag usage. Representative Thatcher of Massachusetts found adjusting the design of the flag "a consummate piece of frivolity"; Representative Smith of Vermont complained that this alteration would cost sixty dollars for each ship in the merchant fleet.[46] Nevertheless, the law went into effect 1 May 1795, and although variants continued to be used as they had all along, this fifteen-star/fifteen-stripe flag has come to be known, in honor of its most famous example and the eventual popularity of the anthem, as the Star-Spangled Banner.

On 14 September 1814 Key took his poem to his brother-in-law, Judge Nicholson, Chief Justice of Maryland, who sent it that same day to the printer Benjamin Edes to create handbills, which circulated in Baltimore all week. The poem first appeared in a newspaper on 20 September 1814, in the *Baltimore Patriot,* which was followed by publication in the *Baltimore American* the next day. Titled "Defense of Fort M'Henry," in the *Patriot* it included this editor's comment: "The following beautiful and animating effusion, which is destined long to outlast the occasion and outlive the impulse which produced it, has already been extensively circulated. In our first renewal of publication we rejoice in an opportunity to enliven the sketch of an exploit so illustrious, with strains which so fitly celebrate it."[47]

In November 1814, *The Analectic Magazine* of Philadelphia printed the poem and noted: "These lines have already been published in several of our newspapers; they may still, however, be new to many of our readers. Besides, we think that their merit entitles them to preservation in some more permanent form than the columns of a daily newspaper."[48] Musicologist Joseph Muller credits Thomas Carr of Baltimore with the first published arrangement, dated October 1814, noting that other publishers copied or reprinted this version until a new arrangement appeared under the auspices of Firth & Hall of New York between 1832 and 1839.[49]

On 6 January 1815 the following advertisement appeared in the *Washington National Intelligencer:* "STAR SPANGLED BANNER and YE SEAMEN OF COLUMBIA.—Two favorite patriotic songs, this day received and for sale by Richard & Mallory, Bridge Street, Georgetown."[50] Beginning on handbills in Baltimore, the poem spread up and down the seaboard over the next several months first via newspapers, and then by magazines and published musical arrangements. Its first dated printing in a collection of popular tunes, a songster, is 1816 in Wilmington, Delaware. Over the next twenty years it did not become firmly established as a regular selection in such songsters, however.

Although many today would complain about the difficulty of range in the melody of "The Star-Spangled Banner," Key cannot be held directly accountable. The tune is an English drinking song, "To Anacreon in Heaven," the theme song of The Anacreontic Society of London composed by John Stafford Smith. Admirers of the British club, led by John Hodgkinson, founded a Columbian Anacreontic Society in New York in 1795 and it is logical to assume the theme song crossed the Atlantic as well;

there is evidence of it being publicly performed in Savannah and published in Philadelphia the following year.[51]

Not only was the song sung in America, but the tune was quickly adapted to several new lyrics, many of them political. On 1 June 1798 "Adams and Liberty" (which begins "Ye Sons of Columbia who bravely have fought") was performed to this tune at the anniversary of the Massachusetts Charitable Fire Society in Boston. The author, Robert Treat Paine, wrote new lyrics for a Boston tribute to Spanish patriots in 1809. Between the first presentation of "Adams and Liberty" and the Battle of Fort McHenry, a large variety of lyrics were written and published to this tune. Many of the patriotic versions began with references to Columbia. In 1813 alone the titles included "For the Fourth of July," "Freedom," "Embargo and Peace," "Union and Liberty," and "Jefferson's Election."[52]

Indications that Key was making a contribution to a popular subgenre are strengthened when one appreciates that the *Port Folio,* a Philadelphia based monthly magazine, offered several premiums for patriotic songs in 1813 and 1814, no doubt in response to the War of 1812. "The Pillar of Glory, A Naval Song," by Edwin C. Holland of Charleston, South Carolina, which took first prize in November 1813, was patterned on "To Anacreon in Heaven," and the winner of a best national song contest, which the *Port Folio* announced in May 1814 and printed in July, was "The Birth-day of Freedom," sung to the tune of "To Anacreon in Heaven."[53] One can be fairly certain that Key had at least casual contact with some of these songs, and this doubtlessly influenced his choice of meter for his poem.

"The Star-Spangled Banner" did not move into the category of popular classics until the attack on Fort Sumter prompted patriots to turn to a song that honored the national banner. It would not become the official national anthem, however, until 1931. Nevertheless, Francis Scott Key made a significant contribution that early September morning in Baltimore harbor, a contribution that would later, by association, elevate his home and his own image into the category of symbols valued in American civil religion.

A less noticeable event occurred a few years earlier, on a hillside in rural Maine. Still, in its own way, this event would have ramifications on the role of the American flag in civil religion that could rival the dissemination of Key's poem that was to follow.

In May 1812, aroused by the political climate of the times, Jeffersonian-Democrats who lived outside of Colrain, in what was, prior to the Compromise of 1820, part of the commonwealth of

Massachusetts, sought a way to demonstrate their patriotism and indicate their willingness to fight, if need be, for the preservation of their independence. All members of the rural community around Catamount Hill attended a gathering at the one community institution, a log cabin schoolhouse. Two local ladies handy with a needle, Rhoda and Lois Shippee, had sewed together a likeness of the national banner, and this was raised over the school, while the entire community watched. No speeches, no prayers, no music or ceremony graced the occasion, although years later Fanny Bowens Shippee, a child present that day, wrote a poem to commemorate the event.[54] With the simple act of raising this flag, the Catamount Hill Association symbolized their commitment to the United States. In connecting the center of public education with the dissemination of American civil religion they took the first step in what was to be a long and fascinating historical relationship between the school and the forces of American civil religion, forces that would raise the flag to the pinnacle of holiness.

3

Flag Culture in the Antebellum Period

As chapter 2 reveals, in the early years of the American republic, citizens recognized the flag as a national symbol that represented the country as an identification marker on naval vessels, and more importantly, after the Navy was temporarily disbanded following the Revolution, on the growing commercial fleet of the United States. Although the American flag was a secondary, decorative element in patriotic artifacts at this time—often serving, for example, as a border in a drawing of Washington or a detail in a representation of Columbia—it was part of the constellation of elements that artists, poets, politicians, and businessmen could draw on in using nationalistic references to advance their various personal and public aims. In the period from the War of 1812 until the outbreak of the Southern Rebellion, the uses of the Stars and Stripes in military and naval life, in painting and ceramic-ware, continued to be part of flag culture; but as nationalism developed and the country expanded, that flag culture also spread, slowly but surely, into several new areas. This chapter will describe that spread, tracing the gradual elevation of the national banner in the emerging civil religion. Using Hughey's definition of a civil religion as discussed in chapter 1, we find ample proof that such an emergent system flourished after the firing on Fort Sumter plunged the Union into Civil War. As a result of that patriotic response, the flag replaced George Washington as the single most important symbol employed to encapsulate the values of American civil religion. Leading up to this replacement, the uses of the symbol in the antebellum period expanded in the field of poetry, in patriotic campaigns, in nativist demonstrations, in fine art, and, as war neared, in life-or-death situations that tested loyalty.

The flag of Fort McHenry earned special honors as "the Star-Spangled Banner" while illustrating a truism that continues to operate in the culture of the United States today: in times of increased nationalism and social stress, various groups will seek

44

new ways to demonstrate their patriotism and commitment to the established social order, either by developing new uses or exhibitions for accepted patriotic symbols or by introducing new symbols. Francis Scott Key's poetic response and its subsequent dissemination are the first application of this principle involving the American flag on a national level, but each subsequent war involving the United States would bring new examples of sacred moments in which the symbolic nature of the flag intensified. The celebration of those moments through music, art, custom, and ritual has become a recurring motif in American civil religion; indeed, as new forms of media have developed the impact has intensified. Back in the second quarter of the nineteenth century, however, the process was comparatively slow.

The rise to popularity of "The Star-Spangled Banner" was gradual. In the antebellum years, tunes such as "Columbia, the Gem of the Ocean" or the Revolutionary War favorite "Yankee Doodle" vied with it for service at patriotic functions. A case might even be made for consideration of the increasing use of "The Star-Spangled Banner" as a measurement of the growing significance of the American flag to the country's emerging civil religion. It is worth noting that twenty-eight years after the song's introduction, in commemoration of Key's death on 11 January 1843, the Supreme Court of the United States saw fit to adjourn for one day in respect for his memory. At that time the *Baltimore American,* a newspaper that logically would promote the regional favorite for national use, made its policy clear in the following comment: "Francis Scott Key, the author of the 'Star-Spangled Banner,' is no more. So long as patriotism dwells among us, so long will this song be the theme of our Nation."[1]

As a gesture of recognition for Key's contribution to American patriotic prose, flags were lowered in Baltimore and Washington, D.C. on the day of his burial. Apparently by this time the tradition of flying a flag at half-staff in tribute to war fatalities or dead military or government leaders had already expanded to include civic figures deemed deserving by those in power.

Military historian Mark Mayo Boatner III believes this tradition originated in the naval practice of dipping sails as a sign of respect. In dipping its sails, a ship reduced speed and permitted other vessels to overhaul it. Well before the Revolution this custom had been abbreviated to the dipping of a flag to other vessels to demonstrate respect. Naval custom also used the lowered flag as a signal of distress, and as flag use became more prevalent on land, the half-mast signal of respect or distress quite logically became the half-staff signal of honor to recently deceased distinguished individuals.[2]

The fifteen-star, fifteen-stripe arrangement of the Star-Spangled Banner no longer adequately represented the nation in 1818, when twenty states belonged to the Union and it was clear more would soon apply for admittance. In March 1818, Representative Peter Wendover of New York rose before a Committee of the Whole in the House of Representatives to legislate a new design for the flag. Wendover began this work by persuading Congress to set up a flag study committee in 1816. While serving on this committee, Wendover received recommendations for altering the flag's design from Captain Samuel Reid of the United States Navy. Reid had also served as warden of the port of New York, and it is he who is credited with the idea of having stripes represent the original colonies and stars represent the current number of states in the Union.[3]

Reid wanted to make a distinction between the marine flag, as used on warships representing the government, and the shore flag, as used on land by government and private citizens or at sea by business and commercial interests. As documented in chapter 2, a variety of designs were still in use at sea in the second decade of the nineteenth century. However, following President Monroe's signing of this act into law on 4 April 1818, the Navy Commissioners issued a circular, slightly modified by President Monroe that September, that made no distinction between these two categories of flag use. The thirteen-stripe (one for each original colony), twenty-star (one for each member of the growing Union of states) flag Wendover argued for in Congress set the pattern for design of the American flag that continues today, both on land and at sea.

In Wendover's appeal to Congress to accept the thirteen-stripe, twenty-star flag, he alluded to the symbolic value a national banner held, even at this early date. "The importance attached to a national flag, both in its literal and figurative use, is so universal, and of such ancient origin, that we seldom inquire into the meaning of their various figures, as adopted by other nations, and are in some danger of forgetting the symbolical application of those composing that of our own."[4] A generation of Americans had grown accustomed to a combination of stars and stripes on their flag; these symbols could be retained, although their number and arrangement might be modified. As Wendover put it, "suitable symbols were devised by those who laid the foundation of the Republic; and I hope their children will ever feel themselves in honor precluded from changing these, except so far as necessity may dictate, and with a direct view of expressing by them their original design."[5]

Although the significance of the stripes and stars already tied into an idealized War of Independence forty years earlier, it is also clear from Wendover's speech that, except for the Navy, which had its longer tradition of appropriate flag use, little attention had been paid to conformity with official rules of correct flag use, even in the highest circles. He commented: "I would refer you to the flag at this moment waving over the heads of the Representatives of the nation, and two others in sight, equally the flags of the Government: while the law directs that the flag shall contain fifteen, that on the hall of Congress, whence laws emanate, has but thirteen, and those at the Navy Yard and Marine Barracks have each at least eighteen stripes. Nor can I omit to mention the flag under which the last Congress sat during its first session, which, from some cause or other unknown to me, had but nine stripes."[6] In concluding his call for more uniformity, Wendover noted that the subject "was not of a character to be classed with those of the highest national importance" but still deserved action. Twice he referred to the national flag as "the star-spangled banner,"[7] an indication of the connection between the growing popularity of Key's poem and the growing significance of the flag in the emerging civil religion of the United States. Wendover used the references to support his rhetorical aim of arousing the patriotic pathos of his audience to persuade them to agreement.

In this decade following the completion of the war with Great Britain, often referred to as the Second War for Independence, educated Americans heightened their call for a literary independence as well. One young poet, Joseph Rodman Drake, himself a success story who had overcome poverty to attain a medical degree at the age of twenty, wrote:

> No native bard the patriot harp hath ta'en,
> But left to minstrel of a foreign strand
> To sing the beauteous scenes of nature's loveliest land.[8]

Drake took up that harp, but died only a few years later, unable to complete this artistic mission. A contemporary and friend of Fitz-Greene Halleck, Drake is today remembered chiefly as a figure in one of Halleck's poems.[9] However, one patriotic poem Drake penned survived, and although not a critical success in his own day, it nicely met the needs of a later generation. "The

American Flag" first appeared in the *New York Evening Post* on 29
May 1819. Later, it was widely disseminated in a McGuffey Reader
for sixth-grade students published in the decade following the
Civil War, and although its author was more intent on distinguishing a classical personification of Freedom, his focus on the flag
throughout the poem no doubt influenced its selection for the
postbellum children's reader. Since the Civil War, patriotic tributes to the flag have become a common poetic topic, but Drake,
along with Key, deserves recognition as one of the earliest contrib-
utors to the genre.

A brief analysis of the structure of Drake's poem confirms that,
although it is one of the first tributes specifically focused on the
flag, it does not endow the flag itself with primary sacred value,
but sees it as a receptacle of such value emanating from the
personification of Freedom (see Appendix).[10] In the first, second,
and final verses of the five-stanza poem, Drake emphasizes the
guardian protectress Freedom, who gives this standard as the
symbol of her chosen land. Verse three deals with "the flag of the
brave," a consideration of the flag as identification for American
soldiers, while verse four describes "the flag of the sea," a consideration of the flag as identification for American sailors.

"The American Flag," although receiving some critical attention
in Drake's day, was ahead of its time in that certain segments of
society concerned with passing along messages of patriotic content
did not yet require the flag as a central focus in creative works. A
scan of the poetry selections in July issues of such pedagogical
journals as *Instructor* or *Grade School Teacher* over the past fifty
years of the twentieth century would reveal that, in works for the
young and those who socialize the young, the flag has been firmly
established as the main focus of American patriotic poetry, perhaps because, since the Civil War, the flag has emerged as the
dominant symbol of American civil religion.

Another result of the War of 1812 was a heightened awareness
of the protection that the American flag, as a representation of the
government of the United States, afforded American citizens
abroad or at sea. Indeed, one of the main factors that brought the
United States into the war with Great Britain was the Royal Navy's
disregard for the rights of American sailors aboard ships flying
the America flag, and the issue of impressment was not only of
commercial concern, but of honor. In the 1820s and 1830s, some
opportunities arose for Americans to turn to the flag for protection in foreign lands. In such situations, when other governments
recognized the flag and granted those Americans safety or asy-

lum, newspaper and magazine accounts of the incidents enhanced the role of the flag in demonstrations of nationalistic pride back home.

The case of the Honorable Joel R. Poinsett, minister to Mexico in 1825–29, exemplifies such nationalism. When Gomez Pedraza was elected president of Mexico, revolt broke out, and armed combatants struggled for control of Poinsett's neighborhood. A widowed neighbor came to him for protection, and while Poinsett reassured her, a bullet passed through his coat and struck the wall of his home. Retiring inside, he was soon greeted by an angry mob, which prepared to storm his home and capture Europeans seeking refuge there. As they began to force the gate open, Poinsett stepped out on his balcony with Mr. Mason, the secretary of the American legation, who unfurled the American flag over the crowd. Perhaps those gathered were not entirely clear as to what this action signified, but it surprised them enough to quiet them and make them lower their raised guns. Poinsett took advantage of the opportunity to claim the protection of the United States government for all in his household and warn the mob just who he was. Throughout the remaining battle for the area and until peace was restored, his home remained safe.[11]

Similarly, a few years later in Lisbon, the wife of the American Charge d'Affaires found her home in the middle of a minor civil war battle as the forces of Dom Miguel fired on armed boats of his brother, Dom Pedro. As her husband was not at home, she took the American flag and waved it out the window. In response to her action, the soldiers ceased shooting and moved away from the area of her home.[12]

As a decorative element on such items as hatboxes, wallpaper, and children's toys, the flag continued to be represented in the ways it had earlier been, but spread to some new uses as well. A huge flag flies from the stern of a merchant ship pictured on top of a hatbox made for Joseph S. Tillinghast of New Bedford, Massachusetts, in the 1830s. Similar to earlier tributes to American shipping, it bears the legend: "Prosperity to our Commerce and Manufacturers." Wallpaper distributed during the same time by John and Charles Cook of Boston balances scenes of a sailing ship at sea with scenes of a steamship on a river; although different modes of transport and in different environments, both vessels conspicuously display the American flag.[13]

During the 1820s and 1830s the flag began to appear in settings or situations beyond its traditional military, naval, and merchant shipping uses. Although it was by no means ubiquitous in daily life and the frequency of its representations does not begin to come close to that of contemporary American society, there are some indications that it was growing in importance as a symbol to express civil religious values.

As Ruth Elson has ably demonstrated in *Guardians of Tradition,* the figure of George Washington was the primary focus of those concerned with socializing young people in the values of American civil religion during the first half of the nineteenth century.[14] Although the flag does not appear in antebellum schoolbooks, it can be found, balanced by a red, white, and blue shield, as an important design element on a Parcheesi board dating from the mid-1830s. And for girls learning the intricacies of sewing, needlebooks with petit-point covers done as small American flags have been found dating from this early period.[15] Were there other aspects of daily life for antebellum American children in which representations of the national banner were evident? As the specialized study of the culture of children continues to grow, perhaps more information can be found in this area.[16] This would contribute to a clearer comprehension of the hierarchy of American civil religious symbols as it has changed over time and lead to insights concerning which groups employed these symbols in the socialization process, and for what explicit and implicit reasons.

During the election of 1840, a new icon developed in the arena of American political symbolism, an icon that often included the American flag as an important element. William Henry Harrison, former governor of the Indiana territory and celebrated military hero of the Battle of Tippecanoe, was the chosen candidate of the Whig party, which drew its support from eastern industrialists, southern planters, and prosperous western merchants. To sell their nominee to workers, farmers, and pioneers, party strategists portrayed Harrison as a frontier-born, cider-drinking fellow who championed the rights of the common man.[17]

Central to this image of Harrison was the notion that he was born and raised in a modest log cabin. (Actually, he was born in a mansion on a Virginia plantation.) A Baltimore *Republican* reporter, trying to defame the candidate, early on suggested, "Give him a barrel of Hard Cider, and settle a pension of $2,000 a year on him, and my word for it, he will set the remainder of his days in his log cabin, by the side of a 'sea-coal' fire and study moral philosophy."[18] Whig politicians turned this remark into the slogan of "Log Cabin and Hard Cider"; the log-cabin motif soon appeared on many banners, bandannas, and broadsides promoting Harrison for president.

An interesting aspect of the adoption of the log-cabin motif by the Whigs—aside from the appeal to Democratic principles for Whiggish ends—was the occasional inclusion of an American flag flying from the roof of the log cabin depicting Harrison's rural roots. There are no indications that in the antebellum period private citizens flew the national flag from the roofs of their homes, especially if these citizens were pioneers on the western frontier. A study of data from 1875 reveals that the practice of flying flags over or beside private homes was even then almost negligible, despite the influence of spreading flag culture and the heightened nationalism provoked by the Civil War.[19] Therefore, it is safe to assume that the inclusion of the flag in the motif was to heighten its nationalistic appeal, to draw on the symbolic resources of the flag as a symbol of civil religion to help justify the log cabin motif, and to accelerate its acceptance as a civil religious symbol on its own.

Whig supporters adopted a variety of materials to show off this motif. A gaudy brooch inscribed "The Peoples Choice/The Hero of Tippecanoe" shows the American flag atop a log cabin.[20] A silk bandanna dated 1840 held in the J. Doyle Dewitt Collection of the University of Hartford pictures a log cabin in a clearing surrounded by trees; a cider barrel and some logs lie before the door, two deer graze undisturbed nearby, and the legend reads simply "W. H. H. O.K." (William Henry Harrison—Okay). Over the cabin waves a disproportionately long American flag. A cotton bandanna from the same year, now held by the William Henry Harrison Home, displays the flag flying from a pole in front of the log cabin, and a quilt from Montgomery County, Maryland, depicts the flag, albeit with only one star, again flying from the roof of the cabin.[21] In each of these representations, an American eagle is shown in flight somewhere nearby, indicating that both the flag and the eagle were recognized civil religious symbols that the Whigs employed to help hallow the image of the log cabin.

The Whigs won that election, although Harrison contracted pneumonia on the day of his inauguration, grew progressively worse, and died after serving as president for only one month. In campaigning for his election, the Whigs went beyond using the flag in the process of log-cabin iconization to using actual flag banners, inscribed with the name of the candidate, to draw on patriotic emotional connections to ensure political support. The

flags tended to have thirteen-star cantons (twelve small stars encir-
cling one large one) and were inscribed in bold black letters on
some of the white stripes, HARRISON AND REFORM or THE
HERO OF TIPPECANOE (the latter usually including a small
portrait of Harrison in the center of the flag).[22]

This evidence suggests that by 1840 the flag was a strong
enough symbol to be used as support in the introduction of new
symbols. Even more significant, identification with the flag was
important enough to help elect a political candidate. From the
days of the Revolution, the flag had been included in political
artwork, and this use did continue—a broadside of the political
song "Harrison and Glory!" for example, written in 1840 by
William Koodwin of New Haven, Connecticut, was topped by a
bust portrait of Harrison, bordered by four flags and a laurel
wreath, with a gentleman farmer/log cabin scenario in the background.[23] The use of the inscribed banners, however, indicated
something new: not putting the flag beside a text or in the corner
of a picture, but putting the text or the picture directly *onto* the
flag itself. Such flags would be carried in political parades and
demonstrations, then saved as popular souvenirs after the votes
were counted and the elections were over.

As stated earlier, Harrison did win that election, although the
contribution of this new type of political advertising probably did
not prove as significant a vote-getter as all the jugs of hard cider
proffered to thirsty constituents by Whig candidates capitalizing
on the slogan. Still, the parading of flag banners was a new
technique that obviously had some persuasive merit. In the election of 1844, not only did the Whig candidates Clay and
Frelinghuysen use flag banners for such political advertisements,
but so did their Democratic opponents Polk and Dallas. It was in
the election of 1844 that it became common practice to include the
names of both the presidential and vice-presidential candidates
on these banners.

The use of these modified flags during presidential campaigns
flourished throughout the nineteenth century. Starting with the
campaigns of Clay and Polk, the stars were sometimes removed
from the canton and replaced with a portrait of the presidential
candidate. On other occasions, the inscription interrupted not the
stripes but the stars.[24] Each new election brought some interesting
variations, but the practice of advertising candidates on the American flag went unquestioned when it was introduced and it quickly
became accepted as common procedure.

During the 1840s, as Whigs and Democrats waved their inscribed flag banners and fought for the vote of the common man first championed by Andrew Jackson, many Americans grew interested in the prospects of national expansion. The lucrative possibilities of agricultural and commercial development, a steadfast belief in the superiority of Anglo-American democratic institutions, the dream of being part of a people chosen by God to demonstrate to the world how a continent should be cultivated and civilized—these factors merged to create a civil religious attitude known as manifest destiny. It was God's will that America should spread from sea to sea—and some said, beyond—and where America went, so went the flag.

Although the flag did not receive the central focus in speeches or representations of the concept of manifest destiny that it would in the propaganda of renewed nationalistic expansionist forces in the late nineteenth century, it was still an important symbol of American possession and accomplishment, so newspapers paid careful attention to such events as the first American flag raised in California, the first American flag to round the Cape of Good Hope on the way to China, or the first American flag to be raised over the president's palace in Mexico during the Mexican-American War, a conflict that, although short, was highly profitable in terms of land acquisition.[25]

The belief that God had chosen the settlers of America for bounty and empire often had a darker side to it: the belief that new immigrants had come to steal away from deserving Americans a share of the wealth. Nativist movements organized in reaction to the influx of immigrants from politically and economically retarded Germany and starving Ireland. For groups such as the American Republican Party (which later became known by the nickname "the Know-Nothings") the national banner acquired an emotional significance as the flag of Protestant white Anglo-Saxon inheritors of the duties and values of those who fought the American Revolution. When these men referred to "America" (they rarely spoke of "the United States") they pictured an idealized society in which General George Washington's successors would keep the land secure for the descendants of those who liberated it. From their perspective, the jobs and neighborhoods of Eastern cities were threatened by an influx of foreigners, and Roman Catholics at that. Historian Jean H. Baker has noted that, as these nativists became a political force, "they soon appropriated the American flag, the eagle, and an etching of Washington for their party."[26]

As the election of 1844 neared, proponents of nativist philosophy moved to take action. The American Republican party candidate received a large vote in a November 1843 election for State Senator in New York City, and the following April, an electorate fearful of the continuing influx of immigrants and their speedy absorption into the ranks of the Democratic party gave a nativist administration control of the city.[27]

Anti-Catholic nativist groups spread down the Atlantic seaboard, gaining strength in New Jersey and Pennsylvania. Drawing converts from the Whig party while frightening noncommited foreign-borns into the Democratic party, the political influence of the Native American Party swelled. In April 1844 tension between the supporters of Native American principles and Irish-born Roman Catholics erupted into three days of violence in the Philadelphia area. A careful examination of this clash, known as the Kensington Riots, shows how an intensification of the Nativist party's identification with the American flag gave them the United States' first nonmilitary martyr to the cause of protecting the national banner from desecration.

For an artifact to be desecrated it must first, logically, be held sacred. Although the Know-Nothings held especially dear the allegorical symbol of America as a healthy, virile, young man, untainted and courageously prepared to defend himself, the three most important elements of nativist iconography were the American eagle, the portrait of General Washington, and the American flag. In reviewing their surviving campaign materials, Baker asserts that "the most detailed nativist representation was that of a rock symbolizing Constitution and Union, surrounded by mechanics, sailors, and farmers, with one citizen carrying a huge American flag."[28] The red, white, and blue flag symbolized for these working class citizens the struggles and achievements of the American Revolution; as a nativist constitution passed in Germantown, Pennsylvania, put it: "Let us come forward, then, and prove that the spirit of '76 is not yet extinct and that we are not degenerate sons of worthy sires." To demonstrate their idealization of their Revolutionary War forefathers, one group adopted the name "Order of the Sons of the Sires of '76."[29] Unfortunately for them, and for many Americans in later generations, the symbol of the flag came to represent not only political ideals but also, regrettably, their rationalized attitudes of religious and ethnic bigotry.

A brief consideration of the chain of events at the Kensington Riots shows the influence of violence upon the process of hallowing the flag. Native American supporters had called a public

meeting in Kensington on Monday, 6 May 1844. Originally sched-
uled for a vacant lot, the meeting was driven by rain into a market
house near the Hibernia Hose House, a fire company manned by
Irish immigrants.

Angry anti-Catholic rhetoric unleashed in an Irish neighborhood was, for its day, not completely unlike the recent American Nazi party demonstrations in heavily Jewish Skokie, Illinois—
a powder keg waiting to be lighted. How the violence was
provoked is arguable. A Whig paper contends that noisy Irishmen
attempted to disrupt the peaceable meeting, and when bystanders
silenced them, the Irish began shooting into the market house
from the upper windows of the fire company.[30] In any event, a
pitched battle ensued. Several area homes were attacked and
battered before the Irish rallied and drove back the Native Americans to end the first day of fighting. "Master street, between
Germantown road and Cadwalader street, was literally strewed
with broken bricks and stones."[31] And George Shiffler, a young
mechanic and supporter of the Native American party, was one of
the first to die.

For reporters and nativist organizers, what made Shiffler stand
out from the eight others who died in these riots was the fact that
he died protecting the flag, thus becoming a martyr not only for
the political aims of the Native American party but also for the
significance of the flag in American civil religion. As one sympathetic nativist recalled the incident eleven years later:

> One young man, about nineteen years of age, was engaged
> throughout the afternoon, in supporting the American flag, which
> hung over the speakers' stand. This rendered him an especial mark
> for the aim of the enemies of the cause he was maintaining. Two or
> three times had the flag fallen to the ground, and as often did George
> Shiffler, with the assistance of several others, again raise it, and cause
> its stripes and stars to float above their heads. But his efforts were
> unavailing, for a bullet at length pierced his heart, and he fell as
> senseless as the flag he supported, to the ground.[32]

Although the last independent clause of the final sentence in this
quote is out of tone in its recognition of the flag as a material
artifact lacking life or sensory responses, the rest of the piece
honors Shiffler for honoring the flag. And, according to
onlookers, "the flag which he had supported was torn and levelled
with the dust, by those who had sworn to protect our country and
her laws."[33]

For the Native Americans, who already felt their public schools threatened by Roman Catholic efforts to discontinue readings from the King James version of the Bible, the death of Shiffler and the simultaneous desecration of the flag demanded revenge. The following day a large group of Native Americans carried the flag Shiffler had guarded through the streets of Philadelphia, calling for an afternoon meeting to determine a course of action. Beside the flag they bore a placard, inscribed in large letters: "This is the Flag that was trampled on by Irish Papists."[34] Those who attended the meeting passed a resolution approving a decision "to make suitable preparations for the internment of the first martyr to the cause of Civil and Religious freedom among us," and all were urged to attend Shiffler's funeral in one united congregation. The desecrated flag was then carried to Kensington and nailed up amid fiery rhetoric by nativist agitators, which quickly led to a renewed attack upon the Hibernia Hose House. That night the Kensington rioters burned and destroyed St. Augustine's church and rectory, as well as a Roman Catholic school and—presumably by mistake—a temperance grocery store. The Roman Catholic Cathedral Church of St. John and St. Mary's Church were also attacked but not razed. Many were injured and several died.[35]

During this riot, identification with the flag in the Philadelphia area came to mean identification with Native American principles. Angry mobsters vowed that all dwellings of Irish Catholics in the Kensington area would be set on fire. "In response, small American flags, and coloured rags, of every description, sewn together to represent such flags, were hastily prepared and hung from the windows of hundreds of houses in the vicinity, to designate the residences of those favourable to the Americans, and to save them from the fury of rabble."[36]

After three days of rioting, city officials managed to restore peace through police protection of Roman Catholic church sites. On Thursday, May 9, as a safeguard, Francis Patrick, Roman Catholic Bishop of Philadelphia, suspended all public worship in Catholic churches "which still remain" until the situation quieted down. That same day a long procession and large crowd of spectators attended Shiffler's funeral march and, although there was a solemn dedication with much displaying of flags, no violence followed.[37]

The outbreak had been quelled but emotions continued to run high. The next Fourth of July, the Native American party held a parade in Philadelphia to commemorate their fallen and display their strength. Delegations participated from Delaware and New

York City, and over three thousand marched. Hundreds and hundreds of American flags were carried, from small hand-held pennants waved by nativist children's brigades to huge silken banners stitched in group efforts by women's nativist support leagues.[38] On this Fourth of July, the Star-Spangled Banner meant to these people not only the glory of the nation's past, but more significantly, their vision of its proper future.

Although today some might scoff at the Know-Nothings' values, one should not underestimate their political clout. Angry reactions to the Compromise of 1850 and the Kansas-Nebraska Act of 1854 swelled the nativist ranks. A Maryland nativist secret society—significantly named the Supreme Order of the Star Spangled Banner—expanded to a national federation of secret lodges in June 1854. This hierarchy was the basis for the power structure of an influential incarnation of nativism, the new American party (the group specifically labeled "Know-Nothings" for their unwillingness to divulge information about their organization, based on these nativist fraternal lodges).[39] In 1854 and 1855, this party carried six states and almost gained control in seven more. If it had not split on the controversial issue of slavery prior to the election of 1856, it might well have emerged as a dominant party in the nation, unfortunately demonstrating an American acceptance of intolerance.[40] As it is, the Know-Nothings set a precedent for the appropriation of the American flag to represent a version of American civil religion that celebrated an ethnically pure minority as an elite of "true Americans." The Star-Spangled Banner as the symbol of a racially pure Protestant America would reemerge, to the consternation of some citizens, as an emblem of the twentieth-century Ku Klux Klan and the post-Holocaust American Nazi party.

Although specific groups such as the Supreme Order of the Star Spangled Banner sanctified the flag in recognition of the American Revolution and the War of 1812, in the antebellum years the general public recognized and respected it as a symbol of America but did not yet hallow it. However, some impetus was given to such a shift in 1846 by the outbreak of the Mexican-American War, a military exercise quite justified for believers in manifest destiny. Just as William Henry Harrison built a political future out of military renown in the War of 1812, so did Zachary Taylor capitalize on participation in the Mexican-American War to eventually win himself nomination and election as President of the United States of America.

Perhaps because he failed to take into account sectional differences and the fact that the war lasted little over a year, Professor Wilbur Zelinsky has probably overestimated its contribution to flag culture in relationship to other events occurring in the first half of the nineteenth century.[41] The war necessarily reinforced traditional military uses of the flag, and it inspired patriotic hoopla, using the flag as a marker for territorial expansion, but it was not a popular war in the northeast. Political outpourings of support came from the regions of the country that would most clearly benefit from the war: preeminently the West, but also to a certain extent, the South. Few material artifacts from the war itself that illustrate uses of flag symbolism exist, and those that do, such as a lithograph of the Americans forcing their way to the main plaza in the Battle of Monterey on 23 September 1846, display the flag in conventional forms.[42]

However, a few examples of the growing focus on the flag to make a political candidate appear more attractive remain from Taylor's successful 1848 bid for the presidency. Several bandannas survive that were designed that year, depicting the general astride his horse, prepared for battle, or in full length dress uniform as the celebrated "Old Rough and Ready." Among these cotton mementos, two stand out as bandannas that emphasize the American flag with Taylor as a minor element, rather than the other way around. Ironically, the flags illustrated, for some unexplained reason in both cases, have seventeen rather than thirteen stripes.[43]

An American flag could attract the attention of native travelers arriving in new, unfamiliar towns; the recognition of a well-known symbol over the door of a hotel could, to some degree, prove reassuring (much as the golden arches of McDonalds, however aesthetically displeasing, can be a comforting, familiar sight to an American traveler in Europe or Asia today). An anonymous watercolor of Eagle Hotel in Bethlehem, Pennsylvania (ca. 1860), shows how a flag-bedecked inn might welcome a traveler.[44] Certainly, innkeepers eager to catch any holiday traffic would be remiss not to fly the flag on the Fourth of July. For example, Harper's Weekly noted on 4 July 1857 that the Burnet House, Cincinnati's most prestigious hotel, decorated its principal entrance with several American flags.

Although it is difficult to state precisely, at one point, approximately in the 1840s, owners of hotels began the practice of inscribing the names of their establishments upon American flags, which were then flown from the roofs or over the doorways of the buildings.[45] Such practices do not seem to have persisted long after the Civil War, however, as a new sensitivity to the significance of the American flag emerged.

In the antebellum period, when creating works of art, illustrators and artists included the flag in situations they deemed appropriate, whether on the cover of musical song sheets or in the more recognized watercolors and oil paintings. As in the Federalist era, these representations usually depicted and corroborated accepted uses of the American flag in the contemporary society. In the 1830s, the sheet music for martial tunes such as the "Philadelphia Gray's Quick Step" or "The Blue's Quick Step," dedicated to various military personnel, included drawings on their covers of soldiers encamped beneath the banner, although in the former case the flag lacks the canton of stars, appearing to be a regimental adaption of the Sons of Liberty's Stripes of Rebellion. After the Mexican-American War, "Smith's March," dedicated to General Pernifor F. Smith, "the hero of Contreras," illustrated a soldier at attention holding the flag. The more somber "On to the Charge!" dedicated to the memory of Major Ringgold, "late of the U.S.—light artillery," depicted his grave. In the picture, memorial statuary of an eagle and a cannon stand near the grave and behind the simple cross marker an American flag, topped with black crepe streamers, rests with its cloth almost skimming the top of the grave.[46] The use of black crepe memorial streamers was a popular Victorian practice and remained so until twentieth-century codification of flag etiquette restricted such additional embellishments.

Representations of the American flag in fine art in the antebellum years indicate many military uses with some commercial and allegorical uses, as well as its customary display on patriotic national holidays. W. H. Creasy's *Stockton* (1849) shows the flag waving over a military installation. Robert Salmon's *Packet Ship 'United States'* (1817) and Jurgen Frederick Huge's *Bunkerhill* (1838) portray its continuing importance as identification for sailing vessels and steamboats. Alexis Chataigner's *Triumph of America* (1815) and the anonymous *Memorial to George Washington* (ca. 1815) illustrate the ongoing use of the American flag as the banner carried or guarded by the female personification of Columbia.[47]

John Lewis Krimmel, a German specialist in genre paintings, emigrated to Philadelphia at the age of twenty-three, and adapted the style of Dutch genre scenes to American life.[48] Several of his paintings include the presence of the American flag at typical holiday gatherings, such as *A Parade Passing Independence Hall, Philadelphia* (ca. 1812) or *Fourth of July in Center Square* (1819). His *Election Day at the State House* (1816) shows local, state, and national flags flying above the active crowd of voters and politicians in the street.[49]

As in the days of George Washington, antebellum portraitists included the flag as a secondary element in paintings of important political figures. John Neagle, son-in-law and student of the great Philadelphia portraitist Thomas Sully, in 1843 painted a striking tribute to Henry Clay, a copy of which hangs today in the House of Representatives wing of the United States Capitol. The great Whig statesman Clay poses between two sets of symbols. On his right, in the background, an anvil, a plow, two grazing cows, and a distant sailing ship combine pastoral harmony with commercial success. On his left, in the foreground, a massive American flag, much larger than Clay, billows down to the floor, and conspicuously enshrouds half of a globe (the Northern hemisphere, most clearly the continent of North America) and appears quite capable of covering the rest. In 1843, there seems to be no dishonor in allowing the flag to touch the floor, as it does in this portrait. After Clay, it is the most dominant element in the painting, and the positioning of his hands unavoidably directs the viewer to concentrate upon the flag after examining the congressman. John Sartrain made engravings of this portrait, produced and circulated by Charles W. Bender & Co. of New York, and needlepoint tapestry reproductions of the engraving became prized possessions of some Whig supporters.[50]

The flag continued to appear in the subgenre of history painting in artworks dealing with military situations. Perhaps influenced by genre studies, history painting in the antebellum years moved away from "the lofty ideal and the old-master manner" to more anecdotal specific scenes.[51] The style flourished in Duesseldorf, Germany, in the 1840s, and the opening of a Duesseldorf Gallery in New York City in 1849 spread its popularity in America. Emmanuel Leutze, born in Wuertenberg but raised in Fredericksburg, Virginia, went to Duesseldorf to study in 1841 and ten years later, while still there, he created his famous *Washington Crossing the Delaware*, a history painting that demonstrates not only the influence of the Duesseldorf style but also the growing importance of the American flag in civil religious iconography.

Leutze's original remained in Germany until 1942, when American bombers destroyed it along with the gallery in Bremen where it then hung. A diligent worker, Leutze had made two later

This 1851–52 painting by Emmanuel Leutze, *Washington Crossing the Delaware*, became a significant image in nineteenth-century American culture, demonstrating the growing importance of the national banner in civil religious iconography. (Photo courtesy of the National Archives.)

versions in 1851–52, however. The second has drawn large crowds at the Metropolitan Museum of Art in New York City throughout the one hundred thirty-four years it has been on display, and the third, which hung in the White House for many years, served as the model for the proliferation of engravings that spread the image throughout the United States in the second half of the nineteenth century.[52]

Even today copies of the painting remain popular choices to decorate schools and public buildings. Although many Americans might not recognize Leutze by name, repetition and media adaptions have made the tableau familiar. Washington faces forward, his foot on the gunwale, as Green Mountain Boys and Gloucester fishermen row him across the Delaware on Christmas Eve, 1776, en route to fight and win the Battle of Trenton, the Continental Army's sorely needed first real victory. Behind General Washington, Lieutenant James Monroe, another future president of the United States, has the honor of holding the thirteen-star

American flag, which is the pivotal image in the artistically balanced arrangement of passengers in the boat.[53]

The painting is, of course, an idealization, historically inaccurate in its use of the American flag: the Battle of Trenton predated the Flag Resolution of 1777 by six months.[54] A vessel bearing Washington would have borne his personal command flag, a blue field covered with thirteen stars. The actual crossing was done in the dark of night, and was accomplished as quietly as possible. The inclusion of James Monroe as flagbearer is a nice touch that can be interpreted as a glorification of the position's responsibility. In the late nineteenth century, some superpatriotic groups came to endow the flag with mystical and supernatural powers in the progressive unfolding of the nation's divine destiny. For them, Monroe's role in the painting as flagbearer could be interpreted as a foreordained step in his preparation for the highest office in the land.

Today the image of the crossing remains more crucial to American civil religion than the actual occurrence. In 1985, when asked why the flag is important to our society, a college freshman replied, "because it was carried in all those Revolutionary battles; it's in that picture of Washington at the Delaware." When he learned that the painting was done seventy-five years after the event and that Leutze had taken liberties with historical facts, he tried to emphasize the significance the picture holds for him: "It doesn't matter if [the flag] was really there or not. What is important is that we think it was there since it represents what our country is all about." For this student, and for many other Americans, historical accuracy is irrelevant when it begins to threaten accepted beliefs about the use of a powerful symbol such as the flag of the United States.[55]

The image of Washington crossing the Delaware, in entering the constellation of American civil religious motifs, has of course been widely reproduced, imitated, and modified, and the practice continues in contemporary society, often adapted to sell beliefs or merchandise. In the world of advertising, stores such as Sak's have built sales campaigns on the tableau and, logically, promotions capitalizing on patriotic holidays—especially Washington's Birthday sales—strategically draw on it.[56] It has inspired numerous artistic adaptions, from an anonymous late nineteenth-century rendition with simpler, stiffer figures that lack the grace of the original to Alex Katz's *American Flag and Soldiers, Boat & River* (1961), which reverses the vessel's direction, limits the passengers to two, and emphasizes vividness of color.[57] The recognition factor for the icon was evidenced in its use in comedy blackout skits on the popular 1960s television program *Laugh-In* or as a teaching device by a singularly successful history instructor in the 1984 film *Teachers,* and its power also serves political cartoonists when they employ the image in a new way to make humorous or satirical points.

Another allegorical use of the American flag in artwork before the war pointed toward a more profound meaning than simple political identification. Charles G. Crehen's painting *Young '76* (ca. 1855) has a haunting quality about it, in part due to the gaze of the Gainesborough-influenced cherubic lad of perhaps seven years of age who is pictured dressed in the garb of an adult of the American Revolution. He holds a sword raised in deadly earnest, and the flag is balanced over his shoulder. Ready for a fight, this young innocent, painted to show the vitality of the nation in its youth, displays a militant resolve to protect the Union forged by that coalition of colonies.

Later, as the North-South conflict escalated, patriotic pro-Unionists placed increasing emphasis on the flag as a symbol. Foreshadowing of what would come later occurred during the Nullification crisis of 1832–33. When South Carolina threatened to declare itself superior to federal laws, emotions ran high, and an error in flag etiquette was interpreted as an insult to the government. In January, 1833, Governor Hamilton of South Carolina left Augusta, Georgia, en route to Charleston aboard the steamer *William Seabrook.* The ship's ensign, according to its captain, mistakenly hoisted the American flag upside down, a recognized naval sign of distress. The mistake was noticed and corrected, but not before Georgians spotted it from shore. They interpreted this as a symbolic statement by Governor Hamilton on the stability of the Union. The editor of the *Augusta Courier* complained: "The indignation we feel in common with an insulted community does not allow us to speak another word concerning such an outrage."[58]

The following February, the Governor of Virginia commissioned the painting of a large state flag to be used to honor the State Guard in a ceremony on Washington's Birthday. Constituents and advisors convinced him such action would belittle the Union, and the painting remained in storage, while the national flag, fixed upon a pole, was flown from the southern end of the Capitol loft in Richmond. As it was, a dissatisfied Philadelphia newspaper, reporting on the festivities in Virginia, admonished the Southerners for inattention to the flag, after it was caught on some lightning rods and torn.[59]

In June 1833, J. E. D. of the *Boston Centinel* [*sic*] celebrated Andrew Jackson's firm stand on and victory over the question of nullification. Although the war would not erupt until twenty-eight years later, the poem illustrates how, throughout this period, the very design of the flag that Captain Samuel Reid had successfully lobbied to legalize in 1818 now made it an increasingly powerful symbol for the continuance of the Union:

> Hail, banner of glory! Hail, banner of light!
> Whose fame lives in story, whose folds cheer my sight;
> Not a star is supprest, not a stripe has been torn
> From the flag of the West, which our fathers have borne.
> Our Union is fast, and our homes ever sure,
> Our freedom shall last while the world shall endure.
> Then hail to the banner whose folds wave in glory,
> Let the free breezes fan her, and whisper her story.
> The tumult has ended, the storm's died away,
> The fiend has descended that led us astray.
> The sons of the West are our brother again,
> And the flag of the blest floats from Texas to Maine.[60]

"The flag of the blest" reinforces the role of the flag as a symbol of America in its civil religious collection of motifs and values. Unfortunately, the capitulation of South Carolina on the 1833 question of nullification was not the end of the tumult; rather, it emphasized the beginning, and although years of careful compromising delayed the eventual outbreak of war, the regional, cultural, and economic differences between the North and the South eventually resulted in Southern states declaring their independence from the Union and forming their own Confederacy.

South Carolina seceded first on 10 December 1860, and in January, Florida, Mississippi, Alabama, Georgia, and Louisiana (in that order) followed suit. By this time, the flag as a symbol of Union took on such intense meaning that actions against the flag, interpreted as actions against the federal government, could quickly lead to death. On 29 January 1861, Secretary John A. Dix sent a famous directive to a clerk ordered to save a revenue cutter in New Orleans harbor before it was confiscated by forces of the state of Louisiana. Dix telegraphed: "If anyone attempts to haul down the American flag, shoot him on the spot." Although the confederates nevertheless took control of the vessel, a quick-thinking sailor managed to secure the flag and send it to Secretary Dix via General Butler. For protecting the flag from capture and dishonor, the sailor was promoted to lieutenant.[61]

War loomed on the horizon. Citizens, both North and South, prepared for the coming battle. For Northerners, it was a "War against the Flag,"[62] and the specific Southern atrocity that provoked it was the firing on the American flag at Fort Sumter.

4

Symbol of the Union: Flag Use during the Civil War

During the years of martial violence from 1861 to 1864, millions of citizens saw their national banner hallowed by the baptism of battlefield fire. Searching for outward expressions of inner commitment to a cause they interpreted as moral and patriotic, Northerners turned to the flag that symbolized that Union they would fight to maintain, giving it increased significance and use in their day-to-day life. An outburst of flagwaving at the onset of the Civil War was followed by a heightened sensitivity on the part of soldiers and citizens alike to the representational nature of the flag. Legends grew involving the flag in various patriotic episodes. After their husbands went off to fight, wives and mothers at home took on the responsibility of explaining the significance of the flag to their children. And in the churches, where voices joined in prayer and supplication for victory, the American flag quietly appeared, not just a secular symbol, but an affirmation of a belief in God's ordained plan for the future reconciliation and growth of the Union. The Civil War fostered a definite practice of civil religion in the North, and in so doing, elevated to prominence therein the symbol of the flag of the United States.

The national flag, in its traditional role as an identification marker for government-held military installations, first took on this heightened significance as it continued to fly over Fort Sumter in the harbor of Charleston, South Carolina, after that state seceded from the Union on 20 December 1860. The day after Christmas, Major Robert Anderson, operating in what he believed to be the best interest of both the North and the South,[1] moved his garrison of federal forces into the fort and awaited further directions from Washington.

Fort Sumter was well situated at the entrance to the harbor. Representatives of South Carolina demanded that the installation be turned over to state authorities; President Buchanan, in-

creasingly influenced by a pro-Unionist cabinet, broke off nego-
tiations with the South Carolinians, putting into motion military
orders to send down men and munitions. The nation tensed for
war for, as Civil War historian Bruce Catton has pointed out, the
North would not go to war over an abstraction, but would fight "to
possess a fort or to hoist a flag on some disputed staff."[2] A
bricklayer in Baltimore typified the public response of the North
when, in a letter of support to Major Anderson, he volunteered to
bring a band of workmen "who would not hesitate to lay aside the
trowel if it became necessary and help defend their country's
flag."[3]

On 8 January 1861, a steamer flying the U.S. flag, the *Star of the
West,* attempted to bring supplies to Fort Sumter, but was fired
upon by Rebel forces from nearby Morris Island and Fort
Moultrie. Major Anderson decided not to return fire from the
fort, and the *Star of the West* put back out to sea. This conservative
action on the part of Anderson angered some of his officers:
"Captain Foster, of the engineers, ran down the stairs in open
fury, throwing his hat on the ground and muttering something
about 'trample on the flag'."[4] Captain Foster was speaking figur-
atively, but he used an analogy that was to grow in tenor and usage
as 1861 progressed: an affront to the government of the United
States was an affront to its flag, and vice versa.

The South Carolinians and their Confederate colleagues were
not without regard for the banner that, until recently, they had
acknowledged as their own. When the Yankee supplies were obviously depleted in April, Brigadier General Pierre G.T. Beauregard of the provisional army of the Confederate states sent a
formal demand for surrender to Major Anderson that ended with
this sentence: "The flag which you have upheld so long and with
so much fortitude, under the most trying circumstances, may be
saluted by you on taking it down."[5]

Shortly after midnight on 12 April, Anderson sent a message to
Beauregard: if no hostile acts were committed against Fort Sumter
or the American flag (my italics), the United States forces, if given
safe transport, would evacuate on 15 April. At 3:20 A.M. Beauregard returned the warning that his men would commence firing
on Fort Sumter in one hour, and he lived up to his word. As soon
as this notice was received, the American flag was raised over the
fort, and daylight broke to display heavy Confederate bombardment of both flag and fort. At noon the flagstaff was shot down.
Although Lieutenant G.W. Snyder and Sergeant Peter Hart

climbed up and managed to fasten it anew to a gun carriage on the fort's barbette, the Southerners determined that the time had come for renegotiations.[6]

Eventually it was arranged: Anderson's forces did surrender, but they were permitted, before leaving, to hoist the flag, salute it, haul it down again, and take it with them as the steamer *Ysabel* carried them away from the Confederate-held fort. This same flag was transported for safekeeping to the well-protected vaults of the Metropolitan Bank in New York. During the war, however, the Sanitary Commission, a northern forerunner to the Red Cross that was administered by socially concerned members of the Yankee gentry class, obtained the use of the Fort Sumter flag, a powerful symbol, as a fund-raising tool across the country. Commission officials took it from town to town and displayed it before large crowds, exciting the crowds by telling them of the "outrage" that had occurred at Fort Sumter. Patriots demonstrated their convictions by trying to outbid each other at the auction of this special flag. Traditionally, the highest bidder would not keep the flag, but ceremoniously return it to the Sanitary Commission, which would then pack it away and transport it to another auction in another city. In this manner the Sanitary Commission raised several thousand dollars, utilizing the Northern outpouring of affection for the flag to help the wounded or suffering victims of the war.[7]

The Sumter flag carried special meaning, and its display across the nation increased both its particular appeal and a sensitivity to the flag in general. Shortly after the fall of Charleston and on the fourth anniversary of the evacuation of Fort Sumter, President Lincoln decreed that the American flag that had last flown over Fort Sumter be returned to the fort and rededicated in a special ceremony that included much ritual honoring the banner as a special object: the crowd sang "Rally Round the Flag, Boys"; army chaplain Reverend Matthew Harris blessed the flag; and Major Anderson raised it anew amid much cheering. The occasion concluded with a singing of "The Star-Spangled Banner."[8]

Such a victorious celebration for Union forces was a long way off from the Confederate acquisition of Fort Sumter in 1861, however, when an emboldened Confederate Secretary of War, L.P. Walker, predicted that the flag of the Confederacy would fly "over the dome of the old Capitol at Washington before the 1st of May." When news of the evacuation of Fort Sumter reached President Lincoln, he issued a proclamation calling for seventy-five thousand volunteers to defend the Union. The North responded with an outburst of patriotic support, a reaction in which the flag took on new uses. Drawing on Morris and Croffet's *Military and Civil History of Connecticut, 1861–1865*, noted flag historian George Preble described the response in this manner: "When the stars and stripes went down at Sumter, they went up in every town and county in the loyal States. Every city, town, and village suddenly blossomed with banners. On forts and ships, from church-spires and flag-staffs, from colleges, hotels, storefronts and private balconies, from public edifices, everywhere the old flag was flung out, and everywhere it was hailed with enthusiasm; for its prose became poetry, and there was seen in it a sacred value which it had never before possessed."[9]

Mary A. Livermore served the Union forces as a nurse during the war. In her autobiography, she recalls how Lincoln's call for volunteers affected life in Boston, where she lived as a young woman: "Flags floated from the roofs of the houses, were flung to the breeze from chambers of commerce and boards of trade, spanned the surging streets, decorated the private parlor, glorified the school-room, festooned the church walls and pulpit, and blossomed everywhere."[10]

Livermore accompanied her father to the door of Faneuil Hall in downtown Boston on Tuesday, 16 April 1861, to receive the gathering volunteers. While there she had an emotional experience focused on the national banner. Although her recollection might have been romanticized by the passage of time between the event and the penning of her memoirs, her story illustrates the new status many Northerners gave to the American flag that spring of 1861.

As the men filed into Faneuil Hall, in solid columns, the enthusiasm knew no bounds. Men, women, and children seethed in a fervid excitement. "God bless it!" uttered my father in tender and devout tone, as he sat beside me in the carriage, leaning heavily forward on his staff with clasped hands. And following the direction of his streaming eyes, and those of the thousands surrounding us, I saw the dear banner of my country, rising higher and higher to the top of the flagstaff, fling out fold after fold to the damp air, and float proudly over the hallowed edifice. Oh, the roar that rang out from ten thousand throats! Old men, with white hair and tearful faces, lifted their hats to the national ensign, and reverently saluted it. Young men greeted it with fierce and wild hurrahs, talking the while in terse Saxon of the traitors of the Confederate States, who had dragged in the dirt this flag of their country, never before dishonored.

I had never seen anything like this before. I had never dreamed that New England, slow to wrath, could be fired with so warlike a spirit. Never before had the national flag signified anything to me. But as I saw it now, kissing the skies, all that it symbolized as representative of government and emblematic of national majesty became clear to my mental vision. . . . It was this holy flag that had been insulted.[11]

That same day the *New York Times* reported that the outburst of patriotism, focusing on the flag, was occurring throughout the North and the West. "Wherever the splendor of the Stars and Stripes, the glittering emblems of our country's glory, meets the eye, come forth shouts of devotion and pledges of aid, which give sure guarantees for the perpetuity of American Freedom."[12] In New York City's harbor, many of the vessels flew all their American flags in support of Lincoln's request. In Albany, crowds gathered on the streets to discuss the war news, and flags were displayed from the armories, hotels, and newspaper offices "as though it was a gala day." Cincinnati and Indianapolis had similar responses; in Baltimore, a militia company known as "The Minute Men" flew a version of the national banner emblazoned with the motto "the Union and the Constitution."[13]

In the smaller town of Troy, New York, on Tuesday evening, 12 April 1861, citizens demonstrated "in favor of the Stars and Stripes," then marched to the home of old General Wool, a respected pillar of the community. He addressed the crowd from his porch, reminding them that he had fought under the Stars and Stripes carried in triumph by Washington and under which Jackson had closed the Second War for Independence at New Orleans. He admonished those gathered: "Will you permit that flag to be desecrated and trampled in the dust by traitors now? . . . My friend, that flag must be lifted up from the dust into which it has been trampled, placed in the proper position and again set floating in triumph to the breeze."[14] Similar rallies and calls for protection of the flag were held in other communities of the free states, and again, what should be noted here is that, in the predictable swelling of patriotism, the American flag clearly dominated as a focal symbol for display, exaltation, and identification of pro-Union sentiment.

In fact, those that did not rush to display it could be suspected of infidelity. After Lincoln's request for volunteers had been received, when the *New York Herald*, a newspaper that suppported the Democratic party, did not immediately display the national flag from its offices, a self-appointed "committee of gentlemen" called on the proprietor and "suggested that if he wished to save his 'institution' from attack" he must fly the Stars and Stripes. An angry crowd began to gather in the street. To placate the crowd, a flag was hung from an upper-story window, and soon after a young boy came running through, bringing a flag attached to a staff, which was promptly hung out a second-story window at the *Herald's* building. There was some grumbling, but the crowd dispersed.[15]

A newspaper office in Philadelphia was not so lucky. There a mob marched on printing offices at Fourth and Chestnut streets, where a secessionist newspaper entitled *The Palmetto Flag* (after the flag of South Carolina) was known to be printed. The mob raised a large American flag across the street, and began throwing bricks and stones at the building. During this assault, the proprietor quickly hung out an American flag, and tossed to the mob copies of *The Stars and Stripes*, a pro-Union paper also published on the same premises. This seemed to appease them, and as the mayor and police took possession of the building, the mob moved down to Third Street, demanding that another newspaper, *The Argus*, display the American flag. In the same city, the next day a mob of a few hundred gathered at the home of Josiah Randall, who brought out an American flag and urged them on against the property of Southern sympathizer William B. Reid. The mayor, with his police force, intercepted them, threatened to shoot anyone who continued rioting, and arrested the ringleaders.[16] In such cases, identification with the flag was not only stressed but demanded to insure the loyalty of major centers of media communication or influential citizens.

In Chicago, on Friday, 19 April, the *Tribune* ran front-page pictures of the "Old Stars and Stripes" and the "Rattlesnake" flag of secession, with the legend beneath them: "Choose Ye This Day, Which You Will Serve." This quote alludes to Joshua's farewell address to the Children of Israel, which he ends by reaffirming his personal commitment to the side of the Lord, although some might follow false idols (Joshua 24:15). Significantly, on the following Saturday and Monday the *Tribune* ran a front-page picture of the "Old Stars and Stripes" there alone. In downtown Chicago, the Wigwam, a well-known local auditorium, was renamed "National Hall," and designated as the center for a "Patriotic Festival" to be held on Saturday, 20 April. The public announcement of the event included this encouragement: "The loyal people are invited to display the national flag during the day from their stores, work-shops, offices and dwellings—to fly it from every steeple, masthead and dome in the city."[17]

The firing on Fort Sumter, although dividing the country, strengthened support for the Unionist cause in the North. Lincoln consulted with his recent political rival Stephen Douglas in preparing the call for volunteers, and Douglas, an influential Democrat, made clear his backing of the president. In Alida, Illinois, the Democrats and Republicans had erected distinct party flagstaffs during the 1860 campaign; when news of the bombardment of Sumter reached them, they cut down the party flagstaffs, "spliced them together," and raised the national banner to the wind on a higher, appropriately named "Unionist" pole.[18]

The schools, a vital center for the socialization of the young into the values and mores of the larger society, also participated in the outburst of patriotic enthusiasm focused on the American flag. On 28 April 1861, in a ceremony that included speeches by local dignitaries, members of Brown High School in Newburyport, Massachusetts, raised an American flag not far from the schoolhouse. On 1 May 1861, in an intermediate school in North Boston, a ten-year-old student brought a small flag forward during morning recess, and the teacher encouraged his classmates, many of them Irish-born, to give three cheers for the flag. And in the afternoon session, to demonstrate their patriotism, many of the boys brought flags from home that they placed over their desks for the rest of the day.[19]

By and large, however, the schools were not yet the important centers for dissemination of flag culture and flag etiquette that they would become later in the century. Although zealous Unionists advocated the flying of flags from all public buildings in response to the attack on Fort Sumter, the public schools did not at this time initiate and endorse this policy throughout the country. Instead, flag ceremonies and demonstrations were quick, emotional responses to the call to arms; however, there is some evidence that the connection between the flag and the schools was strengthened because of the Civil War. At the Ladies' Seminary in Bethlehem, Pennsylvania, on 31 May 1861, the Stars and Stripes were raised over each of the school's three main buildings. To mark the occasion, nearly two hundred students sang "The Star-Spangled Banner," after which they paraded through the town, bearing flags and cheering for the Union.[20] George T. Balch, a New York educator, recalled in 1890 that during the Civil War flags flew on all public schools in the city of New York. He also added, however, that "as time went on and the stirring events of the war passed into history, the exuberance of patriotic ardor became less and less, the flag was more infrequently seen on the schools, until in 1887, but about twenty-five flagstaffs remained on the one hundred and thirty-two public school houses in the city at that date, and most of these were in an unserviceable condition."[21]

The country was much more "flag conscious" as a result of the bombardment of Fort Sumter and Lincoln's call for volunteers. These two events, more than anything else, elevated the national banner to its preeminent position as a symbol of American civil religion, a preeminence it continues to enjoy today. Some might argue that constant use of a sacred symbol diminishes it: for example, during the Civil War years, perhaps as a result of the increased display of flags in places of business, it became a popular practice to use stationery and/or envelopes emblazoned with the American flag or with some other patriotic devices together with the American flag. The samples that remain show the flag as the dominant motif. Those who purchased and used such stationery had patriotic motives—for them, it was no doubt a way of reaffirming their ideological commitments and reinforcing their own political identities. Not surprisingly, a similar industry in the South offered Confederate supporters envelopes emblazoned with the flag of the Confederacy, the Stars and Bars.[22]

As some of the above examples suggest, the elevation of the flag to a higher status increased the popularity of Francis Scott Key's "The Star-Spangled Banner." Other hymns to the flag also appeared as a response to the outbreak of war. On 3 May 1861, as the 69th Regiment of New York celebrated moving their flag from Georgetown into Arlington Heights on the outskirts of Washington, D.C., over one thousand people joined in singing a new song, by John Savage, entitled "The Starry Flag." Harriet Beecher Stowe, noted author of *Uncle Tom's Cabin* (whom Lincoln reportedly greeted with "so this is the little woman who got us into this big war") also wrote a hymn to the flag, sung to the tune of "America," for the solemn raising of the national flag over Andover Seminary. Preble notes that "Our Star-Gemmed Banner," by H.E.T., also captured "the spirit of the times." Especially relevant are the first and last verses—the first for its depiction of the phenomenon of flag display popular in the North, the last for emphasizing the flag's mystical connection to the unfolding plans of Providence:

> God bless our star-gemmed banner,
>   shake its folds out to the breeze,
> From church, from fort, from house-top
>   o'er the city on the seas;

The die is cast, the storm at last
   has broken in its might;
Unfurl the starry banner,
   and may God defend the right!

Then bless our banner, God of hosts!
   watch o'er each starry fold,
'Tis Freedom's standard, tried and proved
   on many a field of old;
And thou, who long hast blessed us,
   now bless us yet again,
And drown our cause with victory,
   and keep our flag from stain.[23]

During the Kensington Riots, George Shiffler became a martyr to the Know-Nothings, as he was willing to give his life to protect the national banner. Now, on a much grander scale, volunteers throughout the Union were coming forward to pledge support of flag and country, and, if need be, offering their lives as sacrifice. Fiery speeches before Northern crowds often played on this theme: a Mr. Westbrook, speaking in New York a few weeks after Lincoln's call to arms, held up a flag, denounced the "traitors" that had disgraced it, and "asked God to record his vow to stand by, protect, and if need be, die for that flag."[24] It was quite natural that the willingness to die for the flag itself became a common theme in the stories and legends of Yankee bravery during the war. This theme was in turn connected to the civil religious faith in a Supreme Being in league with the goals and the aspirations of the Union forces.

As the soldiers went off to battle, they often marched to stirring patriotic tunes. In July 1861, *Harper's Weekly* reported that regiments fording the Potomac at Williamsport held singing contests. When one group caught attention by singing "Red, White, and Blue" ("Columbia, the Gem of the Ocean"), the crossing party that followed launched into "The Star-Spangled Banner," which spread throughout the forces, as soldiers joined in. "The effect was strikingly grand."[25]

The Union soldiers used patriotic tunes not only to set a cadence while they marched but also to entertain themselves at night around the campfire. A songbook for soldiers and sailors published near the end of the Civil War contains a wide assortment of these songs, many of them focusing on tributes to the flag. Some were simple but direct, such as James T. Fields "The Stars and Stripes," which maintained "*Their* flag is but a rag—

Ours is the *true* one; Up with the Stars and Stripes—Down with the new one!" In the tradition of Francis Scott Key, the soldiers often appropriated popular airs and applied new lyrics. "Red, White, and Blue" was transformed to "The Sword, Flag, and Plough"; "Gaudeamus Igitur" became "Our Country and her Flag." Exemplifying such an adaption to honor the flag, on 29 April 1861, D. Bethune Duffield wrote new lyrics for the "Anvil Chorus" from *Travatore* to create the "Flag-Song of the Michigan Volunteers." Whether marching to its rhythmic beat or harmonizing to it around the campfire, Michigan volunteers on their way to future battles must have reflected on the chorus's call to the flag:

> Star-Spangled Banner! our hopes to thee are clinging,
> Lead us to victory, or wrap us in death—
> To thee staunch are we, while yet a breath
> Remains to sing thee:
> Or arms to fling thee,
> O'er this fair land, wide and free.[26]

Soldiers dedicated their lives to the service of the flag, not just on a symbolic level, but in the protection of the physical object, the flag itself. Color-Sergeants carried the national and regimental colors into battle. These piloted the members of their regiments into the fray and served as a guidepost throughout it. It was important that these colors should not fall to the ground, and even more important that they should not fall into enemy hands. Such behavior displays residual traditions, beliefs passed down and transformed from ancient religious practices, when holy men would carry into battle symbolic representations of gods or spirits, known as "proto-vexilloids" to vexillologists. The flag of the United States did not represent the God of the Northern soldiers, but as the following evidence suggests, many of the soldiers did see a strong connection between the will of God and the future of the Union.

In *War Memories of an Army Chaplain*, the Reverend Henry Clay Trumbull of Philadelphia, who served as chaplain of the 10th Connecticut Infantry, maintained it was not uncommon to have two or even four individuals fall while keeping the flag up during a single fight. He spoke affectionately of "the devoted soldier who, catching up the falling colors as they went down again in fight, called out, heroically: 'Here are two minutes more for the old flag!' and dashed ahead into the jaws of death."[27]

Many tributes remain that celebrate the valor of such devoted soldiers, and among them are several examples of homage to soldiers who carried and safeguarded the national flag, especially if the flagbearers died while carrying out this duty.[28] Of the eight corporals making up the color guard of the 99th Pennsylvania under Sergeant Harvey May Munsell at Gettysburg, all but Munsell died in protecting the flag during that engagement. It is interesting to note that the site they defended was the spot from which Lincoln later gave his Gettysburg Address, and in 1886 it was selected as the location for a monument to the war dead of the 99th. One can speculate that the presence of the Stars and Stripes and its defense by Sergeant Munsell's color guard served to hallow the ground and played a role in the later decisions to select the site for the address and the monument; Nicholas Smith, a historian writing about this connection in 1903, emphasized such a correlation.[29]

Such honoring of the dead was an important cultural activity in the United States in the mid-ninteenth century. In fact, the dying words of an individual were taken very seriously. Deathbed conversions and requests were much more common in the literature of the period than they are today, because of different cultural attitudes toward death. And so, it is not surprising that with the elevation of the American flag to new levels of veneration during the Civil War, stories began to spread of dying soldiers reaching out to the flag—for solace, love, and even invigorating strength.

Nicholas Smith reports that the 5th New Hampshire's color guard had a tough time at the Battle of Fredericksburg. Color-Sergeant Reuel G. Austin was wounded, and turned the national flag over to Sergeant George S. Grove, who also was wounded. Sergeant John R. McCrillis stepped in and carried the flag throughout the rest of the engagement—except for one intermission. Captain James B. Perry, wounded and aware that he was dying, could not be removed to the rear because of a flurry of gunfire. Lying on the ground, he told his companions he would die content if he could but see the flag one more time, and when McCrillis received word he brought Perry the flag. According to Smith, Perry died clutching the flag in his hands.[30]

Other recorded examples of soldiers using their last words to glorify the flag testify to the North's sudden passion for the Stars and Stripes, especially as a civil religious symbol that includes a recognition of Divine support for their cause. Edward M. Schneider of the 57th Massachusetts Regiment left Philips Academy in Andover to enlist at the young age of seventeen. He died from a wound received 17 June 1864, but with his dying breath sent this message to his brother serving in the navy: "Stand by the flag, and cling to the cross."[31] In a similar case, Colonel Thorton Brodhead, aware that he was dying, dictated a letter to loved ones: "Two bullets have gone through my chest, and directly through my lungs. I suffer but little now, but at first the pain was acute. I have won the soldier's name, and am ready to meet now, as I must, the soldier's fate. I hope that from heaven I may see the glorious old flag wave again over the undivided Union I have loved so well."[32]

The flag was significant in the demonstrations and parades that supported many of the volunteers as they enlisted in response to Lincoln's call. It was omnipresent in the army camps and on the field of battle. And as some of these soldiers prepared for death, they turned to the symbol that for them now embodied so many of their beliefs and values.

For Union soldiers taken prisoner during the war, the flag could also serve, along with patriotic songs, as a useful symbol in the reaffirmation of their identities as Yankees despite their presence in Southern prisons. For example, in Andersonville, a Confederate prison infamous for its living conditions, whenever news of Union military victories or advances managed to leak in, the prisoners would gather in groups and sing such songs as "Red, White, and Blue" and "The Star-Spangled Banner." Prisoners also made a point of celebrating their traditional Independence Day in whatever way they could. To observe the Fourth of July in Libby prison in 1863, some inmates literally gave the shirts off their backs—contributing a red shirt, white shirt, and blue blouse—for the creation of "an extemporized flag" that their compatriots could honor. And in the stockade in Macon, Georgia, on the same date a year later, the crowd got even more excited. The prisoners gathered around the central structure of the stockade to hear commemorative speeches, but word soon spread that one inmate, Captain Todd of the 8th New Jersey Infantry, had smuggled in a small United States flag when he was imprisoned. The crowd began calling for its display, and took up, in turn, the tunes "The Star-Spangled Banner" and "Rally 'round the Flag." They became so worked up singing and cheering for the flag that the Confederate commandant ordered the artillery manned and the infantry to their guns, while sentencing all inmates to silence in their quarters, before any rioting should commence. In these times of stress the flag was a vital symbol for the prisoners, and the telling of such incidents in the North only further contributed to its importance at home.[33]

Although for the most part it was men who fought for the Union, some women ignored cultural restrictions and participated on the battlefields too. In her account of the war, Mary Livermore mentions one "Michigan Bridget," whose husband was a private in the 1st Michigan Calvary. This remarkable woman not only fought for the North, taking up arms and firing should a nearby soldier fall, but she was also known to rally retreating soldiers and maintain a position, taking up the flag and using it to guide the troops. Livermore's autobiographical memoir includes a contemporary woodcut of "Michigan Bridget" in a pose that owes much to traditional Anglo-American historical painting for stylization. Drawing on the techniques for balancing such a composition that is exemplified in the works of Benjamin West and John Trumbull, the anonymous artist captures a flow of movement, with Michigan Bridget stepping forward with the flowing flag just to the right of center in the tableau. Michigan Bridget's pose in the woodcut also shows a revision of the traditional female war allegory of flagbearer that would become popular across the Atlantic in both French and German memorial sculpture following the Franco-Prussian War in 1870.[34]

Michigan Bridget was, of course, an anomaly. The "woman's sphere" of cultural activity, as it came to be acknowledged in the first half of the nineteenth century, did not include armed combat, but it certainly gave women the moral responsibility for guiding their husbands and children in matters of proper conduct, (especially as the "woman's sphere" was interpreted by such influential figures as Sarah Josepha Hale, editor of *Godey's Ladies' Book* for over fifty years, beginning in 1837). *Godey's Ladies' Book* had a circulation of one hundred fifty thousand by 1858, which was quite formidable for the time, and Hale's editorial policy and perceptions of cultural roles are useful in understanding beliefs and practices of women of her time and class.

Hale subscribed to the notion that the minds of the sexes differed not in strength of intellect, but rather in how that intellect should be awakened and directed. She agreed with many of her contemporaries that women, as guardians of the hearth and home, were innately gifted with a sensitivity to moral and emotional issues and were required to influence husbands and children, through the social institution of the family, to enable all to reach higher plateaus of moral sentiment and enlightened conscience.[35] Thus, when the Civil War came, northern women who subscribed to the popular "cult of domesticity" (which was gradually evolving) had certain obligations, since patriotism is, after all, an emotion. They had to reassure husbands going off to war that they were making the noblest moral commitment (and reassure themselves that they were suffering for the greater good of the nation) and they had to take on the task of instructing the young in the proper expressions of patriotism in time of stress and war. In both of these cases, subsequent to the firing on Fort Sumter, American women became involved with the Stars and Stripes in new and significant ways.

One thing they could certainly do, by drawing on their traditional roles as seamstresses, was to make flags to meet the increased demand created by Lincoln's call for volunteers. Beginning in April 1861, and throughout the war, women who were relatives or friends of soldiers enlisting for military service would join together in groups to produce flags for the men, which were often presented to them in special ceremonies, which usually included tributes to the flag and its symbolism as well as stirring pledges to the Union cause.

Women of New York, for example, responded to the quick call of the 7th Regiment to the defense of the capital in April 1861. They took up subscriptions to produce a large silk flag, on which they worked together to finish, and sent it to their loved ones in Washington. There General Thomas presented it to the regiment, along with a list of the women who had helped to make the banner. It began with the following lines of dedication, which reinforce the civil religious meaning the flag took on during this conflict:

Dedication of a United States Flag
sent by Ladies of New York
to the Seventh Regiment.

The flag of our country, what higher assurance
Of sympathy, honor, and trust could we send?
The crown of our fathers' unflinching endurance,
'Tis the emblem of all you have sworn to defend:
Of freedom and progress, with order combined,
The cause of the *Nation*, of *God*, and *Mankind*.[36]

The same month, in Roxbury, Massachusetts, the women of the city presented a silk flag to the company of men serving under Captain Chamberlain. The Reverend Dr. Putnam of the Unitarian Church delivered a presentation address, after which a little girl in a white outfit (with trim of blue and red) stepped forward to place the flag into Captain Chamberlain's hands. He knelt to receive it reverently, then gave an acceptance speech to those gathered to witness the symbolic transaction.[37]

Such flag ceremonies happened in towns and cities throughout the North that spring, and the practice seems to have become fairly well-established. Although the details of the presentation/ acceptance ceremonies might have varied a bit from place to place, the dynamics remained consistent: participants observed a solemn ritual; patriotic music was regularly involved; women, if they spoke at all, spoke briefly; an official of the military or the clergy, in accepting, would deliver a short speech extolling the historical significance of the American flag, summarizing what it symbolized to those present, and restating the dedication of the fighting men to protect it, both on a specific physical level and on a larger, metaphorical level. In these ceremonies the distinction between the private and the public spheres was clear: it was the women's role to make the flag that served as a constant reminder to the men of their personal patriotic feelings; it was the men's role to accept this offering and vow to cherish and protect it while at war.

Such ceremonies thus helped raise the flag to cult status while also providing an opportunity for women as protectors of the hearth, men as defenders of the homeland, and the community as an integrated unit to demonstrate their commitment to the Union cause. The women of Farmers Valley, a rural hamlet in McKean County in northwestern Pennsylvania, gathered to present a flag to their Home Guard on 19 June 1861. These soldiers would later be mustered into service at Philadelphia as Company H of the 58th Regiment of Pennsylvania volunteers, and participate in several battles, including significant campaigns in Sandy Ridge and Gum Swamp, North Carolina. At the time of the flag presentation, the horror of the war had not yet closely touched the lives of this pioneer stock; the community was caught up in the fervor of the call to arms, and a flag ceremony provided the vehicle for a public demonstration of their values.

Miss L.C. Otto, on behalf of the ladies, offered the flag to the militia, "trusting that the same sentiments which actuated our fathers, whose hands first gave the Stars and Stripes to the breeze, will ever remain the governing principle of your lives." She urged them never to dishonor, disgrace, nor abandon this flag, and called on God to enable them to "become an honor to themselves, their country, and to the Flag we have given them." Captain Asa H. Cory, the leader of the Home Guard, responded. He defined a flag as "a representation of history," and spoke of the Stars and Stripes as "baptized in blood at the birth of our Nation." He recalled as a child hearing his own grandfather tell of his participation in the battle at Lexington, and said that, "in memory of a Washington, a Jackson, and a Taylor" this flag, made and presented by the ladies, would be protected. At the end of his speech, in referring to the national banner, he emphasized it as a symbol of Union: "Our Southern States have discarded this National emblem and insulted and vilified it; yet we trust it will ere long float again over a *united Union*."[38]

One cultural artifact that contains valuable evidence about the special relationship being established between women and the flag at this time is the engraved membership certificate of the Ladies Loyal Union League, the women's branch of a patriotic organization. A series of vignettes by Currier and Ives border the signatures at the center of the certificate, and these drawings reflect the increased significance of the flag in a patriotic woman's life. Two of the vignettes are of battle scenes (one on land, one at sea) and the flag is prominent in both. The four main drawings picture the day-to-day life of a member of the Ladies Loyal Union League. In only one of these drawings is the flag absent, a vignette in which the league member nurses a wounded soldier in a military hospital. In the other three, the flag dominates each picture. While talking with a handsome soldier on the street, the league member gestures at the Star-Spangled Banner flying from a storefront just over their heads. Attending a military parade with other women, she watches Union soldiers walk by carrying flags, as flags fly from buildings up and down the street. And at home, she gathers her children around her to explain to them the meaning of the flag, which hangs from a flagstaff she upholds with her left hand, beckoning the children to her with her right.[39] The message here is clear: the American flag should be seen both in public and at home, and it is a woman's duty to remind men and teach children of its moral significance. The drawings encompass the range of a woman's social interactions: dealing with men, participating in activities with other woman, and caring for children. In any of these social situations, a woman could and should discuss the significance of the flag of the United States.

During the Civil War, popular magazines proved a useful medium for the transmission of patriotic sentiment, and with it, a deeper appreciation of the national flag. In December 1863, *The Atlantic Monthly* published Edward Everett Hale's "The Man Without a Country," which has endured and become a classic, not only

A Civil War view of the recovery ward in Carver General Hospital in Washington, D.C. The thirty-four-star flag closest to the front is a style popular during this period, known as the "Great Flower" pattern. (Photo courtesy of the National Archives.)

because of its literary style but also because of its nationalistic theme. With this work Hale, grandnephew of the Nathan Hale who had but one life to give for his country, also made a significant contribution to the growing collection of stories and legends that embodied the themes stressed in the civil religion of the United States. Many saw Hale's short story as truth, and he later felt the need to explain his fabrication in the *Mississippi Historical Society Publications.*[40]

Hale's story centers on the fate of Philip Nolan, a brash young follower of Aaron Burr who, during his court-martial for treason, blurts out "D——n the United States! I wish I may never hear of the United States again!"[41] The court grants this request, and the story unfolds through details of Nolan's forced life at sea under the guard of the United States Navy. Nolan is allowed to live freely but he is denied any information about the United States for several decades, until a dramatic scene at his deathbed. This denial illustrates how serious such a loss would be, and Nolan participates vicariously in the cult of the flag. He makes his bunkspace into a "shrine": "The stars and stripes were triced up above and around a picture of Washington, and he had painted a majestic eagle, with lightnings blazing from his beak and his foot just clasping the whole globe, which his wings overshadowed." "No matter what happens to you," he warns a young seaman, "no matter who flatters you or who abuses you, never look at another flag, never let a night pass but you pray God to bless that flag." On his deathbed he adds "There cannot be a man who loves the old flag as I do, or prays for it as I do, or hopes for it as I do."[42] Hale intended the story to arouse support for the government in a coming election. It contributed to the cult of the flag that developed in the 1880s and, because of its patriotic theme, entered the canon of acceptable short fiction for the teaching of American youth. It remains a respected selection in this field today.

A review of *Harper's* magazine for the four years preceding the Civil War and the four years during the war reveals the heightened sensitivity to the flag the war generated. Before the war, Fourth of July references and discussions included the flag—if at all—only peripherally. Much more attention was focused on the problem of firecrackers or the reading of the Declaration of Independence.

With the firing on Fort Sumter, however, *Harper's* joined the ranks of those who singled out the national flag as the preeminent civil religious symbol in signifying God's support of the North in this conflict. As the editor pointed out in "Our Flag and What it Symbolizes" in July 1861: "God has given us our guiding law and our moving mind, and he will continue and renew them still. More deeply perhaps than we are conscious, we feel this two-fold gift when we look at the flag of our Union, as we have so often done of late, and our hearts beat quicker, and our eyes fill with tears of joy and hope as we gaze upon its stripes and stars. Those stars speak to us of laws of equity as fixed as the eternal heavens, and those stripes, as they wave in the breeze, tell us of that mysterious breath which moves through men and nations that they may be born, not of the flesh, but of God."[43]

In 1863 *Harper's* included a description of a flag ceremony in which a chaplain presented, on behalf of the ladies of Hascall, Indiana, a flag to the 15th Indiana volunteers. General G.D. Wagner received the flag on behalf of the regiment, and delivered an acceptance speech, while the regiment stood at attention and the entire brigade attended the presentation.[44]

The continued emphasis on the flag as a civil religious symbol to unite the Northern forces throughout the war is neatly illustrated in an anecdote that appeared in *Harper's* in 1864. A four-year-old, blonde Southern girl with all the innocence yet insight of youth was watching a brigade of the Reserve Corps marching through Athens, Alabama, on their way to the aid of General Thomas at Chicamauga. "When she saw the sun glancing through the stripes of red and on the golden stars of the flag [It was customary at this time for the military to use either white or gold stars on their flags], she exclaimed, clapping her hands, 'Oh, pa! pa! God made that flag!—see the stars!'" The child's excitement was picked up by the soldiers, who resolved that "God's flag should conquer."[45] The anecdote was very popular, and was reprinted in *Harper's Weekly*, where the story of her recognition of "the sacred flag" was also retold in poetic verse.[46]

Harper's Weekly, a periodical begun by the successful journal in 1857, included in the same issue a two-page pictorial tribute titled "Our Flag" that, in a manner similar to the Ladies Loyal League certificate, provides useful information for flag usage and emphases at this particular time. [47] The *Harper's Weekly* tribute is perhaps even more significant, for it attempts, in a series of vignettes of varying sizes, to delineate the role of the flag in both military and civilian society in 1864. It would stand to reason that the uses of the flag given in the largest pictures were clearly the most significant, and that those of smaller dimensions portray practices and uses that were considered noteworthy but were not yet as well established or significant as the others.

The vignettes of this pictorial tribute "Our Flag" are presented in four sizes. The largest, central picture emphasizes the flag as a symbol of American values in totality. Entitled "Protector of All Rights," it depicts Lady Liberty bearing the flag into the South. Slaves freed from their chains, awed by her presence, are worshiping her and the banner she carries, while a genuflecting white woman, looking up in adoration, kisses the folds of the banner. On a secondary level, this central picture is balanced by drawings on left and right, which portray the two military services with the flag—one of the army carrying it into battle, the other of a sailor clinging to it aboard a ship. The four corners of the tribute contain four different aspects of the uses of the flag by the military: at the top of the page, the flag accompanies soldiers as they go off to war and as they return; on a more somber note, at the bottom of the page the flag is shown hanging over the bed of one soldier in a military hospital and draped over the casket of another who has died for his country. To fill in space below the main vignette are three smaller drawings that indicate some other uses of the flag in American life. It is shown flying over the tent in a military camp, but it is also presented in non-military uses. In a drawings entitled "At Home," children play at a parade that honors the flag, while "In Church" a large American flag hangs down over a pulpit at which a minister stands, preaching the Gospel.

This final use is one that needs a bit more attention, especially when we consider the significance of the introduction and acceptance of this secular, military symbol into the sacred space of church pulpits and sanctuaries. Such an activity strengthens claims of the flag's increased civil religious authority as a result of the Civil War.

Along with the other trends in new use and renewed respect for the flag, the introduction of the American flag into the churches was spurred by Northern indignation at the attack on Fort Sumter. As part of the patriotic response of Northern civilians to Lincoln's call for volunteers, flags were flown from many church spires in the Northern states. In New York City alone, in the third week of April 1861, there are several accounts of flags being raised over Episcopal, Baptist, Dutch Reformed, and Roman Catholic churches, often to the accompaniment of ceremonial music such as "Yankee Doodle" or "Red, White, and Blue."[48] In some cases the flags were flown out of tower windows, over porticos, or from the roofs of the churches.

This blending of the secular and the religious was, for the most part, unquestioned by aroused patriots. At Grace Episcopal Church on Broadway in Manhattan, the vestry voted to fly a flag from the very top of the church spire, 240 feet above the ground. On 27 April, several persons climbed the stairs to the top of the steeple to accomplish this feat, but became nervous about crawling out onto the roof. Finally two painters, O'Donnel and McLaughlin, carried the flag on a staff and climbed out and up the lightning rod. Securing the flag atop the cross, one of the pair bowed to the assembled crowd below, which let up a cheer.[49] The New York *Commercial Advertiser*, a paper that did not sympathize with the Union cause, provided a lone bit of dissent to the introduction of the American flag above places of worship: "The historian of the day will not fail to mention, for the edification of men of future ages, the fact that the flag, which was once the flag of our Union, floats boldly to the breeze of heaven above the Cross of Christ on Grace Church steeple."[50]

Not only was the American flag physically attached to the symbol of the cross outside churches, but within them, throughout the

North, the flag also entered as a symbol encapsulating belief in Divine guidance of and support for the Union cause. Many sermons preached Sunday, 25 April, dealt with the topic of the war, and in several cases Biblical references were enlisted to legitimate and sanctify the role of the American flag. Examples from the city of New York demonstrate how the introduction of the flag into the church might have been substantiated: "Dr. Bethune took for his text, 'In the name of God we hang out our banners.' Dr. Osgood's text was 'Lift up a standard to the people.' "When the choir in a church pastored by Dr. Bellows sang "The Star-Spangled Banner" the audience applauded, a response a bit out of the ordinary for church etiquette, but then, up until this time, so was the introduction of the American flag. References to the introduction of "The Star-Spangled Banner" into church services occurred in other places as well—it seemed a logical choice for pro-Union services confronting the issue of the war, and it in turn received support from the new emphasis on the flag in civilian life and the intensification of its traditional significance for the military.[51]

Some ministers of the Christian faith took to the cause of war with great relish; indeed, the Southern clergy have been held more responsible than any other group for creating a state of mind in the South that Secession could work and, once the war began, for maintaining and inflating Confederate patriotism. By the spring of 1862, half of them had already joined the military service of the Confederate States of America.[52] Northern ministers were quite influential as well, and as they spoke out on crucial political matters, the symbol of the flag came into the churches. For instance, in Newport, Kentucky, soon after the war began, a Methodist minister known as the Reverend Mr. Black decorated his church with several American flags and brass eagles. He set as hymns for the day "Hail Columbia," "The Red, White, and Blue," and "The Star-Spangled Banner," and preached a sermon that went into graphic detail about the deserved hanging, rotting, and dismembering of Confederate leaders.[53]

It is surprising that church historians, vexillologists, and those concerned with the significance of American civil religion have not done more research on the introduction and diversity of representation and usage of the American flag among the various denominations and religions of the United States.[54] My preliminary investigation suggests that flags were first accepted into church services in response to Sumter and, since then, as war or crises have affected national or regional levels of patriotism, have fluctuated in the regularity of their presence as ornamentation and recognition of the civil government within the sanctuary of "God's house." The usage varies not only over time, but also among the many different denominations and although it departs tangentially from the sociohistorical analysis of the present study, further consideration of this matter could lead to new insights into the complex interrelationships between American church and state and the various social forces that affect them.

The Civil War, however, was clearly a watershed in the developing role of the American flag. And after the war, as the country grappled with continuing industrialization, urbanization, and the social and political ramifications of Reconstruction, that new honoring of the flag provoked by the martial conflict was retained and transformed in certain ways by hereditary and veterans' organizations. Their influence, and the editorial policy of the most widely circulated children's magazine in the country, would be the major forces contributing to the career of the American flag in the second half of the ninteenth century.

5

The Cult of the Flag Develops

Following Lee's surrender to Grant at Appomattox on 9 April 1865, the Union of states (as depicted by the thirty-five stars then on the flag) was nominally restored, although reconciliation proved a long, drawn-out process that in some respects has not yet been completed. The flag came to be included in the fiery rhetoric of Republican politicians, who combined praise of the banner with "waving of the bloody shirt" as, in the decades following the war, they drummed up memories of conflict to humiliate Democratic opponents. Technological changes both in the production of flags and in printing enabled the distribution of flags and flag images on a scale previously unmatched, and the celebration of the centennial of the Declaration of Independence provided an opportunity for citizens to stress progress and reunification using the flag as a positive, ubiquitous symbol. Following that centennial, the career of the flag did not wane. Legends about it developed and spread, while hereditary societies and veterans organizations adopted its hallowed usage into their ideologies and agendas. These groups did much to foster a cult of the flag; as a result, a new concern and respect for the flag can be traced in popular periodicals published for children in the decade before the Spanish-American War.

The Republican party emerged prior to the Civil War from a strong alignment of people with Northern stances on such sectional issues as the future role of slavery and the tariff and, for the most part, it was Republican politicians who waged the war. Therefore, it is not surprising that after the war, to maintain political control, Republican candidates considered it expedient to exploit war issues, keep antagonism alive, and connect the Democratic party to treasonous action or support whenever possible. Constant appeals to the patriotism of Northerners who had fought for the Union could thus be used paradoxically to maintain sectional discord while simultaneously giving bickering Republican factions an area of clear agreement. Seeing such action as detrimental to the public good, some contemporary political analysts labeled this strategy "waving the bloody shirt," but its effective manipulation of slow-dying hatred and distrust proved decisive in Republican victories in the 1860s and 70s.[1]

When Republicans "waved the bloody shirt" they labeled Democrats as unpatriotic threats to the government. In 1870 Senator Zach Chandler of Michigan called the plagues of Egypt down upon such "traitors," and even encouraged women married to Democrats to deny them the pleasures of the marriage bed, so that the party would die out.[2] Oliver Morton, governor of Indiana during the Civil War, summed up Democrats in this fashion in 1866: "Every unregenerate rebel calls himself a Democrat. Every man . . . who murdered Union prisoners . . . who contrived hellish schemes to introduce into Northern cities the wasting pestilence of yellow fever, calls himself a Democrat . . . . In short, the Democratic party may be described as a common sewer and loathsome receptacle, into which is emptied every element of treason North and South, and every element of inhumanity and barbarism which has dishonored the age."[3] Republican politicians worked references to the flag into such orations in two obvious ways: Republican soldiers had fought and died for its glory and honor; Democratic Copperheads had betrayed its trust and symbolism. Robert Ingersoll exemplified the latter strategy in his nominating speech of James G. Blaine at the Republican National Convention in Cincinnati in 1876: "Every man that endeavored to tear the old flag from the heaven that it enriches was a Democrat."[4]

One legacy of the war was that there were more representations of the American flag, and actual flags themselves, to be seen in the United States of the 1870s, to subtly reinforce for Republican voters their commitment to the "party of patriotism." When the Civil War first broke out, the demand for flags outran supplies. In New York City, the price of bunting—the worsted fabric used to make flags—jumped from $4.78 a piece to $20.00, while book-muslin, the material used to make the stars for the canton, went from ten cents to three dollars a yard.[5] Enterprising housewives and other flagmakers turned to substitute materials, while representatives of the business world worked on creating durable, cheaper flags. Technological developments in flag making that occurred as a result of the businessmen's research can best be understood in the historical context of the American bunting industry.

A small home-based bunting industry, created to meet the

needs of the American Revolution, did not long survive the Treaty of Paris, for American flagmakers found it less expensive to import British bunting than to make it in the United States. When it came to purchasing flags for the Army and the Navy, military policy dictated buying from the lowest bidder. American flagmakers purchased British bunting, then competed for sales of finished flags to the different branches of the military. A federal statute of 1856 authorized the president also to "provide at public expense all flags (among other things) he shall think necessary for the several legations, consulates, and commercial agencies in the transaction of their business."[6]

Because of these military and bureaucratic needs, the United States government was an important market for sellers of the national flag and, throughout the nineteenth century, money had been flowing out of the country to English wool merchants for the bunting. Therefore, in 1865 Abraham Lincoln signed a law directing the Secretary of War and the Secretary of the Treasury to buy American manufactured bunting "as their respective services require for a period not exceeding one year, and at a price not exceeding that at which an article of equal quality can be imported."[7]

The establishment of such an early "buy American" law seems an admirable, selfless, and patriotic act on the part of its sponsors, but as Smithsonian textile specialist Grace Rogers Cooper has pointed out, there were certain individuals who foresaw and benefited from the law. A powerful and respected Republican, General Benjamin F. Butler, had already bought an interest in a waterpower site in Lowell, Massachusetts, as well as some nearby manufacturing buildings. In December 1865 he informed Congress that the United States Bunting Company, a partnership he had formed with entrepeneur D.W.C. Farrington, would be happy to supply flags made from American bunting. Apparently Butler and Farrington realized that innovations in combing machines and the currently high tariff on imported British textiles made the launching of an American bunting industry possible. Aided by Lincoln's law and their quick start, they dominated the American bunting industry for several years.[8]

In 1869, working to simplify the process of flag manufacture, Farrington introduced a new method of flag making, "clamp dyeing." Following this procedure, muslin was no longer required to make the stars; their image was created by leaving appropriate sections of cloth color free in the dyeing process. This allowed the

United States Bunting Company to consolidate the two steps of (1) manufacturing the bunting and (2) making the flags from it; clamp dyeing permitted a one-step complete manufacture of the flags themselves. Although this process received much praise at the Philadelphia Centennial Exhibition, continued innovations in the sewing machine made machine stitching of flags, first begun in the United States in the 1850s, increasingly popular in the 1870s and 80s, and the dominant method of flag making by 1894.[9]

Along with a home bunting industry, a silk flag industry based in the United States also developed after the war.[10] Silk flags were more expensive than cotton and muslin flags, but other, cheaper alternatives also existed. Especially popular in the latter category, small printed muslin and silk paper flags were mass produced in the years following the war. Although fragile and easily destroyed, those few that remain reveal the widespread and casual use of the flag for advertising purposes in this period. As a mark of civic responsibility, merchants often purchased flags to give to children, who would presumably develop a sense of patriotism by playing with them.[11] The merchants paid to have advertisements for their businesses imprinted on the flags themselves, generally on the white stripes. One small silk paper flag of this sort includes the following instructions on the extra wide margin on the hoist side of the flag: "Put this on a stick for the children." The white stripes are imprinted, from top to bottom, with the lines shown in figure 1.[12]

Ithaca Sign Works of Ithaca, New York, made another flaglet of this type. Its white stripes were imprinted with the advertisement shown in figure 2.[13]

During the Civil War patriotic Yankee mothers encouraged their daughters to make small homemade flags for play or gifts. The professional manufacture of such miniature flags received a real boost in the decades following the war from the heightened patriotic interest created by the decision to celebrate the Centennial of 1776 in conjunction with the first World's Fair in the United States, an exhibition to be held in Philadelphia. Flag souvenirs record the historic event, again, with data imprinted on the stripes. Flag-related merchandising developed to serve a public eager to celebrate one hundred years of growth, putting aside more recent memories of fraternal bloodshed and strife. Even in small towns in Oregon, a long way from Philadelphia in 1876, merchants were pushing "star-spangled stockings" as a must for

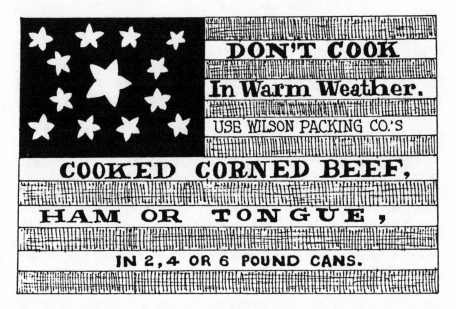

Fig. 1

"patriotic ladies."[14] At the Exhibition itself, souvenir Stars and Stripes fans were popular items that also proved useful in the heat of a Philadelphia summer.[15]

Although 1876 was the year of one of the most controversial presidential elections in our nation's history, and the compromise that put Rutherford B. Hayes in the White House a matter of complex deals and political maneuverings, the nation reflected a positive mood at the Centennial Exhibition, that of "a young, expansive, energetic and extremely confident country."[16] More than nine million visitors passed through the exhibition gates from opening day on 10 May 1876 to closing on 9 November 1876. The largest crowds, however, did not gather to see mechanical innovations, foreign cultural contributions, or even the freak show just outside the main gate, although all were popular exhibits. Rather, the most popular exhibit was a display of the camp equipment that George Washington had used on his campaigns,[17] which suggests the sense of national heritage the celebration of the Centennial inspired, as well as the continuing popularity of the first president as the most eminent hero in the nation's patriotic tales and legends.

Although it did not draw the crowds that Washington's equipment did, a prominent display highlighting the history of the flag of the United States also received attention at the Centennial. J.C.

Julius Langbein, a gentleman scholar who attended the celebration, noted that "in the east end of the main building at the Centennial Exposition in Philadelphia is a design of the progressive manner in which our National Flag was evolved out of the multitude of heraldic suggestions furnished by the American Colonies."[18] Exposition officials also displayed the Stars and Stripes elsewhere at park festivities—the main entrance of the main building, for instance, flew four eleven by eighteen-foot national ensigns. Flag designs also turned up on commemorative quilts, tablecovers, and bandannas made for the celebration.[19]

Just as political candidates would have their names and pictures printed directly on campaign flags in the nineteenth century, so too, to mark the Centennial, promoters imprinted flag banners of silk or cotton with inscriptions advertising the Philadelphia Exhibition or with the image of George Washington surrounded by the words "Centennial 1776–1876."[20] Variations in the arrangement of stars on the field of blue still flourished in this period, and some flagmakers became quite creative in their preparation of special Centennial banners. One, for example, maintained the standard thirteen stripes of red and white, but used seventy-six stars to spell out, in two rows on the canton, "1776/1876." Colorado had joined the Union in 1876, and although its star was not supposed to appear officially on the canton until 4 July 1877 (in keeping with the federal enactment of 1818), this centennial flag-

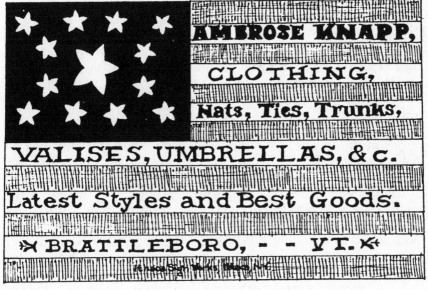

Fig. 2

maker took the liberty of including it early, so that each of the thirty-eight states was represented twice, once in the "1776" and once in the "1876," to achieve the symbolic total of seventy-six stars.[21]

The high point of the centennial year was, of course, the Fourth of July. In New York City, public buildings, businesses, churches, and homes were all "profusely decorated with flags, streamers, and buntings." Small towns organized ceremonies that might include flag raisings at sunrise and lowerings at sunset, the singing of "The Star-Spangled Banner," and patriotic oratory. In the small town of Scio, Oregon, J. Bryant led a committee on flag decorations, while Ira Taylor toasted the flag at a community dinner. In even smaller Sweet Home, Oregon (population twenty-five), residents discovered too late that they had failed to procure an American flag for their observation of the Fourth—so they made one from Centennial stockings that some of the girls had succumbed to purchasing.[22]

Although Philadelphia's Fourth of July celebration was grander than Sweet Home's, it evidenced the same dedication to the national banner. A gala parade began at 8:30 on the eve of the holiday, working its way through the streets of the city so that the head of the procession reached Independence Square at midnight. One scholar, William Pierce Randel, estimates that two hundred fifty thousand tourists joined native Philadelphians for this event. At midnight, after a pause of solemn silence, the new Liberty Bell made its debut, ringing thirteen times. The crowd then shot off guns, blew whistles, and created a raucous din as if it were New Year's Eve. In Independence Square, an orchestra and chorus struck up "The Star-Spangled Banner" followed by the Doxology.[23] Here, as elsewhere in the United States on the Centennial Fourth, Americans combined praise of the flag with praise of God.

In honor of the national celebration, thirty-nine upper-grade pupils in the Irving School in Des Moines, Iowa, students of Lou Wilson, created *1876: A Centennial Offering*, a collection of original stories, essays, poems, and illustrations "dedicated to the memory of the boys and girls of 1776" with a preface that requested the manuscript be sealed up, preserved, and shared in the future with "the boys and girls of 1976."[24] Included among essays on Henry Wadsworth Longfellow, Edgar Allen Poe, Sir Walter Scott, far-off lands, and Anglo-American history, is a piece by Nellie C. Saylor entitled "Stars and Stripes."

Saylor gives a straightforward explanation of the evolution of the Grand Union flag to the flag described in the Resolution of 1777, then modified by Congress in 1818. She quotes the federal legislation, and attributes the blue canton to the Scottish "Covenant" flag, no doubt consulting history texts that were then available. Although, as has been discussed in chapter 2, all early flags certainly did not have the stars arranged in a circle, Saylor accepts this detail as fact: "The stars were then disposed of in a circle, showing the perpetuity of the Union, the circle being the sign of eternity." The recent Civil War no doubt led to this symbolic emphasis on union, but another factor must be considered in trying to understand why Saylor accepted the thirteen-stars-in-a-circle variant as the only version of the first flag. Archibald M. Willard painted the famous painting *The Spirit of '76* in 1875 in preparation for the coming centennial. In this well-known work of art, an elderly drummer is accompanied by a drummer and a fife player, as they march before a Continental army flagbearer, who carries a flag matching Saylor's description. As noted earlier, for reasons of design, balance, and perhaps ignorance, nineteenth-century painters of eighteenth-century events had not always been scrupulous in their attention to historical accuracy where flags were concerned. Willard's painting achieved rapid popularity; advancements in lithography and printing enabled hundreds of thousands of copies of the work to be distributed throughout the country even before the actual painting went on display at the Centennial Exposition. In fact, the Exposition officials asked Williard if they could display the painting because it met the needs of a public that had become fascinated with its heritage during the promotion of the centennial observance.[25] It would not be extreme to suppose Saylor had seen copies of this print—perhaps even in the classroom, for the image certainly became a popular choice for decorating school walls, and has remained so to the present.

Saylor prefigures a sense of the nationalism to come at the end of the century with her statement "It [the flag of the United States] is found in every land, and on every sea, where the foot of man has been. And there is no nation who dares to offer it insult. The haughtiest sovereigns dare not refuse to salute its free folds as it passes by their strongholds of power." Before concluding her essay with the final stanza of Drake's "The American Flag" (which, it will be remembered, was reprinted in a McGuffey's Reader after the Civil War), Saylor took the time to question why she and her contemporaries loved the flag of the United States. She decided "Because it represents the government and institutions of our

Designed and distributed to celebrate the American Centennial, copies of Archibald M. Willard's *The Spirit of '76* reinforced beliefs in the thirteen-stars-in-a-circle variant as the common first flag, although historical evidence suggests many motifs for star arrangement were in use. (Photo courtesy of the National Archives.)

country . . . Under it God has enlarged and prospered our nation as never nation was before."

For Saylor, as for many of her generation and since, a connection between God and her country was one of the meanings symbolized by the flag. The idea of a benevolent God building a brighter earthly future for America would continue to be a significant aspect of the complex patriotic ideology held by citizens of the United States. The endurance of this particular belief can be contrasted with shifts in other cultural attitudes. For instance, the illustration following Saylor's essay which harkens back to an antebellum emphasis in children's literature on the transience of all human existence,[26] is a morbid drawing of Death, with the caption "There is a reaper and his name is death." These children were receiving and creating a variety of cultural messages, and although the drawing of Death would not mean the same thing to the intended young readers of 1976 as it did to its creators, much of the praise heaped upon the flag would sound familiar and correct.

The centennial of the Flag Resolution, 14 June 1877, did not draw the kind of attention that the 1876 celebration did, yet the flag had become significant enough to deserve special recognition on this occasion. The federal government requested that the flag be flown from all public buildings on June 14th in observance of this centennial.[27] The city of Boston held the most elaborate celebration of the day. The flag flew from public and private buildings and from ships in the harbor. At noon patriots gathered to fire a special military salute on Boston Common, and that evening Old South Meeting House was packed to hear patriotic oratory and to see the Star Spangled Banner that had actually flown over Fort McHenry. Julia Houston West sang the familiar anthem to that flag, with the audience joining in on the chorus.[28] Although it did not yet have the name, the first "Flag Day" had been observed. In the following decades, as patriotic ritual intensified, the event would become a national holiday, officially recognized by Congress in 1949.

The reawakened respect for the flag, inspired by the historic celebrations, lingered after the centennial passed. In 1879 Benjamin Foltz of Rockford, Illinois, privately published a small pamphlet of two poems on the glory of the flag. Inscribed to the Hutchinson family, this pamphlet approaches the flag from two perspectives: "The Banner We Love" describes the emblem's majesty and lasting significance, while "The Old Flag Insulted" warns those who would desecrate it that retribution awaits.[29] As the nineteenth century drew to a close, patriotic citizens and organizations moved beyond the simple institution of more flag rituals to lobby for legislation to punish those guilty of flag desecration.

Certain flag historians, motivated by zealous patriotism, but unfortunately lacking precise sources, disseminated some unsubstantiated information about the American flag that became accepted as fact in the years following the centennial. Although their dates of origin varied, one going back to the year the Civil War began, all three legends gained popular acceptance during the centennial period, and each, although unsupported by sufficient historical data, met certain needs of the public. First was the claim that the design of the flag came from Washington's coat of arms, second, the story that the flag of the *Bonhomme Richard* (believed by some to have been the first Stars and Stripes) had been rescued and passed down in the Stafford family, and third, the story that Betsy Ross designed and created the first Stars and Stripes at the personal request of George Washington.[30]

The significance of the figure of George Washington in the collection of symbols and values that Americans drew upon in patriotic references had been slightly overshadowed by the new degree of emphasis on the national flag as a result of the Civil War. The celebration of the centennial, as has been earlier demonstrated, provided an impetus for a resurgence of interest in and references to "the Father of our Country." Connecting Washington to the origin of the flag had a combined effect of glorifying both symbols.

English playwright Martin Farquhar Tupper made the connection popular in his centennial drama *Washington*. In this play, written in anticipation of the 1876 festivities, the character of Benjamin Franklin, referring to Washington's family coat-of-arms, says, "the leader's old crusading blazon . . . multiplied and magnified . . . in every way to this,/Our glorious national banner."[31] In *St. Nicholas*, the best loved and most fondly remembered children's magazine of the second half of the nineteenth century, editor Mary Mapes Dodge also granted the coat-of-arms myth credibility. With a circulation fairly constant around seventy thousand copies per issue,[32] her magazine reached many school children, and she regularly invoked the image and legends of Washington to instill patriotism. In 1882, *St. Nicholas* published an article by Edward W. Tuffley entitled "Origin of the Stars and Stripes" that credited Washington with the decision to transfer the design of his coat of arms to a banner for the new nation. This same piece also gave some credence to the Betsy Ross legend, for

Washington makes this decision in a back room of a Philadelphia upholsterer named Ross. Emphasis in this article, however, is clearly on Washington as national patriarch, and Tuffley indicates the flag should be especially honored as a symbol because Washington was responsible for it.[33]

Earlier, in 1861, in Trenton, New Jersey, upon the death of her mother, an elderly spinster name Sarah Smith Stafford came forward and claimed that her father, James Bayard Stafford, had been the sailor who rescued the American flag from the sinking *Bonhomme Richard* in its Revolutionary War battle with the *Serapis*. When the flag had been shot down, her father had jumped into the ocean, grabbed it, and then swam back to the ship, where a British officer cut him down. James Stafford survived, however, and another sailor delivered the flag to John Paul Jones, who transferred it to the *Serapis* when his men successfully captured the British vessel. Miss Stafford had in her possession a handwritten note—dated 13 December 1784—from a "Secretary Pro-tem James Meyler" awarding her father this flag in recognition of his brave service.

Later scholars have proven that the flag of the *Bonhomme Richard* was lost during the battle, as mentioned by John Paul Jones in his own recollection of the incident, and that the "Meyler" letter was probably a fabrication. Other inconsistencies and the basis of the story on family tradition indicate the Stafford flag is inauthentic.[34] Although the authentic *Bonhomme Richard* flag went down with the ship, Stafford's announcement came in the year of the attack on Fort Sumter, and organizers used her flag to draw crowds at Sanitary Fairs in New York and Philadelphia and at the Trenton Fair of 1862. When the Civil War first broke out, she sent a small piece of the flag to Abraham Lincoln, for inspiration.[35] Such an action was no doubt motivated by patriotism, but it also must have given her a sense of pride, importance, and power.

This "*Bonhomme Richard* flag" also drew crowds at the Centennial Exhibition in Philadelphia. Upon Stafford's death in 1880, she willed it to her brother, Samuel Bayard Stafford, of Lanham, Maryland. He was an invalid, but his wife, who resided in Cottage City, Massachusetts, took charge of the banner. Never allowing it out of her sight, Samuel Stafford's wife carried this to a national encampment of the Grand Army of the Republic in 1887 under the escort of the Malden (Massachusetts) Grand Army of the Republic post. There, Civil War veterans honored it as "the first Stars and Stripes ever made."[36] On behalf of the United States, President McKinley accepted the flag from the Stafford family,

The Stafford flag, purported for years to be the battle flag flown from John Paul Jones's ship the *Bonhomme Richard*, drew large crowds at Sanitary Fairs during the Civil War and later at national encampments of the Grand Army of the Republic. Until the 1930s, it was hallowed in the Smithsonian Institution. (Photo courtesy of the Library of Congress.)

and for many years it was hallowed in the Smithsonian. Although historian Theodore Belote endorsed this flag as that of John Paul Jones, suspicions grew, and in the 1930s the Smithsonian called in a panel of experts, headed by Professor Charles Callon Tansill of Georgetown University, who assessed the evidence and deemed the Stafford flag fraudulent.[37] Subsequently, curators withdrew the flag from public display, but for several decades American citizens had honored it and considered it a relic that helped tie them to their historic past.

The third of the flag legends that were prominent during and following the centennial was the strongest and most enduring. Indeed, it persists today, with a tenacious following even among the members of the North American Vexillological Association, a group nominally committed to historical accuracy in flag scholarship. The legend that Betsy Ross, a diligent and quick-thinking Philadelphia seamstress, made the first American flag at the personal request of General Washington, took hold first in Pennsylvania but spread throughout the United States in the final quarter of the nineteenth century. It not only served to glorify the emerging cult of the flag, it provided educators the opportunity to introduce an active female character into the pantheon of political heroes. Here was a productive woman whom young girls could emulate, a woman who demonstrated that knowledge of domestic skills served an important need in the American social order, and although she was only a simple seamstress, the legend showed that her practical and efficient nature motivated her to replace the six-pointed with the less cumbersome five-pointed star.

Certainly the woman known as Betsy Ross existed. Moreover, it is true that she made naval flags for the state of Pennsylvania. The details of her legendary role in the creation of the first "Stars and Stripes," however, come from a paper delivered by her grandson William J. Canby before the Historical Society of Pennsylvania in 1870. Canby claimed a congressional committee headed by Washington called upon Ross in Philadelphia in 1776, requesting her to make the new flag. His information was based on a conversation he had held with her twenty-one years earlier, when she was an old woman of eighty-four and he was a lad of eleven. After Canby delivered the paper, he secured affidavits from some of his aunts that supported his story and added more details, such as Betsy's contribution of the five-pointed star to the design of the flag.[38]

The veracity of the story went unquestioned for many years, and generations of school children grew up learning the legend of Betsy Ross as history in patriotic textbooks, poems, and plays.[39]

Indeed, they still learn it, although many Americans now rightly consider the story a harmless fabrication. As Jane Mayer points out in her 1952 historical novel for juveniles on Betsy Ross, Betsy "might" have made the first flag, and the important thing is that "someone" did.[40] A 1960 Rand McNally Giant Book presents the legend as history, with this small disclaimer on the inside front cover: "The charming story of Betsy Ross has grown to be an American tradition. Since it is not definitely known by whom the first flag was made it could have come about in this way."[41]

Why has the legend been disputed? No evidence remains of the flag committee Canby describes, nor is there any proof that Washington knew Ross, nor that Congress adopted any flag before 14 June 1777. Of twenty-two scholarly studies that had been done on this issue by 1965, fifteen rejected the Betsy Ross legend, five left it unproven, and two found it believable.[42]

The argument of the faithful continues to be "as long as you cannot prove she didn't make the first flag, I intend to believe she did." This can be seen, in part, as the effective and successful socialization of the young into a belief in the legend of Betsy Ross. Although the *St. Nicholas* magazine article cited earlier credited Washington for designing the first flag, in the same children's magazine, barely ten years later, two more articles appeared that demonstrate the rise in popularity of the Betsy Ross legend in the late 1880s and early 1890s, and with it, a sharpening sensitivity on the part of the writers and editors to encourage a patriotic commitment to the flag by the young readers.

In 1892, in "The Five-Pointed Star," Charles F. Jenkins explained Betsy's supposed role in modifying the type of star used on the national banner. In 1893, in "The Stars and Stripes," Henry Russell Wray went even further. The flag had become "America's dearest emblem," "the sacred national emblem." Betsy, its creator, was "the finest needleworker in America." She came from "good colonial stock," and Wray took time to describe her Philadelphia home, reputedly built by William Penn himself.[43]

That home was destined to become a shrine. Amid the patriotic fervor aroused by the Chicago World's Columbian Exposition of 1893, C.H. Weisgerber painted a romanticized portrait of Betsy Ross sewing the first Stars and Stripes, which was exhibited for the first time at the Exposition. It depicts the imaginary meeting of Ross and the congressional committee, and Weisgerber created her idealized likeness based on a composite of pictures of some of her female descendants. He also followed Willard's lead in showing the stars in a circle. The work, entitled "The Birth of Our

Nation's Flag," became famous just as Willard's "The Spirit of '76" had, and prints of it were mass distributed throughout the United States at a cost affordable to most citizens. Inspired by the popularity of the painting, Weisgerber started a movement, the American Flag House and Betsy Ross Memorial ·Association, incorporated in 1898, dedicated to purchasing her home and restoring it for historic and patriotic interest. For a subscription of ten cents, members received "a lithographed certificate of membership in the organization that included a picture of the house of Betsy Ross, her grave in Mount Moriah cemetery in Philadelphia, and a color reproduction of the Weisgerber painting." Over one million copies of the Weisgerber painting were distributed through this subscription drive alone. The legend spread, and with it the design of the "Betsy Ross flag," which subsequently became the standard representation of the first flag in twentieth-century American history textbooks.[44]

These legends became part of the growing body of practices and beliefs associated with the flag of the United States. Its symbolic connection with a Divine plan for the future of the Union had been reiterated by writers of the Civil War period, its ties to a shared historical heritage emphasized during the centennial celebrations. In the closing decades of the nineteenth century, certain groups and individuals believed the national banner to be a useful symbol in conveying to young people proper respect for government and traditional social institutions. Children were to learn early to associate the flag with the republic and with the history of that republic as interpreted by those stressing this symbolic association. Twentieth-century historians, such as Wallace Evan Davies and John Higham, have labeled this focus on the Stars and Stripes "the cult of the flag." This cult emerged in the 1880s, gained strength throughout the 1890s, and was securely entrenched by the turn of the century.[45] Before examining how the influence of the cult caused shifts in the way the American flag was presented in children's magazines in this period, it would prove advantageous to briefly consider the background and motivation of the groups that became most influential in bringing about a heightened appreciation of the flag: the veterans' organizations and the hereditary societies.

Both groups had precursors in the decade prior to the Civil War, the War of 1812 Veterans and the Mount Vernon Ladies Association. Neither group was very large by postwar standards. The Mount Vernon Ladies Association, founded in 1856 after South Carolinian Ann Pamela Cunningham appealed "to the ladies of the South" to raise the two hundred thousand dollars necessary to purchase George Washington's home, drew the support of many prominent social matrons, and before the advent of the Civil War, had branches in twenty-nine states in the North and the South. Aided by Edward Everett and the Masonic Order, the women managed to raise the funds and secure the property to establish it as a patriotic shrine.[46] This first major accomplishment by a women's patriotic and historic society is also noteworthy in that it focused on "the Father of our Country."

In the fifteen years following Lee's surrender at Appomattox, it was the veterans' organizations rather than the hereditary societies that grew rapidly. Groups such as the Society of the Army of the Tennessee, the Society of the Army of the Cumberland, and the Society of the Army of the Potomac drew up charters in the five years following the Civil War. The most prominent, however, came to be the Grand Army of the Republic, the G.A.R. This organization expanded its membership in the late 1860s, declined some in the early 1870s, and then experienced a spurt of growth in the 1880s. Its membership peaked in 1890 with over four hundred and nine thousand registered members.[47]

The tradition of the G.A.R. maintained that Benjamin Franklin Stephenson founded the organization in the spring of 1866 in Springfield, Illinois. A druggist and doctor, Stephenson was disgruntled with the treatment of war veterans, and believed that if they organized they could more effectively lobby for pensions. A scholar researching the G.A.R., Mary R. Dearing, has shown this to be another example of a romanticizing of history; she argues persuasively that Illinois Governor Richard J. Oglesby and his associate General John A. Logan masterminded the formation of the G.A.R., hoping to use it to wield political influence and obtain a Senate seat for Logan.[48]

Although the organization was subject to political manipulation on the state and local level, it did come to serve as a recognized outlet for the veterans' views, and the national encampments—annual conventions—became particularly effective occasions to spread the cult of the flag. The New York department of the G.A.R. caught the national organization's attention when, in January 1889, it proposed a state law requiring flags on all schools. The G.A.R. became directly involved with flag presentations in this manner: DeWitt C. Ward, a New York school trustee, had purchased American flags and publically presented them in formal assemblies at "perhaps half a dozen schools" in the city of New York. Charles F. Homer, a G.A.R. member, attended one such ceremony and was impressed by its effect of "inculcating a spirit of patriotism" among the immigrant children in the audience. He told his Lafayette Post brothers about the experience, and convinced them on 4 May 1888 to pass a resolution to adopt the practice and present an American flag to the City College of New York. This was done with great ceremony 8 June 1888. "Let this dear old Flag be more sacred in your eyes, more entitled to your homage, more dear to your hearts," said Lafayette Post Commander Floyd Clarkson to the college students—many of them immigrants or children of immigrants—when he presented the flag. The Reverend Dr. John R. Paxton, a veteran of Gettysburg and Petersburg, added: "whatever nation you belong to by birth, whatever tongue your mother taught you, whatever your color or your race, no matter, there is only one flag . . . Now let us come and gather under its blessed folds. Let us be tangled in the stars and covered with the stripes." City College President Alexander G. Webb was caught up in the patriotism of the experience, too, and subsequently joined the Lafayette Post.[49]

This flag presentation received favorable press coverage, and inspired members of the George H. Thomas G.A.R. Post in Rochester, New York, to plan a flag extravaganza for the following Washington's Birthday, during which, amid pomp, oratory, and songs such as "Red, White, and Blue," "Flag of the Free," and the obligatory "The Star-Spangled Banner," the G.A.R. bestowed flags on every public school in the city.[50] Other posts followed suit. In August 1889 the national encampment voted that "posts should present the emblem to every public school that did not have one." In 1892, G.A.R. Commander-in-Chief William Warner re-emphasized the practice: "Let the 8,000,000 boys and girls in our elementary schools be thus imbued with a reverence for the flag and all it represents. Then the future of the Republic is assured, and that flag shall forever wave." During the 1890s, twenty-six of the state and territorial encampments of the G.A.R. eventually passed similar resolutions, but they usually requested the government to purchase the flags, rather than actually offering to pay the cost themselves.[51]

Should any educators or school boards find the presence of a flag on school grounds objectionable, the G.A.R. members were prepared to exert pressure. In one documented case in 1892, William Thompson and John Luckett, school directors in Franklin, Illinois, forbade schoolmistress Minnie Blough to place a flag in front of the schoolhouse where she taught. Chicago and Rockford G.A.R. members grew angry when they learned of this, and a rumor spread that one of the directors was an unnaturalized immigrant, the other a draft dodger who had fled to Canada during the Civil War. The veterans warned that if the flag were not raised over that school "there would be trouble"; they purchased a flag and planned an elaborate flag-raising ceremony. "I don't know of any penalty attached to raising an American flag over an American schoolhouse," said a member of the contingent, "and I guess the G.A.R. has as good a right [as] anyone to assist therein." The veterans marched together into the town only to discover the directors, alarmed by the response their decision had provoked, had installed their own sixty-foot flagpole complete with flag in the schoolyard the previous day. They also flew another flag on a ten-foot pole from the peak of the schoolhouse, and to make certain no angry veterans should become violent, Thompson raised a flag pole in the front yard of his home and flew the Stars and Stripes there as well. The G.A.R. contingent, which had drawn a crowd of three hundred, claimed victory and went ahead with their flag raising ceremony, moving it to the yard of William Van Wert, across the street from the school. Still more flags were flown from a nearby windmill and a nearby Methodist church during the ceremony, which included speeches on the veterans' patriotic commitment, a reading of "Barbara Fritchie," a short lecture on the history of the flag, and the closing hymn "America."[52]

Although they supported the introduction of the flag into the public schools, members of the G.A.R. also lobbied to introduce it into churches, emphasizing the national banner as a mystical symbol of the connection between Providence and the future of the United States. At a soldier's reunion in Iowa in 1887, Colonel Hepburn called for teaching children more respect for the flag, since "it is to our institutions what the cross is to the Christian religion." George W. Gue, pastor of the First Methodist Church of Rock Island, Illinois, and Chaplain of the Department of Illinois G.A.R. for 1889, convinced the Central Illinois Conference of the Methodist Episcopal Church to pass the following resolution on 30 September 1889: "Resolved, that we, as a conference, do recommend that the American flag be placed in our churches and Sunday-schools as an emblem of our Christian civilization."[53]

In 1890 Gue published *Our Country's Flag*, a large collection of poems, pictures, and patriotic quotes celebrating the Stars and Stripes as a sacred symbol. One illustration, entitled "Our Country's Flag Over Every Schoolhouse and Church," shows a large Stars and Stripes atop an imposing three-story school building and another flying from the spire of a Gothic church. Especially for the volume, Gue convinced J. C. O. Redington to write a poem entitled "The Flag O'er Our School-House Is Floating." This poem, one of the earliest tributes to the flag in the public schools, interpreted the flag flying over the school as a symbol of the sacrifice of Union soldiers during the Civil War, and the flag within the classroom as a cheerful reminder that "rests aching heads." Another poem in this collection, "Our Country's Flag on God's Sacred Altars," by J. W. Temple, called for a blending of religion and patriotism by introducing the national banner into churches. Such a triumph for civil religion would, according to Temple, bring "Christ's kingdom" to Earth.[54]

The veterans' patriotism and their efforts to lobby on behalf of the flag can be understood by the devotion to the Stars and Stripes they developed during their service in the military. The hereditary organizations, however, were composed of descendants of early settlers or soldiers. As Davies has pointed out, many of the members of these hereditary organizations came from families whose statuses or holdings were being threatened by the rapid changes of urbanizing, industrializing America. As part of an established component of the social order, these well-meaning citizens looked with some apprehension at the rising immigration from central and southern Europe, for here was a population unfamiliar with the liberties and responsibilities of the Anglo-American civic tradition. To the hereditary organizations, both the foreign-born and the young needed to be trained in what the members considered to be proper American behavior. One can speculate that unsettling events such as the spread of Populism, the Homestead Strike, or the financial Panic of 1893 inspired many to seek some solace in groups emphasizing a reverence for the contributions and accomplishments of their ancestors, and with that, a reaffirmation of their own place in society.

This intense interest in ancestral activities first received serious attention during the centennial. In 1876 a New York merchant and gentleman historian, John Austin Stevens, unsuccessfully tried to organize on a grand scale male descendants of Revolutionary War veterans. He did achieve this goal seven years later, during celebrations of the centennial of the Constitution. This group, the Sons of the Revolution, soon suffered from "schismatic differentiation," and in 1889 William O. McDowell organized a splinter group, the Sons of the American Revolution (s.a.r.), which, he felt, would move beyond holding social functions to make significant contributions to patriotism.[55] The concept spread quickly, and several auxiliaries or similarly hereditarily based groups soon organized, most notably the Colonial Dames of America (1890), the Daughters of the American Revolution (1890), the U.S. Daughters of 1812 (1891), and the Society of Mayflower Descendants (1894).

McDowell's commitment to organized patriotism was extraordinary. He was instrumental in the formation of the Daughters of the American Revolution (D.A.R.) and worked unceasingly to develop new patriotic displays. He raised funds and by 1893 had erected a Liberty Flagpole at the Navesink Highlands in New Jersey so that the first thing sighted by those aboard an ocean vessel heading into New York would be an American flag. His efforts to raise similar Liberty Flagpoles in other countries failed, but his project to create a replica of the Liberty Bell to tour the United States in 1893 (in conjunction with the Columbian World's Fair festivities in Chicago) proved popular and successful. "I believe it to be every citizen's duty to give some part of each day to patriotic work," he wrote a friend in 1889. Beyond this, he felt God had selected and guided him to encourage American patriotism. He claimed that his decisions came "so clearly from a controlling Power more than human, and the dividing line, where the Divine directing control ended and the human part came in, to me has been so indeterminable that I am slow to use the word 'mistake' for fear I might be judging that which no human mind can judge."[56]

The 1880s had witnessed the growth of the women's club movement in America, as industrial and domestic changes gave middle-class women an opportunity for a new type of bonding outside the home. Certainly the women's hereditary societies offered their members a chance to converse, to feel part of a select group, and to socialize—but the members also made an oft-repeated commitment to spread patriotic respect for the United States of America.

The D.A.R. eventually emerged as the most influential of these societies. In 1895, at a Minnesota State Conference held at the Central Presbyterian Church in St. Paul, Bishop Gilbert, playing host to the ladies, reminded them of their responsibilities: "This is an era of patriotic societies. What does it mean? Not a fad that will last but for a brief time, but the development and culmination of a spirit that has been growing for many years, and it was inevitable that the outburst should occur. This declaration of universal hospitality that we have sent out, and which has brought all men to our shores, is a good thing. We do not want people to be prevented from coming, but we ought to place certain restrictions upon those who come. America for the Americans, and whoever enters the country must become an American."[57]

That same year Mrs. James B. Clark, State Regent of Texas, explained the aim of the D.A.R. in this manner: "The perpetuity of our Government, the safety of our institutions, depend upon the sentiment with which they are regarded by the majority of our citizens and the fidelity with which the principles are cherished upon which our liberties are based. And here is our mission: to cultivate this sentiment, to illustrate this fidelity." She called upon the club members to concentrate their influences "upon the foreign element in our midst. . . . How indoctrinate them with the political truth which makes us free indeed? . . . Very commendable efforts in this direction have already been made by the placing of Washington's portrait in the city schools of several cities, by the display of the national flag on school buildings, and the singing of patriotic songs by school children."[58] Almost immediately from its inception, the D.A.R. joined the G.A.R.'s campaign to place flags in all public schools. The Sons of the Revolution, the S.A.R., and the Women's Relief Corps (the ladies auxiliary of the G.A.R.) also lent their support.

In the early 1890s, the D.A.R. sponsored a contest to write a national hymn, since some members found the origin of the melody to "The Star-Spangled Banner" in a drinking song improprietous, and others found objectionable the fact that it was originally an English tune. By 1895 no entry that had been submitted was considered adequate for sponsorship. Member Janet E. Hosmer Richards urged her colleagues to advocate and support recognition of "The Star-Spangled Banner" as the national anthem not only by the D.A.R. but by the U.S. Congress itself. She argued that no alternative could surpass the flag as the subject of the national anthem. "Daughters of the American Revolution!" she wrote, "In this soul-stirring hymn we have embodied a sentiment which will serve all true Americans for all occasions. In times of peace, dear flag, we hail thee! In time of danger, inspired by this anthem, we will gladly rally to thy defense and shed our life's blood, if necessary, in order that we may proudly proclaim, after the heat and hardship of the struggle, 'Our Flag is still there!' "[59]

Both the G.A.R. and the D.A.R. realized the importance of training the young in the cult of the flag. One method of reaching the young and training them in proper respect for the flag was, of course, the introduction of the cult of the flag into children's literature. Even prior to the rise of the cult, a children's novel exists from the Civil War period that reflects the patriotic emphasis on the flag engendered by that conflict. The setting for *The Old Flag* is a Connecticut farm on Independence Day, 1840. On the front cover a flag flies atop the barn to mark the occasion. As the story unfolds, an old sea captain, who developed an intense love for the flag while sailing beneath it, advises an impressionable youth: "Now boy, I tell you, if anybody ain't willing to shed the last drop of his blood to keep that old Flag aflying, he's too mean a coward to live in a free country."[60] The anonymous author places an 1864 attitude in an 1840 setting, but this action also allows the presumed 1864 young male reader to envision someone who might well be his father having this experience.

A review of *St. Nicholas* magazine from its inception in 1873 until the Spanish-American War in 1898 reveals shifting uses and applications of the American flag in illustration and prose as a result of the developing influence of the cult of the flag. Although such an analysis cannot stand for all children's literature, it can show the changes in one important periodical, and demonstrate how editors, writers, and publishers participated in the dissemination of the beliefs and practices associated with the cult of the flag.[61]

In the 1870s, aside from a brief flurry of attention for the Centennial Exhibition, patriotic references in *St. Nicholas* usually point to the exemplary role model for young Americans, George Washington. When the flag is mentioned or illustrated, it is an incidental detail. One article does appear in 1876 entitled "Our Flag," but this turns out to be a history of some state flags and various quasinational flags of the Revolution, which are duly illustrated. However, after a description of regimental flags from the Civil War carried in parade, the article ends with an emphasis on the national emblem: "and my eyes grew misty as I saw that [flag] of my state,—but I shall not tell which that was, for every state flag waved by the side of the great United States flag, as much as to say, 'We are not for ourselves but for all.' "[62]

In the 1880s the flag begins to appear more often and more prominently in illustrations. Significantly, in 1888, *St. Nicholas* artists begin the practice of working the American flag into the graphics of patriotic story titles. This suggests a deliberate use of the flag to enhance the impact of the stories. "Ringing in the Fourth" is the first example of this inclusion, soon followed by "A Pig That Really Caused a War," showing a porker sniffing a flag that is draped on the story's title. "The Routine of the Republic," a serial on civics, also opens with a flag flying over its title, and the practice of including the flag in such graphic design becomes more frequent as the cult of the flag gains strength and legitimacy.

During the 1880s, in stories where the flag is peripheral to the plot, it still seems clear that respectful appreciation of the flag is expected. In one story, an offense against the flag is equated with an offense against the country; in another, a homesick lad in Germany remarks, "But Harry, we are American all the rest of the time—regular 'star-spangled banner boys' aren't we?" And in 1885, in a civics serial by Edmund Alton, an early hint of flag etiquette is passed along to the young readers: "Whenever, therefore, an American sees this glorious ensign of his country, the stripes recall to his mind the birth of the Republic, with the events that surrounded it; the stars suggest its wonderful development in size, in resources, and in power; and in homage to the national grandeur and protective authority which it represents, wherever he beholds it,—whether in mid-ocean floating at the head of a passing ship, or waving aloft in the streets of foreign lands,—he lifts his hat to it with a patriotic feeling of filial love and price."[63]

In the 1890s the diligence of the D.A.R., the G.A.R., and other patriotic groups firmly established the cult of the flag. Beyond even more of the conscious inclusion of the flag in passing references in stories, illustrations, and graphics, the influence of this movement can be found in a new type of patriotic story in *St. Nicholas*. In these stories, the American flag becomes a central prop, often granted a "persona" more God-like than human. In "The Studlefunk's Bonfire," for example, the flag mysteriously saves a boy named Joe trapped in a burning house on the Fourth of July—the flagpole bends over to him when he finds himself cut off on the second story; he takes hold of the banner, pulls himself out of the blazes, and shimmies down to safety. Another example of this genre is "A Story of the Flag," by Victor Mapes, the editor's nephew. In this piece a young American in Paris replaces the weather-beaten flag on Lafayette's grave, then, while attending a Bastille Day parade, sees the president of France bow to the Stars and Stripes he holds in his hands. The hero experiences a rite of passage into patriotic maturity; returning to the United States, he makes his bedroom into a shrine of sorts honoring his souvenir flags.[64]

The central question of "Dee and Jay" concerns which girl will be chosen to carry the Star Spangled Banner during the opening ceremonies of a gymnastics exhibition. Alice Balch Abbot, the author of this story, digresses for a bit to point out that young ladies desire to show their love of the flag. "Oh you boys, who glory in patriotic festivals . . . do you ever think of the envy in the hearts of your sisters, as they stand by the roadside? What would they not give to march in the ranks, wield the drumsticks, carry the flaming torches, or, best of all, the fluttering folds of the 'red, white, and blue!' "65

Perhaps the most touching tale in *St. Nicholas* exalting the cult of the flag is Pauline Wesley's "Toby Hinkle, Patriot," published in July 1896. The Stars and Stripes embellishments on the title of the story exhibit how a showy display of the flag which an earlier generation might have labeled ostentatious was now accepted. Toby is a young cripple living on the outskirts of a town called Swamp Corner. Swamp Corner has a liberty pole, but the town has voted against Toby's father's idea of purchasing a big, new flag for a still-far off Fourth of July celebration. Although it will mean months of arduous work, Toby decides to take the job on himself. He reasons that his infirmity affords him plenty of free time to work, and with determination he begins his task. As the weeks go by, more and more townspeople drop in to check his progress. His patriotism becomes contagious and the town raises money for fireworks, "speechifying," and the hiring of a brass band to celebrate the inauguration of the new flag. Because Toby is a cripple he cannot attend the ceremony; however, the band and all the Swamp Corner residents come to his home and serenade him with "The Star-Spangled Banner." Although a cripple, Toby reminds his neighbors of the crippling effect a lack of patriotism can have upon a community, and he offers for reverence what the author of the tale considers the finest outlet for expressing their patriotism, a Star-Spangled Banner.

In the 1890s *St. Nicholas* also published poems glorifying the flag, with passages such as "Each stripe has a meaning you yet cannot guess; Each star is more sacred than words can express" or "This blessed banner overhead possesses heavenly powers!"67 The personification of the flag in some of the previously cited prose and its mystical connection to the deity hinted at in these and other poems both encourage readers of *St. Nicholas* to support the cult of the flag.

In 1891 "Honors to the Flag" reviews some modes of expressing veneration for the flag attributed to army and navy men, explicitly intended for imitation by *St. Nicholas* readers. One form of respect advocated is the taking off of one's hat to the flag. Interestingly enough, this social function is stressed as necessary even when no other people are around.

As the 1890s progress, the magazine continues to stress emulation of the military's overt patriotism, but the emphasis on teaching this responsibility shifts to the educational system. By 1897 *St. Nicholas* describes a "Swearing Allegiance to the Colors" military ceremony noting that public schools teach students how to salute the flag during opening exercises. In "Honors to the Flag in Camp and Armory," a significant bit of information suggests how, in a period of five years (from 1892 to 1897), the proper social reaction to the American flag had undergone—and was still undergoing—a definite transition. "A few years ago when *St. Nicholas* told of 'Honors to the Flag,' a man or a woman in New York who rose in an armory at 'retreat,' or who saluted a regimental flag, would have been remarked. Now anyone who does not do these things will soon be considered as unmannerly as a man who should wear his hat in the house or in church."[68]

This evidence from *St. Nicholas* illustrates the impact the cult of the flag had upon patriotic stories and essays, presenting the symbol of the national banner to young people with a sense of hallowedness that was previously unmatched. How successful was this new emphasis on the flag in inculcating patriotism? Such a question is hard to answer, but English novelist Sir Walter Besant, commenting on a visit to the United States at this time, said that "nothing he saw in America impressed him so deeply as the devotion of our young people to their Flag . . . and that a nation which as a whole felt as we seemed to feel about our colors from the time we left our mothers' knees, was one that could withstand the world in arms."[69]

The shift that came about in saluting the flag from 1892 to 1897 was largely influenced by the contributions another children's magazine made to the cult of the flag in this period. As chapter 6 will show, the editors and staff of *The Youth's Companion*, reacting to the G.A.R.'s call for the flag in the public schools, responded not only with a nationwide campaign, but with a ritual to make firm the connection between the public school and the American flag: the Pledge of Allegiance.

6

Flag Ritual Comes to the Public Schools: Development and Dissemination of the Pledge of Allegiance

Even as the veterans' organizations and the hereditary societies began to have some success in establishing the custom of placing an American flag in schoolyards and classrooms, the next step in the developing relationship between the flag and the public schools began: the call for patriotic ritual in the classroom. In the initial years of the movement, the focus had been on establishing the presence of the flag in schools. The concerted effort of one New York reformer, George T. Balch, proved influential in the development of patriotic ritual for the classroom, and his pioneering efforts opened the way for more widespread contribution to flag ceremony from the most widely circulated children's periodical of the day, *The Youth's Companion*. This journal topped off a campaign to place flags in all schools of the nation by Columbus Day, 1892, with the first nationally organized recitation of the Pledge of Allegiance. An analysis of the background, development, and dissemination of the pledge reveals that this significant act, learned and repeated time and time again by millions of Americans, originated as supporters of the cult of the flag capitalized on the attention given to the Columbian National Exposition in Chicago by politicians, patriots, and the media.

George T. Balch was a New York City auditor who in 1886 received the assignment of reviewing the accounts and administration of the city health department. While pursuing this project, he became interested in what he and a host of others called the "tenement-house problem," the living conditions of many of the recent immigrants. After leaving the staff of the New York Commissioner of Accounts in 1887, Balch wrote a history of the causes and growth of this problem in New York City during the period 1839–88.

Concerned about the potential social disruption of Americaniz-

114

ing an urban population he referred to as "human scum, cast on our shores by the tidal wave of a vast immigration," Balch became convinced that public education provided the best means for "the elevation of the masses." He visited a New York City public school's morning exercises in April 1888, and discovered there an "innovation . . . introduced by one of the School Inspectors only a few months before": patriotic ceremonies that involved revering the presence of an American flag. This fifteen-minute experience brought together Balch's desire to "regenerate" the immigrant population with a viable ritual. In later explaining his relentless dedication to spreading the use of flag ritual in the public schools, Balch recalled, "The exercises, which I witnessed for the first time, made a profound impression upon me, and I thought I saw the germ of a patriotic movement, which, in the hands of wise and judicious teachers, could be made to produce results, the far-reaching consequences of which it would be impossible to prognosticate at this time."[1]

In January 1889, Balch began a two-month, official analysis of the Children's Aid Society's twenty-one industrial day schools, which trained at that time an immigrant population of approximately five thousand students. This resulted in *Methods of Teaching Patriotism in the Public Schools*. Based on his work with .the immigrant population of New York but designed for application in all schools, Balch's handbook was written to instill patriotism in the young. At this time, Balch's official title was Auditor of the Board of Education of the City of New York. It is worth noting that the "School Inspector" who introduced the flags into the city schools was Colonel De Witt C. Ward of the Seventh District, and that Balch inscribed his manual to J. Edward Simmons, then president of the Board of Education of the City of New York. Balch credited Simmons for being the first presiding officer who "suggested and earnestly advocated special attention to instruction in Patriotism, as an integral part of the curriculum."[2]

Balch believed that material aids were fundamental in the encouragement of nationalistic sentiment and, although part of his plan called for the incorporation of the Great Seal of the United States into Good Citizenship Badges (with variants to distinguish student, teacher, or principal), his overwhelming focus remained on the American flag, which he singled out as "the sole symbol of the greatness of this nation, in all its majesty and its sovereignty."[3] Although flag designs—indeed, small flags—might also be used as Good Citizenship Badges, Balch proposed the distribution of flags to students as *rewards* for good citizenship. He also urged schools to dedicate, with ritual and ceremony, a flag mounted on a staff that would serve as the official school flag. Outside, in the school-yard, Balch suggested still another ceremony to dedicate a signal flag, that would fly over the building or grounds, adapting a custom already practiced by Congress to indicate when the institution was in session.

His use of the flag as a reward derived from the practice of Colonel De Witt C. Ward of presenting the class with the highest marks in punctuality and attendance with the school flag on a rotating basis each week. Although evidence suggests Ward began this practice in 1888, there are indications that he had been involved in "patriotic labors" since 1883. Perhaps Ward became involved with patriotic activities during the celebration of the centennial of the Constitution, which also ushered in the founding of the Sons of the Revolution. Such a possibility is strengthened by the fact that both were marked by ceremonies in the city of New York. In any case, Balch appropriated Ward's idea and developed a hierarchy of award flags: the "Scholar's Flag" would be "mounted on a staff and displayed for a specified period on the desk of the best conducted pupil in each class" while a larger "Class Flag" would be "mounted on a staff and displayed for a specified period in the class-room of the best conducted class." Balch stressed that possession of the prized American flag should be won not by superiority in scholarship, which was based on God-given gifts, but rather by good conduct, which he defined as including the following characteristics: "punctuality, regularity of attendance, personal neatness and cleanliness, cheerfulness and evenness of temper, truthfulness, ready obedience to rules and instruction, respectful bearing toward superiors in knowledge and years, and studiousness."[4]

It is no coincidence that Balch's plan encouraged the use of the flag in spreading not only love of country but also a code of moral behavior. He spoke quite candidly about the use of the flag as a tool in the Americanization of the foreign element. In a patriotic primer he was working on at the time of his death in April 1894 (it was published the following year through the efforts of Wallace Foster), Balch included a catechism of fifty-seven questions and answers for students to memorize. According to this catechism, "the first step in learning how to govern ourselves is to learn how to obey." The primary aim of the public school is "to train us in such habits of behavior as will best fit us to become GOOD MEM-BERS OF CIVIL SOCIETY and PATRIOTIC AMERICAN CIT-

IZENS"; it also serves a secondary function "to instruct us through the arts of reading and writing in the use of books."[5]

The series of catechism questions culminates in an explanation of "The American Patriotic Salute," the first known organized flag salute designed for use in American public schools. Balch did not want the salute forced on students; he wanted them to encourage the practice themselves, once their school had obtained a signal flag. This, too, should not come about by administrative force but rather by a student-called election of unanimous consent. "Should the voting fail to be unanimous, the whole matter might be laid over for another month, or for such time as the Principal may think advisable, to enable the more loyal Americans to persuade and convince their opponents." He suggested the use of Scholar's Flags and Class Flags for a few months, and then when interest had been stimulated, to make the procurement and dedication of a school flag and/or a signal flag a "public affair," attended by representatives of the Grand Army of the Republic. "The American Patriotic Salute" should serve as a high point of such ceremonies and, in another allusion to the veterans' organization, those students reciting it would become members of the "Grand Army of Patriotic Americans."[6]

In giving "The American Patriotic Salute," students touched first their foreheads, then their hearts, reciting together "We give our Heads!—and our Hearts!—to God! and our Country!" Then, apparently with their right arms outstretched and slightly elevated, palm down, in the direction of the flag, they completed the salute: "One Country! One Language! One Flag!"[7] Looking back from the present, one recognizes how this rite parallels European totalitarian salutes from the first half of the twentieth century— during World War II, Gridley Adams, the Chairman of the National Flag Code Committee, saw the connection and persuaded Congress in 1942 to pass a joint resolution that "the pledge of allegiance to the flag be rendered by standing with the right hand over the heart."[8] In America in 1891, however, the extended arm salute bore no taint of evil. It was one illustration of a nationalism campaign supported by the hereditary societies and veterans' organizations, along with their monitoring of text-book accounts of the Civil War (which, incidentally, they felt should be known instead by the title "Pro-Slavery Rebellion"), and their encouragement of an annual school visit by G.A.R. members on the Friday before Memorial Day, to remind the students of the significance of the occasion.[9]

The shift in main responsibility in the area of patriotic instruction, from the home to the school, began in the late 1880s and intensified during the decade of the 1890s. In its early phases, drawing in part on the work of Balch, this shift received encouragement from the G.A.R. and its auxiliary the W.R.C. The flag offered a tangible object to incorporate into any schoolhouse patriotic ceremonies, a fact not lost upon the committee formed by the national encampment of the G.A.R. in 1891 to work on propaganda in this area. Spearheaded by Duncan Milner, a Presbyterian minister from Manhattan, Kansas, this group adopted a title that demonstrated their objective: "the Committee on a Systematic Plan of Teaching the Lessons of Loyalty to Our One Country and One Flag." Their auxiliary equivalent, the W.R.C.'s Committee on Patriotic Teaching, soon discovered and advocated the use of Balch's patriotic primer. It appears likely that these groups might even have been instrumental in the publication of Balch's primer, for it was published in Indianapolis, home of *The American Tribune,* a privately financed periodical that strove to serve the G.A.R. audience during its decade of publication 1890–1900.[10] The introduction to the first edition of the primer notes the interest that "noble, patriotic women" have taken in "the cause of intelligent citizenship" since the national flag had been "adopted as an auxiliary in instructing our youth in patriotism."[11] A few years later, a representative of the New York department of the W.R.C. reconfirmed their involvement: "the W.R.C. is deeply interested in the good work of teaching the children patriotism and reverence for our flag and stand ready to furnish flags, charts, and patriotic primers to help them."[12]

Kate Brownlee Sherwood, the W.R.C.'s 1894 delegate to the National Council of Women, a federation of women's organizations, convinced that body to let her chair a committee dedicated to the teaching of patriotism in all schools. Sherwood's emphasis on flag salutes in such a project is neatly illustrated in a children's song she wrote for inclusion in the Balch primer. Set to the tune of "Dixie," her "Salute Old Glory" replaces the familiar refrain "Away, away, away down South in Dixie" with "Awake! awake! awake! salute Old Glory!" (for complete lyrics, see Appendix). She dedicated this text "to the 10,000,000 little American citizens who are saluting the flag as part of their school exercises and who are invited to join in the work of the Patriotic League for intelligent citizenship."[13]

The primer itself demonstrates the emphasis the cult of the flag had achieved in patriotic writings by 1895. It includes brief essays and poems on the two great heroes of American nationalism—the ever-influential George Washington and the martyred Abraham Lincoln. The bulk of the text, however, is full of patriotic quotations and extracts that return again and again to the flag as the ultimate symbol of the nation. The book concludes with two long series of quotes designed to display for the young the powerful significance of patriotism and the flag by presenting a variety of emotional definitions from responsible role models.

Balch's salute called for a pledge to God and country; his primer also sought to mingle these allegiances in the early training of the young, which was a goal for many women encouraging the adoption of the flag into school ceremonies during these years. The opinion of Julia S. Conklin of Indiana, as quoted in Balch's primer, epitomizes this attitude:

> The first lesson of patriotism should be taught at the mother's knee when the innocent lips are taught to lisp 'Our Father, who art in Heaven.' Teach them to love the word 'country.' Teach them that the nobler act of a noble life is to die, if need be, in its defense. Then insist that the lesson at the school be befitting the children of American citizens. Let the American flag be constantly in sight—in the home, in the street, in the school house, in the church. Let our love of God be mingled with our love of country. Let the flag be placed with the Holy Bible, one the emblem of loyalty and that freedom which God intended for his creatures, the other the teachings of humanity and God's divine love for his children. Let the cross, precious emblem of our Saviour's suffering, be entwined with the starry fields of the American flag, which represents the blood bought liberties we enjoy."[14]

Also quoted in Balch's primer, W. F. Kuhn of Missouri echoed the combining of Christian and national symbols in the teaching of the young: "our country's flag must find a place in your ranks, side by side with your grand standard of the blessed Emmanuel, the Prince of Peace."[15] Although not always stressing the mingling of patriotic and Christian ceremony, many educators rallied to support the introduction of flag salutes into classroom practices, among them the editors of *Education,* a Boston-based professional journal.[16] As early as 1890, Illinois State Superintendent of Public Instruction, Dr. Richard Edwards, said "Let the flag wave over every schoolhouse." "Make the best use of the public schools by making systematic instructions in patriotic citizenship the chief part of the course of study" advised Thomas Hunter, President of New York Normal College, while Eliza A. Blaker, Superintendent of Indianapolis Kindergarten and Domestic and Normal Training Schools, suggested "teach the youth in the kindergarten to respect and honor the flag of their country; it will be the stepping-stone to loyal Christian citizenship. Instruct them to reverently salute the flag of the Union . . . the effect of the salute will be magical."[17]

The G.A.R. proved very influential in urging the presence of the American flag in the public schools, and its auxiliary, the Woman's Relief Corps, with the support of other women's organizations, came to the forefront in advocating patriotic ritual involving the flag as a regular student activity. Balch's salute achieved some prominence in city schools, but its usage remained limited. The national acceptance of a new ritual associated with the flag required some sort of promotional campaign focusing on an occasion of patriotic interest. Supporters of the cult of the flag found the occasion in the opening ceremonies of the Columbian National Exposition in Chicago. The campaign to promote this occasion was a carefully organized effort by the staff of the most popular children's magazine of the day, *The Youth's Companion*.

Daniel Sharp Ford edited *The Youth's Companion* from 1857 until his death in 1899, and under his guidance the periodical achieved, by 1885, the highest circulation of any magazine in the country, with a total of 385,000 copies. By 1894 that number had passed the half million mark.[18] Just as was shown in the children's magazine *St. Nicholas* in chapter 5, the expanding uses of the symbol of the flag in *The Youth's Companion* in the late 1880s and early 1890s are demonstrated by the conscious introduction of the flag into graphics and patriotic illustrations, a shift to the flag as the central focus of patriotic pictures rather than as a secondary or marginal element, and the inclusion of stories and articles devoted to the flag, often granting it a "persona."

One such story, "George Washington II," published in 1891, centers on a Fourth of July adventure, and has as its hero a model youth named after the Father of our Country. Because of his name and the high moral tone of his character, young George becomes intensely involved in patriotic activities. To celebrate Independence Day he makes himself a sash from an old weatherworn flag, and wears it to a riverside parade, accompanied by some of his schoolmates. (At this time there was no social taboo against using old flags for clothing; drawings remain of children wearing flags as sashes as early as the Civil War.) The boys crowd out on a pier to get a better view of the passing parade, and one fellow falls into the river and is in danger of drowning. Without pausing to think, George Washington II tears off his sash and throws it to his companion, who is safely pulled back to the pier grasping the former flag. Young George is declared a hero and given as his reward the new flag raised at the special Independence Day exercises.

Another story deals specifically with the dedication involved in obtaining a flag for a country school. In Marion L. Cummings's "His Day for the Flag," schoolchildren give up their one free day, Saturday, to perform odd jobs in order to raise money to purchase a school flag.[19] Ford published this story in 1892, the year in which *The Youth's Companion* culminated a three-year campaign to place flags in all the public schools of the United States. This process supplanted the earlier work of the veterans' organizations and paved the way for later lobbying on the part of the hereditary societies. An analysis of it reveals the influence of a major periodical in bringing about a shift in cultural attitudes and uses associated with the national flag.

The Youth's Companion moved beyond a vocalized support for public schools and the patriotic veneration many believed the flag deserved, to an organized campaign to carefully bind the two together for generations to come. This transition occurred after a decisive shift in editorial policy during the fall and winter of 1889. An editorial published just as the school year commenced outlined the earlier policy. This unsigned editorial spoke out against the contemporary fuss being made over flag rituals. Entitled "Teaching Patriotism," the editorial asserted that true patriotism went far beyond reciting invocations or making gestures of homage; it was a spirit instilled in the individual's mind through the acquisition of truth and knowledge about his homeland. The editorial rejected the idea that the American flag should be flown over every schoolhouse in the country while school was in session. Daily flag-raisings and flag-lowering were demonstrations of patriotism more appropriate to forts or ships at sea. Teaching patriotism went deeper than respect for the flag; it was the teaching of moral duties to keep society pure and good.[20]

Supporters of the cult of the flag, such as Balch, who is anonymously referred to as "a gentleman from New York" in this editorial—and credited with the idea of placing flags in public schools—concurred with the need to teach moral duties, but maintained that flag rituals and flag veneration were both useful means to help remind impressionable students of the high code of values patriotism demanded of them. One staff member of *The Youth's Companion,* James B. Upham, saw the situation this way, and by the beginning of 1890 had developed enough support for his ideas on the active promotion of the cult of the flag to engineer a decisive reversal of this earlier restrained policy.

Upham was born in New Hampton, New Hampshire, in 1845, into a family that had been regularly supplying New England deacons for six generations.[21] Growing up in an environment that conditioned him to place high values on education and religious piety, he took seriously his responsibility, as a writer for a prestigious journal, for passing on the social beliefs of his class to a younger generation. He joined the staff of *The Youth's Companion* in 1872; his uncle, the editor Daniel Sharp Ford, placed him in charge of the premium department. Upham's successful management of this department was no doubt responsible in part for *The Youth's Companion's* rapidly expanding circulation during the subsequent decades. By 1886 Upham was a partner in the business.

One of the first projects Upham initiated at *The Youth's Companion* to promote the cult of the flag was a national essay contest, which he advertised only four months after the unsigned editorial that questioned the cult of the flag. It was during these months that the journal's editorial policy shifted. Upham ran the promotion for the contest, simply titled "The Flag and the Public Schools," in the 9 January 1890 issue, beneath an illustration of a large flag flying over a two-story red brick schoolhouse.

Erroneously claiming the idea for placing flags in the public schools had originated in an earlier issue of *The Youth's Companion,* the magazine asked "the privilege of floating an American Flag (at its own expense) over one public school-house in each of the forty-two States." Students were invited to write an essay on the topic "The Patriotic Influence of the American Flag when Raised Over the Public Schools." Schoolteachers were to select the best essay from each school (not to exceed six hundred words in length) and forward it to *The Youth's Companion* before an April 1 deadline. The staff of *The Youth's Companion* would select one winner from each state in time for the schools to dedicate the flags to celebrate Independence Day. The patriotic promotions of Balch and the G.A.R. were spreading at this time, receiving some attention in the press. Upham must have convinced his uncle Daniel Ford, the publisher, that if the contest generated enough interest it would be good not only for the national morale but for *The Youth's Companion* as well.[22]

To celebrate the importance of the public school in the dissemination of the cult of the flag, and in honor of the essay winners who were to dedicate their new banners on that day, *The Youth's Companion* opened its Fourth of July issue in 1890 with an epic ode entitled "Raising the School House Flag" (see Appendix). Surrounded by smaller illustrations depicting the War of 1812, the Revolution, the Capitol, and such notable patriots as Washington, Jefferson, Franklin, and Lincoln, the poem was flanked by a prominent picture of a group of young American schoolchildren cheering the raising of a flag. Hezekiah Butterworth, assistant editor of *The Youth's Companion* and author of the Zigzag travel series, popular with many young people at that time, wrote the poem. In "Raising the School House Flag," Butterworth combined the mystic covenant between God and America that many believed the flag signified with support of the public schools and a reawakening spirit of expansive nationalism. A refrain repeated throughout the poem is evidence of this jubilant combination:

> Flag of the sun that shines for all,
> Flag of the breeze that blows for all,
> Flag of the sea that flows for all,
> Flag of the school that stands for all,
> Flag of the people, one and all—
> What is thy meaning in the air?
> O banner, answer me![23]

In that same issue, *The Youth's Companion* published the names of the winners of the contest and the public schools they attended. Pupils from forty-one states and six territories entered the contest; *The Youth's Companion* regretted it could not send a flag to every school that participated. It did praise the caliber of the responses, concluding, "The happy connection between the flag and the school has never been better expressed, it cannot be better presented, than in this passage from one of the essays: 'The hope of the nation is the public school, and the emblem of the nation is the flag. Let the two be united.'"[24]

Three months later in an advertisement the periodical announced that it had published a souvenir edition of the illustrated Butterworth poem, printed on heavy paper suitable for framing. To maintain interest in the cult of the flag, *The Youth's Companion* sent a free copy of this edition of "Raising the School House Flag" to every school that had entered the essay contest earlier that year. Moreover, it offered to send a free copy of the poem to every public school in the United States that had already joined the movement by raising a flag on its grounds. And as the 1890s began, schoolhouse flag-raising ceremonies became increasingly more commonplace; *The Youth's Companion* noted that they were an activity "with which our readers young and old are familiar."[25] Throughout the 1890s, the G.A.R., the W.R.C., and other patriotic groups continued to encourage the practice.

On 20 February 1889, State Senator Allan P. Lovejoy introduced into the Wisconsin state legislature a bill authorizing school boards to purchase school flags at public expense. Sent to the Committee of Education, the bill was approved, returned to the legislature, and became state law in April 1889. That same month a Pennsylvania state law *requiring* the practice was defeated on the third reading, but the legal precedents for both voluntary and compulsory placement of flags in public schools had been set. Sixteen years later, *The Youth's Companion,* continuing its support for the cult of the flag, advertised that it would send free copies of school flag laws to any individuals or organizations in states that had not yet made school flags compulsory, celebrating the fact that the following states and territories had already done so: New Hampshire, Massachusetts, Rhode Island, Connecticut, New York, New Jersey, Pennsylvania, Ohio, Michigan, Illinois, Wisconsin, North Dakota, Washington, Wyoming, New Mexico, Arizona, Idaho, and Oklahoma. The states of the Confederacy are noticeable in their absence from this list, indicative perhaps of the strong ties the cult of the flag had to the role of Union soldiers in the Civil War. Eventually, the majority of states, both North and South, would enact some type of legislation encouraging or demanding the inculcation of "patriotic" values—using the American flag as a focal symbol—in the public schools.[26]

Circumstances proved advantageous for the movement to place flags in all public schools when a specific occasion arose that became a focus for the country's growing nationalism. Organizers had discussed for years the possibility of a national commemoration of the four hundredth anniversary of Columbus's discovery of America. Various sites were suggested, but Congress approved Chicago as the location for the Columbian Exposition, a grand world's fair that would give the United States the opportunity to display to other nations its advancements in technology while celebrating its history and development.

It occurred to Upham that, although Congress had made provisions for the official dedication of the Exposition grounds on Columbus Day, 1892, nothing had ever been done to insure a planned celebration of the day throughout the entire country. In 1946, Margaret S. Miller's *I Pledge Allegiance,* one of the few published accounts that gives any details of Upham's involvement, claimed that while lying under a pine tree in East Epping, New Hampshire, enjoying a languid summer vacation in 1889, James B. Upham suddenly had an inspired thought: he would engineer a national public school celebration in conjunction with the official exercises in Chicago.[27] The exposition celebrated material progress; Upham's ceremony would be one of patriotic devotion, marking the significance of the day by emphasizing the virtues of universal public education and the rising cult of the flag. To achieve this he had to ensure that flags would fly in public schools from the Atlantic to the Pacific.

Although the manner and time of Upham's conception of this plan are debatable, Louise Harris, who has devoted years of her life to writing books glorifying the editorial policies of *The Youth's Companion* and its contributions to American patriotism, states that the idea was Upham's.[28] By January 1891, the offers of the free illustrated souvenir edition of "Raising the School House Flag" to any schools raising their own U.S. flags included the request that teachers notify *The Youth's Companion* as to when their schools first raised the flag. *"Has your school* raised a United States Flag?" queried *The Youth's Companion. "We wish to know.* All public schools flying the United States Flag will be entitled to *special honors* in the *National Columbus* Public School celebration Oct. 12, 1892."[29]

By May 1891, a new two-color edition of the souvenir poem was run off to meet the increasing demands. At this time *The Youth's Companion* offered a clever scheme to patriotic students in schools that still did not have flags. "If your school has not yet raised a flag and yet wishes to, let us know it and we will mail you *free one hundred School Flag Certificates.* With these certificates scores of schools have raised money for a $10 flag in one day's time."[30] The promotional copy instructed students to sell the certificates to members of their community at a cost of ten cents each. The "shares of patriotism" the students sold were simple paper certificates (see figure 3) that *The Youth's Companion* produced in mass quantities.

This method proved highly successful, and as the months went by, *The Youth's Companion* ran this and similar advertisements more and more regularly. By the beginning of the school year in 1891, *The Youth's Companion* claimed that thousands of schools had already adopted this system. The magazine offered flags sixteen feet long for ten dollars, flags nine feet long (for smaller schools) for five dollars. These advertisements always urged students to

This Certificate
entitles the holder to a
SHARE
in the patriotic influences
of the
SCHOOL FLAG

Fig. 3. Facsimile of School Flag Certificate

get ready for the National Columbian Public School Celebration, and *The Youth's Companion* continued to provide the souvenir edition of "Raising the School House Flag" as a bonus.

In an editorial published for the Independence Day issue in 1891, *The Youth's Companion* patted itself on the back for the increasing success of "our Flag movement, which is still sweeping the country" and committed itself to an intensification of the program: "Though there are still many schools which are not as yet provided with the flag, the time does not seem far distant when no public school shall be too poor, too remote, or too indifferent to have the stars and stripes floating above its roof."

To support the positive effect of the cult and the need to support its growth, the editorial included testimonials from enthusiastic teachers across the country. From Minnesota one school official wrote, "The flag has come to mean something, whereas before it was a meaningless piece of cloth." Presumably she meant it had been meaningless for those too young to recall the outburst of flag waving during the Civil War. A teacher in Missouri remarked a transformation in the children's feelings: "Now they seem to think it is their flag—an effect that never could have been produced by talking." "Almost every day after the flag-raising one could hear the children cheering the old flag" came a message from Maine, and in other parts of New England the flag in the school was hailed for an unexplained benevolent influence. "I notice it is easier to govern the children since the flag was raised," wrote a teacher from Connecticut; another in Massachusetts said,

"It has been a grand step toward making brave, manly boys and womanly girls."[31]

The Youth's Companion wide circulation and persistent efforts to place flags in public schools broadened and intensified the campaigns begun by the veterans and other patriotic societies, even as *St. Nicholas* and *The Youth's Companion* worked G.A.R. activities into patriotic essays and stories.[32]

The major influence for spreading the movement throughout the country from 1890 through 1892 remained *The Youth's Companion*. Because of this, when Charles C. Bonney, president of the World's Congress Auxiliary to the Columbian Exposition, learned that Upham had begun work on an organized national celebration of Columbus Day, 1892, in the public schools, he officially entrusted *The Youth's Companion* with management of the plan. In an announcement issued on New Year's Day, 1892, Bonney called for local celebrations of the event in communities across the country, noting that it would be highly appropriate for the public schools to be the centers of such activities. After the official appointment, Daniel Sharp Ford promised to put the full resources of *The Youth's Companion* behind the movement, and W. T. Harris, U. S. Commissioner of Education, promised additional support.[33] Upham placed one of his assistants in charge of the entire project, a young man only recently hired by *The Youth's Companion*, Francis Bellamy.

Bellamy, born in 1855 and raised in Rome, New York by a mother who wanted him to be a professional, was ordained a Baptist minister at the age of twenty-four. In 1884 he accepted the pulpit of the Dearborn Street Baptist Church in Boston, a church that listed among its most generous benefactors one Daniel Sharp Ford. Ford liked the young clergyman, and when Bellamy realized his views on helping the working class had become too liberal for a Baptist minister at that time and resigned his office, Ford offered him a job at *The Youth's Companion*. Shortly after he joined the staff, Bellamy took charge of *The Youth's Companion's* campaign for the Columbus Day celebration.

In February, 1892, Bellamy presented this campaign to the National Convention of Superintendents meeting in Brooklyn, and this body appointed him chairman of an Executive Committee on the National Columbian Public School Celebration. Educators of national prominence filled out the rest of the committee: John W. Dickinson, Secretary of Massachusetts State Board of Education; Thomas B. Stockwell, Commissioner of Public Schools of Rhode Island; W. R. Garrett, Superintendent of Public Instruction of Tennessee; and W. C. Hewitt, Superintendent of the Michigan Educational Exhibit at the World's Fair. The National Convention of Superintendents also approved a general committee of all the heads of education in the several states to further the work of the Executive Committee in their various states. Although the educators offered their names and support, Bellamy and the staff of *The Youth's Companion,* who had done so much to promote the project, were to continue to develop and organize the celebration, with committee approval only required for major decisions. The May 1892 issue of *Education* urged national support from teachers and superintendents for the approaching ceremonies, noting that *"The Youth's Companion* has been very active in bringing about this celebration."[34]

Bellamy and his publicity director, Harold Roberts, pulled out all the stops to ensure that their message would reach as many citizens as possible. Their propaganda blitz included state and local school superintendents, educational and religious journals, popular newspapers, G.A.R. posts, and every minister in the country. In March of 1892 *The Youth's Companion* published a "Message to the Public Schools of America" from the Executive Committee headed by Bellamy. Briefly explaining the development of the plan for a national Columbus Day celebration (and crediting the idea to *The Youth's Companion),* the message called on the public school students to lead their communities in a patriotic extravaganza: "It is for you, scholars of the American Public Schools, to arouse a sentiment in your schools and in your neighborhoods for this grand way of celebrating the Finding of America. Educators and teachers will meet you from their side. But it is for you to begin . . . . The Public School of to-day sways the hundred years to come."[35]

The Youth's Companion invited the thirteen million public school students of America to participate in this historic patriotic movement in a methodical fashion. First, they had to convince their teachers and superintendents that they were in earnest, then have their schools vote to participate in the celebration. Almost certainly Bellamy took this strategy from Balch's book; an article praising the voluntary elections of immigrant children in New York City to institute flag salutes in their schools had appeared in *The Youth's Companion* just two months earlier.[36] Obviously, although Balch received no credit, his dream of what might be achieved through spreading flag rituals throughout the schools stood its best chance for fulfillment with the involvement of such an influential journal.

Once schools voted in favor of the celebration, Bellamy instructed them to form local committees to organize the observance well ahead of time, invite the Civil War veterans to participate, and actively seek support from local religious and civic organizations. "The local press will be the most valuable of all supports," noted Bellamy. "Ask your local paper to print this message." *The Youth's Companion* would later supply an "Official Programme" designed to achieve national uniformity in the ceremonies yet allowing for local variations.[37]

Aided by publicity director Harold Roberts, Bellamy made certain that other areas of the media would support *The Youth's Companion* in its campaign to make a success of the Columbus Day Public School Celebration. From March on, the pair deluged the press with copy to propagandize the idea. Roberts himself interviewed Bellamy for an article in *The Boston Herald*, outlining and reiterating the goals of the project. They also kept the State Superintendents of Education aware of developments by form letters, local superintendents and G.A.R. posts by circulars. They formally requested every minister in the United States to preach on the relation of free education to American life before the schools closed in June for summer vacation. To keep fresh material in the press, Bellamy traveled to Washington and New York, interviewing influential politicians and getting their support, in print, for the planned Columbus Day event. He managed to include interviews praising the flag and the planned events from such notables as General John Palmer (Commander-in-Chief of the Grand Army of the Republic), Grover Cleveland, Henry Cabot Lodge, Theodore Roosevelt, and President Harrison.[38]

The Youth's Companion also became involved in the dissemination of flag ritual information by flag merchandising companies as a bonus when customers bought flags, a promotional activity that has continued to the present day. In April, 1892, *The Youth's Companion* ran a long advertisement for W. Anderson and Company, a Boston firm that sold flags and apparently supplied the steady demand for them created by the schools selling *The Youth's Companion's* school flag certificates. This advertisement offered five sizes of standard bunting flags, the same quality as used by the federal government, with a price range from $3.25 to $13.00. Each flag purchased came with appropriate Flag Exercises for a ceremonial public raising, free of charge. As the target date drew near, the planners introduced new forms of impetus. In June, 1892, *The Youth's Companion* announced that it would present a beautiful medal to any student initiating efforts to obtain a flag for any public school that did not yet have one. By September, it boasted that twenty-six thousand schools had obtained flags through its certificate promotion scheme, and the tone calling for participation grew forceful: "Your school will not let itself be left out of the celebration. It must have a Flag."[39]

That summer Bellamy went to Washington and successfully lobbied for a presidential proclamation supporting the introduction of the cult of the flag into the public schools. He called on many leading congressmen of both parties, requesting their support for *The Youth's Companion's* campaign, and he persuaded the President to sign into law the act of Congress establishing Columbus Day as a national holiday. Rhetoric inspired by *The Youth's Companion* certainly found its way into the presidential proclamation: "Let the National Flag float over every school house in the country, and the exercises be such as shall impress upon our youth the patriotic duties of American citizenship."[40] In the few months remaining before the national celebration, *The Youth's Companion* repeatedly emphasized the president's support of the project.

"The Official Programme for the National Columbian Public School Celebration of October 21, 1892" appeared in the September issue of *The Youth's Companion*. It offered detailed instructions for conducting the ceremonies in honor of the four hundredth anniversary of Columbus's discovery of America, including proclamations, odes, addresses, songs,and prayers (see Appendix). The entire exercise climaxed after community war veterans raised the American flag: then each school's pupils, in unison, responded with a patriotic salute to the flag. For this occasion Francis Bellamy, aided by staff members of *The Youth's Companion,* wrote something that would become taken for granted and accepted so that millions would grow up memorizing and uttering it for generations to come, although few would recognize its origin. To climax the years of campaigning to get flags in the public schools and to wed the cult of the flag to the public schools by introducing a simple ritual that could be followed daily, *The Youth's Companion* chose to highlight the national celebration by introducing "The Pledge of Allegiance."

The original wording and procedural directions for "The Pledge of Allegiance," the crux of the official ceremony in Chicago and in countless schoolyards across the entire country, were as follows:

At a signal from the Principal the pupils, in ordered ranks, hands to the side, face the Flag. Another signal is given; every pupil gives the military salute—right hand lifted, palm downward, to a line with the forehead and close to it. Standing thus, all repeat together, slowly: "I pledge allegiance to my Flag and the Republic for which it stands: one

Nation indivisible, with Liberty and Justice for All." At the words, "to my Flag," the right hand is extended gracefully, palm upwards, towards the Flag, and remains in this gesture till the end of the affirmation; whereupon all hands immediately drop to the side. Then, still standing, as the instruments strike a chord, all will sing AMERICA— "My Country, 'tis of Thee."[41]

Many New Englanders looked upon "America" as the "national hymn" at this time. In 1831, Dr. Samuel F. Smith had written its lyrics, which were set to the melody of the national anthems of Great Britain, Liechtenstein, and Austria.[42] First used in a Sunday School celebration for Independence Day in Andover, Massachussetts, the hymn spread with New England missionaries and school teachers in the antebellum period. Since *The Youth's Companion* was published in Boston, it is not surprising that Bellamy selected this song to bridge the ceremony from the flag salute into the prayers, poems, and addresses to follow. At the close of the exercises, he instructed communities to include pageants, addresses, and patriotic songs as they saw fit, and "The Star-Spangled Banner" was doubtlessly used as a closing hymn by many celebrations throughout the country. Bellamy encouraged participation of the G.A.R. and other veterans' organizations in the ceremonies, aware of their involvement in the spread of the cult of the flag. He also succeeded in persuading Edna Dean Proctor, who had earlier published in *Bugle Echos* "The Stripes and the Stars," a patriotic tribute to the flag of the Union as it flew during the Civil War, to write a special poem in honor of the flag for the Columbus Day celebration. Her "Columbia's Banner" (see Appendix) served as "The Ode" for the event throughout the land. *The Youth's Companion* not only disseminated official programs, it also printed detailed instructions for organizing parades, encouraging press coverage, and sparking community involvement for the event.[43]

Following the National Columbus Day celebration, *The Youth's Companion* continued to support the cult of the flag, offering souvenir editions of the official program for a penny apiece and maintaining its veneration of the flag in stories and illustrations. Owing to the efforts of Upham and Bellamy and their staff of workers, who were supported by a network of educators, veterans, and clergy throughout the country, Columbus Day became a regular holiday, the Pledge of Allegiance was introduced on a national level, and public schools throughout the land supported the cult of the flag, stressing its themes with rituals and ceremonies. For at least another decade, Balch's salute continued in use in places where the W.R.C. had distributed his primer, and it was especially suited to primary grade students as late as the mid-1920s, but the Bellamy salute, because of its historic national exposure, eventually emerged as the pledge that would persist and become part of the National Flag Code. Although the later conferences that established that code would change the wording slightly, to emphasize the Americanization of foreign elements in the 1920s, and Eisenhower would change it again, to emphasize the importance of recognition of Divine guidance of the U. S. in 1954, in essence the pledge would remain the same. Once introduced into daily schoolroom ritual, it would be removed only in cases of extreme social provocation.[44] George T. Balch's vision of spreading such activity throughout the United States came to fruition, and the practice flourishes today, close to a century later.

In 1898, the day after the United States declared war on Spain, in a spirit of patriotic fervor, the New York state legislature passed the first "flag salute statute." Pushed through by State Senator Coggeshall, the law mandated daily flag salutes in all public schools: "It shall be the duty of the state superintendent of public instruction to prepare, for the use of the public schools of the state, a program providing for a salute to the flag at the opening of each day of school, and such other patriotic exercises as may be deemed by him to be expedient, under such regulations and instructions as may best meet the varied needs of the different grades in such schools." Similar statutes passed the state legislatures of Rhode Island in 1901, Arizona in 1903, Kansas in 1907, and Maryland in 1918.[45]

Thus the pledge of allegiance was transformed from an exercise to Americanize immigrants into a ritual mandated by law. First the American flag found placement in and around the schools. Shortly thereafter, pledges and rituals developed to institutionalize not only the presence of the banner, but also an organized glorification of it. Legislation to encourage or enforce sanctification of the national flag quite logically led to the next development in American flag culture: moves by the hereditary societies, the veterans' organizations, and other enthusiastic supporters of the cult of the flag to discontinue uses of the flag that they felt were now improper. Chapter 7 will take up the complaints of flag desecration that grew in number as the century drew to a close, and examine how the next phase of the cult of the flag demonstrated cultural reactions to changing uses of the symbol in industrializing, urbanizing, expanding turn-of-the-century America.

7
The Emergence of Legislation against Flag Desecration

As the cult of the flag burgeoned and flag rituals became firmly entrenched in the public school systems of the United States, other uses of the image of the national banner also proliferated, some not always to the liking of the members of the hereditary societies. The tradition of inscribing the American flag with names of particular political candidates, dating back to 1840, flourished in the late nineteenth century. The spurt of flag-related commercial products that sold well during the centennial years resurged with increased vigor to serve a growing market while hunger for economic expansion and the rhetoric of jingoism spurred the country into the Spanish-American War. As advertisers learned from politicians the selling power of the revered symbol, supporters of the cult of the flag organized committees and associations to introduce federal legislation opposing what they labeled "flag desecration." At this time the flag also served as a significant symbol in much of the nationalistic art and music of the era, and "The Star-Spangled Banner" began to receive official recognition from the military as the "national air," while customs associated with its observance spread through the larger society. Further, as the United States entered the twentieth century, Jacob Riis, representative of foreign-born yet patriotic Americans, eloquently pointed out the sacred and intense significance the flag embodied for the millions of citizens who pledged their allegiance to it.

Following the Civil War, the flag appeared not only as a potent symbol in the diatribes of Republicans waving the bloody shirt, but also, of course, as an emphatic physical presence on the rostrums and stages and in the parades and rallies of both parties. As reviewed earlier, Old Glory certainly had served as a decorative element in political meetings or holiday celebrations before, but the Gilded Age was an era in which those with newly acquired wealth and power enjoyed demonstrating their positions with opulence and show; this often translated into a "more is better" attitude when incorporating the national flag into political decoration. For instance, in preparation for the Democratic National Convention of 4 July 1868, organizers hung more than one hundred flags throughout Tammany Hall in New York City, looping and festooning them as borders to emphasize architectural elements and shields bearing images of patriotic heroes. At the inauguration of Grover Cleveland in 1884, the platform on the steps of the Capitol was draped with mammoth flags, folded and fastened in their overflow. Both practices, later condemned by the Flag Conferences of 1923 and 1924, were not atypical for the period.[1]

During the heated presidential campaign of William McKinley against William Jennings Bryan in 1896, McKinley's shrewd manager, Mark Hanna of Ohio, attempted to capitalize on the popularity of the cult of the flag by reemphasizing the earlier connections suggested by those who "waved the bloody shirt." Hanna organized a "Patriotic Heroes Battalion" of revered Republican generals to whistle-stop through ten states of the Midwest and West, averaging seven stops a day, on a train decorated with two thousand yards of bunting. In lieu of a caboose, the end of the train employed a flatcar carrying a cannon and two thirty-foot collapsible flagpoles. Beneath flags flying from these august positions, seventy-year-old General Daniel E. Sickles, a powerful figure in the G.A.R., would climax each stop with an oration reminding the audience of the G.O.P.'s devotion to the Union and the flag. As the train pulled out of the station, a bugler would sound taps and a McKinley supporter would fire from the cannon a closing salute to the flag.

The success of the project encouraged Hanna to declare a special Flag Day for 31 October 1896, connecting the cause of patriotism with the specific economic and political aims of the Republican Party. Since the centennial of the Flag Resolution, Flag Day had been observed only sporadically, growing in popularity as the hereditary societies lobbied for its recognition. The Connecticut branch of the Sons of the American Revolution began the effort in 1890 and by 1895 the national organizations of the Sons of the Revolution, the Daughters of the Revolution, the Colonial Dames, and the Sons of the American Revolution all worked toward this goal. Hanna's idea, however, involved a different use of Flag Day: to identify the banner with one political party.

A Republican newspaper supporting Hanna's proposal, the *Chicago Tribune*, maintained that people should "unfurl Old Glory . . .

and testify thereby . . . their opposition to the Popocratic policy [Bryant's platform] which tends to discredit it." The Democratic committee worked to stop a Republican monopolization of the symbol by urging all its members to fly their flags that day as well. Although members of both parties demonstrated their patriotism by flying the flag that day, the attempt to appropriate it for one partisan ideology by creating a special Flag Day illustrated the power political strategists recognized in the symbol.[2]

One political use mentioned earlier that flourished in this period was the inscription of candidates' names on American flags or the introduction of their portraits either on the canton or the general field of stripes. Such alteration converted these flags from replicas of the national standard to partisan banners. Even before the Civil War, some Americans distinguished between the honor accorded the American flag and that given to such a partisan banner; an 1856 selection from the journal of Benjamin B. French, a government official from the District of Columbia whose house stood on a site now occupied by the Library of Congress, reveals: "Benny and his associates are erecting a flag staff, on which a plain American flag is to be hoisted. I approve it but will have no partisan flag floating on my premises."[3]

Shortly after the Civil War, one presidential candidate reportedly spoke out publicly against the practice of inscribing campaign legends or portraits upon flags. According to a source published thirty years later, while General Ulysses S. Grant was out soliciting votes in 1868, he rode into Galena, Illinois, and noticed GRANT and COLFAX imprinted on an American flag suspended over Main Street. "He requested that the flag be taken down or the names removed, saying, 'There is no name so great that it should be placed upon the flag of the country.'"[4] Perhaps Grant's years of military training had taught him a special reverence for the banner he had seen in camp, in battle, or on triumphant parade. However, General McClellan, the Democratic candidate for president in 1864, was also a military man with a reputation respected nationwide, and he did not seem to mind the use of his name or image on flags. Nor, for that matter, did Abraham Lincoln, who often referred reverentially to the flag as he called for commitment to an undivided Union, yet apparently accepted the widespread custom of imprinting political messages and images upon the banner.

If Grant was disturbed by the practice, it did not bother him enough to alert his followers. At least eight different variants of "Grant and Colfax" partisan banners from the election of 1868 survive, some using the names, some the portraits, and some a combination of the two, all superimposed on the flag of the United States. Still other variants were produced by Republican supporters for Grant in the 1872 election, which he won against Horace Greeley.[5] Looking back from a modern vantage, one is tempted to speculate that Grant's attitude on the matter was romanticized by those lobbying for flag desecration laws in the 1890s. In a letter dated 15 June 1895, General J. C. Smith, then in Europe, declared that Grant made the remark to him while walking down the street in Galena. Smith recalled his personal reaction as "startled . . . yet pleased" and erroneously claimed that, from that day forward, Grant's name was never directly inscribed on a flag, but only attached on a separate strip of canvas.[6] If Grant did make such a statement—and Boleslaw and Marie Mastai claim it was portraits on flags he meant to abolish[7]—the fact that he had been a military hero tied in nicely to appeals for support from the hereditary societies to the G.A.R., who had transferred into civilian life the military practice of inscribing particular names of posts, regiments, and even specific battles on flags.

Whatever Grant's views on the subject were, partisan banners remained a political tool employed in every presidential campaign by both parties through the rest of the nineteenth century.[8] One variant method that proved economical consisted of attaching candidates' names on silk cloth to the bottom of flags flying horizontally. The silken names came prefitted, produced by the flag companies, and were interchangeable. Thus, supporters could switch parties, or use the same flag every four years, and only have to buy new names, saving or disposing of the formerly used attachment. As the consumer culture coalesced and emerged in the closing years of the nineteenth century, the reusable partisan banner offered citizens an opportunity to save the integral part of the symbol, the American flag itself, and adapt the attachments to meet their needs. Advertisements for such attachments displayed both Republican and Democratic examples on the cover. For example, Cheney Brothers' American Silk Flags, of South Manchester, Connecticut, ran an advertisement in 1880 for silk campaign flags with attachments labeled "GARFIELD and ARTHUR" or "HANCOCK and ENGLISH." In 1904, the John B. Varick Company of Manchester, New Hampshire, advertised all wool, standard, U. S. bunting American flags, with attachments labeled "ROOSEVELT and FAIRBANKS" or "PARKER and DAVIS."

Although the attachments offered an alternative to imprinting flags indelibly, the latter practice continued to be widespread. Such partisan banners often flew outdoors, where many passers-by might see them and connect the candidates with the flag. The 1892 catalogue of Reuben Wood's Sons included this information: "Cotton Bunting U. S. Flags. Candidates' Names Printed on Flags. These Flags are Much Used on Rope Stretched ACROSS THE STREET. Printed on Turkey Red and Indigo Blue. Absolutely Fast Colors and Resembles a Silk Flag A LITTLE WAYS OFF. Price, with Printing: 6 feet long, $2.00; 7 feet long, $2.50; 9 feet long, $3.00."[9]

Politicians were not the only citizens to realize the value of connecting their names with the national flag. The use of flags in commercial advertising accelerated as the cult of the flag grew. Those with products to sell recognized the increased attention and reverence the flag received and moved to capitalize on its power. Flag business cards became fashionable; printed advertisements displayed flags with a wide variety of nonrelated products; and flag-printed paraphernalia, expanding on the ideas for souvenirs that had marked the celebration of the centennial, demonstrated that entrepreneurs and businessmen believed patriotic responses to the flag would encourage consumers to buy their products.

Following the centennial, flag business cards employed flags unabashedly. Lacking the skills of a modern-day Madison Avenue executive, in 1878 the anonymous creator of a business card for a Louisiana firm, McFerran Shallcross and Company, realized the power of including a representation of the flag on the card. Since the firm sold "Magnolia Ham," the card depicts Uncle Sam standing beside a giant ham that stretches from the floor to his chin. He holds it with one hand, and points to it with the other. Behind him, a large American flag blowing in the breeze fills the card, with the inscription: "The Magnolia Ham is an American Institution."

Other business cards from the closing decades of the nineteenth century indicate the same tendency to associate a wide variety of seemingly nonpatriotic products with the American flag. The card of the Western Wheeled Scraper Company of Aurora, Illinois, includes the Stars and Stripes in a picture of different models of heavy equipment. The Merrick Thread Company card illustration shows a daring tightrope walker, presumably walking on Merrick thread, balancing halfway between a church spire and an American flag. Printed in blue upon the red stripes is the message: "Merrick's American Standard Sik [sic]

Cord."[10] The latter example obviously appeals to both patriotism and piety in that it connects the two, as many supporters of the cult of the flag wished it to do.

Since print advertising reached such a wide circulation in the United States, flags appeared in many popular periodical and magazine advertisements during the 1890s. *Harper's Weekly*, for instance, might include a representation of the American flag in an advertisement for William's Shaving Stick one month, then include it in an advertisement for Pear's Soap the next.[11] Similar to the items on the business cards, the products advertised often had no clear connection to the national government, and the patriotic sales pitch (rather naively done by today's standards) totally depended on identifying the flag in close association with the product. Even *The Youth's Companion* began running advertisements using the flag to sell unrelated products in 1890, coincidentally the same year that Upham began his campaign to place flags in public schols. The first such example from the magazine appears in November, 1890; it shows a small child waving an American flag near a large bottle of Scott's Emulsion, a cod liver oil that regularly bought advertising space in *The Youth's Companion*. Flags sporadically turn up in the magazine's advertisements for the rest of the decade, particularly in the Fourth of July issues, with both Everett Pianos and Ayer's Sarsaparilla cashing in on the symbol. Although this practice did not become as popular in *The Youth's Companion* advertising as it did in other mass market periodicals of the day, the very existence of the practice in the same journal that lobbied so ardently for increased respect for the American flag indicates that as national advertising developed in relation to the emerging consumer culture, the flag was at first considered an appropriate symbol to use to sell a product. There was no legal restraint to control with which products the flag should be associated, so although it appeared in national advertisements for products such as cod liver oil and sarsaparilla, the image was also used commercially to sell whiskey, lager beer, and tobacco.[12]

By 1896, the U. S. Patent Office had issued twenty-five trademark patterns employing the American flag, and in the five months from July to December 1896, six more companies applied for use of the flag in trademarks. These trademarks represented a wide variety of commercial products: bacon, pickled pork, biscuits, wall paper, soap, leather, patent medicines, cotton fabrics, tinned goods, and other diverse commodities.[13]

Browne Trade-Marks, a guide book for beginning advertisers in fin de siècle America, encouraged the practice. Although the use of flags was certainly not a most crucial issue to managerial strategists who sought to sell their products to the emerging consumer culture, Browne offered these thoughts on the use of such symbols in trademarks: "National flags are sometimes blended with other objects to catch the eye. They are admirably adapted to all uses of heraldic display, and their rich glowing colors appeal to feelings of patriotism, and win purchasers of the merchandise to which they are affixed. . . . One flag printed in green may catch the eye of the son of the Emerald Isle; . . . another flag, with stars on a blue field and stripes of alternate red and white, may secure a preference for the commodity upon which it is stamped."[14]

The commercial exploitation of the symbol was taken one step further in the promotion of products bearing not only flag trademarks or flags in their advertisements, but representations of the Flag of the United States covering the products themselves. Such items blatantly appealed to consumer patriotism. Conservatism and patriotism for the hereditary societies did not extend to accepting every feature of business practice; a hereditary society committee, disturbed by what they saw as desecration of a sacred symbol for private economic gain, compiled a list of offensive products on sale in 1896 that fit this category: the aforementioned partisan banners and posters, patriotic envelopes, awnings, neckties, hosiery, towels, napkins, handkerchiefs, minstrel coats, ballet skirts, boxing trunks, clown costumes, professional bicyclist apparel, picture mats, hammocks, pillows, cushions for yachts and chairs, quilts, equine fly nets, and dog blankets.[15]

Such widespread commercialization of a sacred symbol, it was feared, would diminish its value. After all, the high honor accorded the flag in the society, triggered by the firing on Fort Sumter, had emerged only a generation earlier, and the cult of the flag, as sponsored by the veterans' organizations and hereditary societies, had been stressing the sanctification of the symbol for less than ten years. Therefore, some supporters of the cult of the flag reacted with alarm to the commercialization of the national banner. It had been the veterans' organizations who had pioneered the introduction of the flag into the public schools, and the women's patriotic organizations who had spearheaded the subsequent movement to develop ritual around the flag in the schools, yet when the need arose to confront the forces of expanding American commerce and industry, it was the men's hereditary societies who organized and vigorously lobbied to protect the symbol from what they considered desecration.

No doubt many of the members of these societies had undergone or were presently undergoing status shifts in a culture experiencing rapid change due to industrialization, urbanization, and immigration.[16] The soldiers had worked for the commemoration of Memorial Day and the glorification of the flag for which they had risked their lives; the mothers had worked for the nurturing of the young in a proper moral code that included patriotic ritual focused on the flag, and now the male descendants of early American settlers struggled to keep crass materialistic forces from appropriating the symbol that signified a glorious past. As one member of the Sons of the American Revolution put it, such legislation of the symbol might restore some social control to those descendants:

> Expansive America—the growing power of civilization—absorbing new races, needs a flag law. Our public officials, acting under a flag openly degraded, battle with the lath of a manikin against the spirit of lawlessness and license, which this disrespect encourages in the leaders of mobs and misguided strikers of labor unions. Outlawry and hoodlumism are rampant.[17]

Although the male hereditary societies directed these efforts to forceably restrict commercial and political uses of the flag of the United States, they gained the support of the veterans' organizations and the women's patriotic societies.

Even before these various associations became involved in lobbying for antidesecration legislation, some individuals working alone pushed for change on the federal level. As early as 7 January 1880, perhaps in reaction to commercial and political adaptions of the flag motif that took place after the centennial observance, Representative Barber introduced a bill into the House of Representatives "to protect the national flag from desecration." This bill opposed the printing, stamping, or impressing of any words or designs on the flag (or representations of the flag) for "advertisement of merchandise or other property, or of any person's trade, occupation or business." It set the range of fines for violators at fifty to five hundred dollars. After being read twice on the floor of the House, Barber's bill, referred to the Judiciary Committee, disappeared from the Congressional Record.

Ten years later, Congressman Caldwell of Cincinnati introduced the following bill:

> Be it enacted by the Senate and House of Representatives of the United States in Congress assembled, that any person or persons who shall use the National flag, either by printing, painting, or affixing on

said flag, or otherwise attaching to the same, any advertisements for public display or private gain shall be guilty of a misdemeanor, and on conviction thereof in the District Court of the United States shall be fined in any sum not exceeding fifty dollars, or imprisonment not less than thirty days, or both, at the discretion of the court.[19]

This bill passed the House on 29 September 1890, but subsequently failed in the Senate. During the next four years, supporters of the cult of the flag concentrated their efforts on introducing flags and flag rituals into the public school systems, and no flag desecration bills were introduced. The growing commercialization of the symbol, however, motivated members of hereditary societies to begin campaigns to enact such legislation in 1895.

The movement appears to have originated in Illinois. In Chicago in February 1895, Captain Philip Reade, head of the Illinois Society of Colonial Wars, appointed Charles Kingsbury Miller chairman of a Flag Committee, responsible for compiling a list of names and addresses of all persons and corporations employing the emblems of the national flag or the Great Seal of the United States in the pursuit of private profit. Because of the high degree of shared membership among the various hereditary societies, Miller was soon appointed head of a similar Flag Committee for the Illinois branch of the Sons of the American Revolution, and reported on his progress to both organizations.

Reade worked zealously, giving speeches before meetings and writing influential leaders of various patriotic organizations to enlist their aid, and soon won the support of branches of the Sons of the Revolution, the D.A.R., and the G.A.R. Meanwhile, Miller's committee produced a pamphlet detailing some of the uses of the flag by politicians and businessmen that the committee found distasteful.[20] The mailing list that the flag committee created for the distribution of this pamphlet demonstrates who Miller believed to be most influential in winning public sympathy for the cause against flag desecration: "all Congressmen, governors, mayors and postmasters of large cities, presidents and librarians of colleges, prominent clergymen, editors of leading daily newspapers, public libraries, principal social clubs, historical societies, G.A.R. posts, and the heads of patriotic and hereditary societies."[21]

The June 1895 issue of *Spirit of '76*, a year-old journal edited in New York by William H. Brearley and catering to all those interested in hereditary society activities, asserted that the flag must be protected by law from such "unworthy uses" as saloon awnings, advertisements, and as "drapery or decoration for any place of an immoral character." This editorial suggested that those who were disrespectful to the flag were the same type of people who were disrespectful to God: "there will probably be men enough until the millennium who will be base enough to break their country's laws, treat its flag with disrespesct, and take the name of their Maker in vain, unless they are restrained by force."[22]

The G.A.R., although instrumental in the diffusion of flags throughout the public schools of the land, proved equivocal at first on the question of legislation against flag desecration. In 1889 the New York Grand Army had called for a law against the use of the American flag in advertising, but the following year the Colorado Grand Army held that "the use and display of the United States flag is the right of every citizen" and therefore supported owners of gambling houses and saloons who wished to use the flag to advertise their establishments. After Reade and Miller initiated their campaign, they won the support of the national leadership of the G.A.R., and in 1897 this group, as well as the Loyal Legion, the S.A.R., and the D.A.R., appointed its own flag committee to take up the question of flag desecration.

Soon there were more than two hundred flag committees— on various local, state, and national levels—passing resolutions against what they considered to be disrespectful uses of the flag (its use in modern advertising often offended them the most). In 1898 representatives of the flag committees of the S.A.R., the D.A.R., the Order of Founders and Patriots, the Society of the War of 1812, the Loyal Legion, the Naval Veterans, and the Society of the Army of the Potomac united to form the American Flag Association, based in New York. Headed by Ralph E. Prine, and prodded by Reade, this group dedicated itself to coordinating efforts to pass federal legislation against flag desecration.[23]

Representatives of the American Flag Association, as well as representatives from the distinct flag committees of specific branches of particular hereditary societies, visited congressmen and senators. Members of hereditary societies distributed circulars requesting endorsements among boards of trade, labor unions, business clubs, political clubs, and fraternal societies. Journals such as the Boston *Daily Herald*, the New York *Daily Mail and Express*, the Charleston (South Carolina) *Daily News and Courier*, the Chicago *Daily Times-Herald*, the Des Moines *Daily Register*, the Detroit *Daily Journal*, and the *Christian Advocate* printed supportive editorials. The Boston *Daily Transcript* reported: "The approval of this patriotic movement to secure a flag law is almost as general as was the recent approval of the appropriation of fifty million dollars for any immediate emergencies that might confront the country. Let congress give us a flag law." The Manchester, New Hampshire, *Daily Union* concurred, calling for a flag law so "that the most beautiful flag in the world be freed from the contamination of trade and that it continue to wave as a symbol of deeds of glory and not the almighty dollar."[24] Nevertheless, proposed federal legislation never made it out of the judiciary committees. This stalemate persisted due to the political stances of the heads of the Senate and House judiciary committees, respectively, Senator Hoar of Massachusetts and Representative Henderson of Iowa.

Legally, it was illogical to outlaw the commercial use of flag images while the Patent Office continued to issue the rights to such trademarks. To deny the Patent Office that prerogative and abrogate the previously granted trademarks and copyrights would require more legislation and probably entail appeals from the involved firms. Beyond this, Senator Hoar explained his reluctance in this fashion: "I took up that matter with a very earnest desire for some legislation. But as we reflected on the different plans that were brought to our attention, and we made our own suggestions, the difficulties multiplied. I am afraid that the great political parties of the country would not consent that the practice of hanging out the Flag with the names of the candidates attached should be abandoned."[25] Representative Henderson of Iowa voiced an economic motive for his position. When Representative Barrett of Massachusetts produced petitions circulated by the patriotic societies with one hundred thousand signatures calling for antidesecration legislation, he claimed Henderson replied that "he hoped the American people would continue to wrap hams in the flag, not to teach patriotism, but to teach ham eaters to eat American hams."[26]

In their persistent lobbying, those calling for such legislation continued to stress the holy value of the Flag and its special relationship to a Divine plan for the nation. Miller declared, "Our patriotism must not be endangered, nor our national pride humiliated, by the widespread desecration of the flag. These three sacred jewels, the Bible, the Cross and the Flag, command the national reverence." He also wrote, "the emblem of our republic should be kept as inviolate as was the Holy of Holies in King Solomon's temple."[27] For all their strategic dissemination of circulars to politicians, clergymen, and commercial and labor leaders, however, the American Flag Association and the hereditary societies' flag committees failed to bring about enactment of such federal legislation. Nevertheless, concerned supporters of the flag had created a national clearinghouse for their aims, the American Flag Association in New York, and this group, along with the flag committees of the various patriotic societies, frustrated in these efforts on the national level, altered their strategy. They quickly found state legislatures much more amenable to restricting uses of the national banner for personal or private profit.

The first state law restricting the use of the flag by advertisers, merchants, and politicans became effective in South Dakota in 1897. The Illinois state legislature followed suit in July 1898. Illinois was, after all, the home state of both Reade and Miller; their organizing and influence doubtlessly instigated this legal action. Subsequent legislation passed in New York provided the model law on flag desecration; Theodore Roosevelt, then Governor of New York, signed the action into law after the New York state legislature passed it on George Washington's Birthday, 1899. For supporters of the cult of the flag, Washington's Birthday had become a significant occasion for the promotion of the flag as a sacred symbol, tying together once again the patriotic images of the father of the country and the flag, while disseminating myths and legends concerning either and often both.[28]

Once states began legislating against commercial use of the American flag, the future of flag laws lay in the jurisdiction of the courts, which had to determine the constitutionality of such restrictions. Attempts to enforce the Illinois law and the New York law were both thrown out of court, but persistent lobbying by the patriotic organizations led to more state flag laws and more legal battles in court. Finally, in a landmark decision in 1907, the Supreme Court upheld the right of individual states to determine the accepted uses of the American flag within their borders and prohibit those uses found unacceptable.

The arrests and subsequent court battles on this issue began in Chicago. On 4 August 1899, F. L. Rossbach, manager of the Washington Shirt Company in Chicago, was charged with using the American flag for advertising purposes. He argued that his trademark (which included the image of the American flag) had been registered in the nation's capital on 25 May 1898, and he produced a license that granted him the exclusive right to use the trademark for thirty years. A Chicago judge dismissed the case against Rossbach, and in so doing raised this question about the goals of the cult of the flag: "Wherein is the flag desecrated by making a lithograph or a picture thereof as a trade-mark? If the common use of the flag is to abate veneration of it, why did our solons pass a law making it compulsory upon those in charge to fly the national emblem from the flagstaff of every school house?"[29]

Also in Chicago, at approximately the same time, a cigar seller named Ruhstrat was convicted for including the image of the flag of the United States on his cigar boxes. One label depicted the flag next to Lincoln, another depicted it next to the Capitol building, and still others showed it entwined in a wreath around a portrait or off in the corner of the label. Ruhstrat appealed, and the Illinois court that heard his appeal in 1900 declared the statute unconstitutional since it "did not demonstrably promote the safety or welfare of the society."[30]

In New York City, home of the American Flag Association, police chief William S. Devey issued an announcement on 19 July 1900: "all American flags, whether of cotton, silk, printed, painted, illuminated in electric lights, or of any other kind which contain anything in the way of an inscription or advertisement will be hauled down by the police department." Devey ruled that barber shop poles were exempt, but in his indictment he specifically included advertisements for "Yankee Doodle Toothpicks," "Star Spangleline for the Bath," and "Uncle Sam Pills."[31] As these examples indicate, the flag was part of a larger complex of national symbols appropriated by advertisers; nevertheless, although supporters of the cult of the flag might disapprove of such use of the images of Yankee Doodle and Uncle Sam, it was the preeminent symbol of the flag alone they wished to protect through antidesecration legislation.

Like Chicago, New York also had enough flag advertising to create a situation in which someone convicted under the flag law appealed to a higher court. In 1902 James H. McPike, manager of a cigar business, was arrested and incarcerated in New York for selling "Betsy Ross" cigars. (The boxes, made in Philadelphia, depicted the legendary Betsy and the flag.) While McPike was in jail, the Appellate Division, although divided on the issue, granted him *habeas corpus,* which released him from imprisonment while the Court of Appeals judged the constitutionality of the law. In 1903 that court decided that the state could make flag desecration a misdemeanor, but that the portion of this particular law that "discriminated against businessmen" was "not defensible," and that, in any case, it was unconstitutional to apply it to a product such as "Betsy Ross" cigars, which clearly predated the statute in its origin.[32]

By 1905 Nebraska had established a law against flag desecration based on the New York model. Its test came very soon when a businessman named Halter was arrested for selling beer bottles that had tiny flags on the labels. Halter did not find such action disrespectful; he predictably argued that the federal government, not states, should decide what is proper use of the national flag. Since the flag was a federal symbol of the country united as one, it should not come under state jurisdiction. At the time this involved an interpretation of states' rights. Halter did not conceive of the possibility that someday flag use would be interpreted as a "freedom of speech" issue involving individual rights; in fact, his defense attorney even went so far as to accept the right of the federal government "to protect the flag in time of peace as well as in time of war, even to the killing of the person or persons who might haul it down, should it become necessary to resort to such harsh means." This case went through appeals and reached the United States Supreme Court in 1907. At that time the Supreme Court not only upheld the Nebraska law, it approved the right of any state to pass such legislation. In his opinion, Justice Harlan approved the dissemination of the cult of the flag: "a state will be wanting in care for the well-being of its people if it ignores the fact that they regard the flag as a symbol of their country's power and prestige, and will be impatient if any open disrespect is shown towards it."[33] He also maintained that forbidding the flag to be used as a beer advertisement in no way obstructed anyone's personal liberty. From 1907 on, each state could use this case to support its legislature's particular interpretations and mandates for proper flag use within the state's borders.

Although it had profound implications, the use of the flag in advertising was only one small category of its widespread usage at the end of the nineteenth century. For instance, a great display of flag flying, flag waving, and flag saluting helped the citizenry feel a part of the war to "liberate" Cuba. It was a rather quick and successful thrust by the United States, an eagerly expanding world power, against the Kingdom of Spain, a weakened colonial master. Congress declared war on 28 April 1898, and by the end of July Spain was sueing for peace. According to the terms of the Treaty of Paris, finalized on 10 December 1898, Spain turned the Phillipines, Guam, and Puerto Rico over to the United States. Cuba remained under American military administration until 1902. Caught up in the patriotic fervor of expansionism following Independence Day of that year, Congress also annexed the Kingdom of Hawaii, which had been declared the Republic of Hawaii by American businessmen four years earlier. Noted historian

In a quick war that raised the cult of the flag to new heights, the United States defeated Spain in 1898. Here the American flag is hoisted over Guantanamo in Cuba on 12 June 1898. (Photo courtesy of the Library of Congress.)

Walter LaFeber has argued convincingly that this rapid expansion by a country championing itself as the fountainhead of democracy was not rooted in a desire for more stars on the flag: "The United States obtained these areas not to fulfill a colonial policy, but to use these holdings as a means to acquire markets for the glut of goods pouring out of highly mechanized factories and farms."[34] In its securing of such markets, the United States military carried the flag into several new foreign areas, reemphasizing its original military use to mark government possession of land and property. And in the spirit of healthy expansionism, a popular attitude toward such flags was "the bigger the better."

Over the arsenal in Havana, for instance, on New Year's Day, 1899, patriotic Americans raised an American flag one hundred twenty feet long by forty-three feet wide. When Admiral George Dewey, "the hero of Manila" and therefore the most touted military celebrity of the day, returned to the United States in his flagship the *Olympia,* it flew a pennant over five hundred feet long, which necessitated trailing the "Red, White, and Blue" in the ship's wake.[35] Such action did not seem to draw complaints from the supporters of the cult of the flag, many of whom cheered the coming of the Stars and Stripes to foreign shores.

One G.A.R. department commander put it this way: "Wherever oppression, ignorance, or any other craft has been oppressing mankind, and they rise and demand the protection of our flag . . . let us give it to them, even if we have to carry it into the very heart of China." New York's Lafayette Post of the G.A.R., which had proved so influential in the veterans' movement to place flags in public schools, decided that the foreign children now under the protection of the flag would be inspired by its regular presence in their lives; therefore, the Lafayette post sent the G.A.R.'s National Aide on Patriotism to Puerto Rico with six hundred American flags to fly over the public schools of the island. Later, the post sent seven hundred flags for distribution in schoolhouses throughout the Philippines.[36]

Students in the United States, meanwhile, began participating in a ceremony that encouraged not only patriotic devotion to the flag as a symbol but also a sense of bonding with many other students in a communal display of commitment. The creation of "living flags" was not a routine, daily ritual in danger of losing meaning through repetition; it was reserved for special occasions, such as the Fourth of July, a visit of the President or Governor, or, as the holiday grew in importance, Flag Day. One group influential in sponsoring the creation of "living flags" by students was the D.A.R., who would "create" living flags, for example, in places such as the steps of the United States Capitol. Such a ceremony was meant to instill in the children a sense of reverence for the place and also for the symbol of which they became, for a few minutes, a physical component. Arranged in rows, the students—in keeping with contemporary attitudes toward patriotic display, the more the better—would hold aloft pieces of red, white, or blue bunting to form a massive, "living flag." Later variations involved children dressing in red, white, or blue outfits. Boleslaw and Marie Mastal describe a "living flag" ceremony in New Orleans, a tribute to President William McKinley on 2 May 1901, that involved "one thousand colored students of the Southern University."[37]

Participation in such spectacles was not a viable option for many Americans living in rural areas, but wherever there was a piano, people could gather to hear some of the patriotic tunes so popular during and after the Spanish-American War. The outburst of nationalistic songs that flooded the sheet music market in 1898 was precipitated by the most popular and enduring work of this period, significantly titled "The Stars and Stripes Forever."

John Philip Sousa, who had become known as "the March King" during his tenure as head of the United States Marine Corps Band from 1880 to 1892, had already written marches, such as "The Washington Post," that had become the best-selling sheet music both in the United States and Europe. He combined his talent for creating a lively martial air with a sensitivity to the spreading influence of the cult of the flag when, in 1896, he composed "The Stars and Stripes Forever." This stirring march was distributed nationally in 1897 and met with immediate success; it became a staple of every Sousa concert from 1897 until his death in 1932. According to Sousa's biographer Paul E. Bierley, recordings of "The Stars and Stripes Forever" sold more copies than any other composition "for many years."

In describing a typical Sousa concert in Philadelphia, Bierley emphasizes that the closing slot on the program was reserved for "The Stars and Stripes Forever": "On the opening bar the electric light flag above the band, with its red, white, and blue bulbs, is turned on. The audience rises."[38] Not only in Philadelphia, but throughout the country, audiences would rise for this particular tune, according it the honor of a national anthem. Its vigorous strains inspired confidence and communicated strength, nicely catching the nationalistic mood of many Americans and translating it into a song dedicated to the flag of the United States.

Other sheet music from 1898 reveals the use of the flag in a wide variety of patriotic illustrations. Frank Thompson's "U. S. Naval Review Two Step" depicts an officer in a ship's rigging, with a massive American flag in the background. "Old Glory"—lyrics by John Northern Millard, music by George Newell Lovejoy—has a cover illustration that says much in its simplicity: it shows only the title and the flag itself, a message considered strong enough to sell the sheet music to unfamiliar consumers. Walter V. Ullner's "The Birth of Our Flag March" has three flags on the cover, one of them, with thirteen stars in a circle, being handed to members of the Flag Committee by a white-haired Betsy Ross. Published in New York, this music offers another medium for the dissemination of the Betsy Ross legend, and exemplifies the American tendency to intensify concern for the flag and its associated legends during wartime.

Three other music sheets from 1898 depict Columbia, or as she also came to be known, "Lady Liberty" or "Miss America," carrying a huge, flowing American flag as her standard. The image of

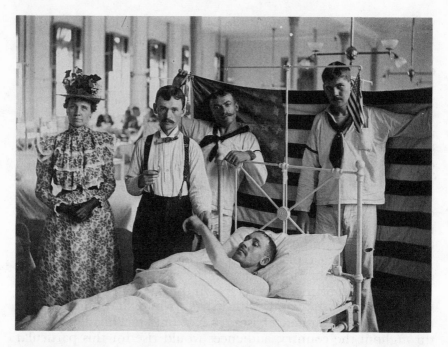

John Philip Sousa's "The Stars and Stripes Forever" was one of the most popular tunes in the country when this group posed at the Brooklyn Naval Hospital for this photograph entitled "Taking the Patient's Pulse." (Photo courtesy of the Library of Congress.)

this female personification of the nation now appeared in a variety of forms. The matronly protector of the Union, as pictured in *Harper's* during the Civil War, continued on the cover of E. T. Paull's "America Forever! March." A collection of patriotic tunes entitled *Music of the Union* bore a cover illustration, imprinted on a background of two flags, of a younger, stronger Columbia, more indicative of a classical reference to Artemis than the earlier version, which correspondingly might be compared to images of Athena. Still a third image of the Lady with the Flag appeared on the cover of J. Edmund Barnum's "Miss America Two Step"; here she was an elegant young woman dressed in contemporary fashions, gracefully posing with her banner beneath a rose-covered trellis.[39] Although it lies outside the perimeters of this study, a comprehensive analysis of shifting uses and images of Columbia, quite apart from this analysis of cultural shifts in flag use and representation, might offer insights into changing cultural perceptions of the role of women in expressing, disseminating, and representing patriotism.

One such shift for women, for instance, was proper behavior when hearing a band play "The Star-Spangled Banner." During the two years prior to the Spanish-American War, a custom had spread of seated audiences rising in the presence of the national flag when it passed on review.[40] In the early 1890s, as one of many actions in support of the cult of the flag, the Commander of the Grand Army of the Republic had urged his followers to rise at the opening bars of "The Star-Spangled Banner." There are indications, however, that the veterans did not feel comfortable doing so when the rest of the audience, unfamiliar with the new custom, did not bother to follow suit. The 1894 national encampment in Rhode Island tabled a resolution requiring members to stand during this particular song. In July, 1895, a privately produced newspaper in Indianapolis, specifically geared to a G.A.R. audience, lamented the fact that audiences usually did not stand for "The Star-Spangled Banner"; it urged the veterans to set an example: "A little persistency for a year or two will establish a rule whose observance will become universal and enduring."[41]

It appears the custom became fixed, for both men and women, during the increased nationalism of the Spanish-American War. "The Star-Spangled Banner" was not the only song accorded this honor at the turn of the century, however. As noted earlier, patriotic citizens also stood for "The Stars and Stripes Forever" and sometimes they stood for "America." Although the general public might not always have been able to discern different statuses between the songs, in 1895 the Army officially recognized "The Star-Spangled Banner" as appropriate to be played at morning flag raisings. In 1904, at the instigation of Admiral Dewey, President Theodore Roosevelt ordered the work played by all Navy bands at both morning and evening ceremonies. These military approvals, coupled with the support of the D.A.R. and other hereditary societies, ensured a quasi-official acceptance of "The Star-Spangled Banner."[42]

The increased respect for the anthem was a by-product of the cult of the flag, which had successfully become the major force in shaping American patriotic ritual. The veterans' organizations and hereditary societies had done their jobs well. It is possible to analyze the methods they used and the success they had in placing flags in schools, encouraging the pledge, or halting the use of the American flag for commercial profit. It would be much harder, however, to determine how successful the cult of the flag was in actually achieving its goal of instilling patriotism in the young and the foreign-born. Nevertheless, the testimony of Jacob Riis, an eloquent immigrant from Denmark, demonstrates that, if nothing else, these groups succeeded in establishing recognition of the flag of the United States as a symbol of special power and unique emphasis.

Born in 1849, Riis came to New York City in 1870 with limited journalistic experience and even less money. Eventually he won himself a position as a police reporter, serving the *New York Tribune* from 1877 to 1888 and then the *Evening Sun* from 1888 to 1899. While tracking down stories of accidents or crimes, he often visited the tenement slums of the immigrant populace, and eventually dedicated the rest of his life to improving their living conditions. Through articles, lectures, and a series of books, Riis became a well-known advocate of social reform.

In 1901 Riis published an autobiographical work significantly titled *The Making of an American*. In the closing vignette of the book, he demonstrated the redemptive and healing powers that the American flag had come to possess in his mind. Even if one accepts this as a bit of creative literary indulgence, the use of the flag in this manner illustrates how an immigrant, writing to an American audience at the beginning of the twentieth century, chose to substantiate his American identity—the final chapter is entitled "The American Made." Although the passage is a bit long, it is presented here in its entirety, to allow Riis the opportunity to present his relationship with the flag in his own words:

I have told the story of the making of an American. There remains to tell how I found out that he was made and finished at last. It was when I went back to see my mother once more and, wandering about the country of my childhood's memories, had come to the city of Elsinore. There I fell ill of a fever and lay many weeks in the house of a friend upon the shore of the beautiful Oeresund. One day when the fever had left me they rolled my bed into a room overlooking the sea. The sunlight danced upon the waves, and the distant mountains of Sweden were blue against the horizon. Ships passed under full sail up and down the great waterway of the nations. But the sunshine and the peaceful day bore no message to me. I lay moodily picking at the coverlet, sick and discouraged and sore—I hardly knew why myself. Until all at once there sailed past, close inshore, a ship flying at the top the flag of freedom, blown out on the breeze till every star in it shone bright and clear. That moment I knew. Gone were illness, discouragement, and gloom! Forgotten weakness and suffering, the cautions of doctor and nurse. I sat up in bed and shouted, laughed and cried by turns, waving my handkerchief to the flag out there. They thought I had lost my head, but I told them no, thank God! I had found it, and my heart, too, at last. I knew then that it was my flag; that my children's home was mine, indeed; that I also had become an American in truth. And I thanked God, and, like unto the man sick of the palsy, arose from my bed and went home, healed.[43]

The transformation to "an American in truth" occurs, climactically, when Riis recognizes the flag as his own; for his devotion, he is miraculously cured. Although not a candidate for the Sons of the Revolution and ineligible for membership in the G.A.R., Riis nevertheless rejoices in the cult of the flag, demonstrating one example of the success of such groups that worked to spread an increased sensitivity to its use and interpretation. The meaning of the flag had become significant enough to those with power to change the society so that laws were passed and enforced to ensure its daily presence in the lives of malleable young people and to prohibit its exploitation for personal rather than patriotic reasons. America entered the twentieth century with an assortment of flag rituals and uses far more complex than that of the society only fifty years earlier: a body of flag poems, songs, stories, and legends had emerged; flag salutes and dedication ceremonies had become a staple of patriotic celebrations. The cult of the flag had secured the national banner the highest honor in the constellation of patriotic symbols employed in the culture. World War I would only serve to emphasize this status even more, and spur a movement for a detailed code of flag etiquette, a code to teach all Americans the proper ritual, ceremony, and uses of the flag of the United States.

8

A Civilian Code of Flag Etiquette

During the first quarter of the twentieth century, customs associated with the flag of the United States became more standardized throughout the society as leaders of veterans', fraternal, and various other civic oriented organizations gradually codified flag etiquette. Before the National Flag Conference representatives first achieved this standardization in 1923, a variety of cultural uses continued to influence the spread of the cult of the flag. George M. Cohan demonstrated that flag-waving patriotism could prove a financially successful element in the Broadway musical. Young people's movements such as the Boy Scouts and the Girl Scouts provided opportunities to mold the character of the youth of the nation, and flag etiquette became a staple in such organizations. The outbreak of World War I in Europe aroused American nationalism and the United States' entry into that war in 1917 triggered an unprecedented demand for flags, which in turn led to the establishment of many new flag manufacturing companies. During the war patriots designed flag pageants to keep the young supportive on the home front, and at this time the flag of the United States made a significant entry into ceremonies of the world of organized sports as well.

A more ominous reaction to the war on the homefront was the adoption of the Uniform Flag Law by several states. Phrasing in this law, in part similar to Espionage Acts designed to protect the nation from infiltration of pro-German propaganda and support, ironically led to some severe penalties for citizens who did not conform to accepted demonstrations of reverence for the flag. During these years that cult reached its zenith in mystical ceremonies invoking a holy power of the American flag; groups such as the Masons or the Eastern Star accorded it homage, but the ultimate expression of the cult of the flag appeared in *The Religion of Old Glory* by William Norman Guthrie, a 1918 tract arguing for nondenominational public religious ceremonies celebrating the national banner. Although Guthrie's proposed ritual was an outburst of wartime patriotism, it exemplifies the symbolic power accredited the American flag during these years. Following the Great War, the National Flag Conferences of 1923 and 1924 responded to a growing concern for an established code of flag etiquette; at the same time, the reemergence of the Ku Klux Klan illustrated the continuing appropriation of the American flag by nativist elements. Stimulated by the Flag Conferences, retired Army Colonel James A. Moss established the United States Flag Association, a socially conservative organization dedicated to instilling love of country through love of flag, while quietly supporting an agenda of political policies aimed at sustaining the established socioeconomic order. Moss's organization was the progenitor of such organizations that thrive today—while the Klansmen marched with their flags and the civic leaders discussed the proper way to hang the national banner from a window, a new network for spreading the cult of the flag was emerging, connecting media, conservative politicians, and private industry.

The Broadway musical was one cultural category in which the use of the flag underwent some noticeable changes in the early twentieth century, and the man most influential in instigating this shift was George M. Cohan. Coincidentally born on the Fourth of July in 1878, Cohan grew up in a vaudevillian family and was raised with an appreciation for popular theater. By 1910 he earned himself the title of "The Man Who Owned Broadway," for he took the profits he made from several successful musical shows he both wrote and starred in and poured this capital into building and purchasing theaters in New York's theater district. One of the basic ingredients in the success of Cohan productions was Cohan's repeated invocation of patriotic themes, often culminating in flag-waving routines. This strategy is nicely illustrated in two of his early hits, *Little Johnny Jones,* his first blockbuster that played Broadway 1904–1905, and *George Washington, Jr.,* its follow-up show in 1906.

Little Johnny Jones recounted the adventures of a brash, young jockey from the United States who goes to England and demonstrates Yankee superiority in winning an important horse race. Much of the play is set in England, providing Cohan, as Johnny, several opportunities to champion the American national character. The classic tune "Give My Regards to Broadway" serves as the finale to this production, but the patriotic highpoint of the show occurs in the middle of the first act, when Johnny, preparing for the race, launches into "I'm a Yankee Doodle Dandy." Flag-waving by supporting actors encourages his rendition, and the Stars and Stripes are again waved exuberantly when he wins the race. While establishing himself as a dominant force in the world of American musicals with *Little Johnny Jones,* Cohan learned an important lesson from the success of this play: patriotism fills theater seats.

He took this knowledge one step further with *George Washington, Jr.* While riding in a funeral procession with a Civil War veteran, Cohan remarked on the man's devotion to a tattered flag of the United States, a relic from the war forty years earlier brought out of storage for the ceremonial occasion. The elderly veteran spoke of his participation in Pickett's Charge at Gettysburg, and told Cohan, "it was all for this. She's a grand old rag."[1] Cohan recognized sincere and profound patriotism, and went home to write a song about the American flag and proper devotion to it. After he had already penned the song, he fashioned *George Washington, Jr.* as a vehicle around it. The story involves a brash (again) senator's son who loves an all-American belle from Virginia. Unfortunately, his father has arranged a marriage for him with an English noblewoman, who is secretly a detective in the pay of an evil U.S. senator. For true love, the hero, George Belgrave, forsakes his family and his name—but not his country—to become George Washington, Jr. Some of the settings include Mount Vernon and Washington D.C. It is in the latter location that the character of an old veteran hands the hero a tattered American flag, which provokes George Washington, Jr.— played by George M. Cohan—to sing "You're a Grand Old Rag":

> . . . Hurrah! Hurrah! We'll join the jubilee,
> And that's going some, for the Yankees, by gum!
> Red, White and Blue, I am for you;
> Honest, you're a grand old rag!
>
> You're a grand old rag, you're a high-flying flag
> And forever, in peace, may you wave;
> You're the emblem of the land I love,
> The home of the free and the brave.
> Ev'ry heart beats true, under Red, White and Blue;
> Where there's never a boast or brag;
> But should auld acquaintance be forgot,
> Keep your eye on the grand old rag.[2]

Audiences reacted warmly to this tribute to the cult of the flag and it quickly became a classic showstopper. Long after *George Washington, Jr.* was virtually forgotten, "You're a Grand Old Rag"—changed to "You're a Grand Old Flag"—remains a standard finale for high school, community, and holiday productions throughout the United States. A theater critic's complaint the third night of the show, charging that calling the national banner a "rag" was an act of desecration, provoked Cohan to quickly change the line, since his purpose was to invoke patriotic support, not opposition.[3] His successful incorporation of the cult of the flag into musicals began a tradition that persists in the theater: it is a generally accepted rule that a patriotic pitch can often win an audience, and due to the influence of the cult of the flag, a patriotic pitch virtually requires the use of the national banner. In the words of the 1953 song by Howard Dietz and Arthur Schwartz, "That's Entertainment," which summarizes various time-honored theatrical methods of audience appeal: "The gag may be waving the flag, that began, back with Mr. Cohan, Hip Hooray! the American Way!—That's Entertainment!"[4]

Although not meant as entertainment but as a means of appealing to an audience to increase sales, when *The Journal of American History* debuted in 1907, this illustrated periodical included a seven and a half by nine inch silk flag inserted into each copy. Not to be confused with the later *Journal of American History* (which developed out of the *Mississippi Valley Historical Review*), the original *Journal of American History*, published in New Haven, Connecticut, announced in its premiere issue the purpose of "collecting the various phases of history, art, literature, science, industry and such as pertains to the moral, intellectual and political uplift of the American nation—inspiring nobility of home and state" so it would be a "testimonial of the marked character of the builders of the American republic."[5] Behind the silk flag, a memorial of the Star-Spangled Banner made by the Cheney Mills at South Manchester, Connecticut, was an insert page with the quote: "Oh, say does that Star Spangled Banner yet wave/O'er the land of the free and the home of the brave." The lead article for the first issue followed, a summary history of the flag of the United States, written by Mrs. Henry Champion. Six silk paper reproductions of various colonial and early versions of the American flag accompanied her article, which credited Betsy Ross for the first version of the Stars and Stripes and noted that, by 1907, thirty-one states and territories had passed laws against flag desecration.

The evolution of the flag offered a useful, significant theme to trace the historical "progress" of the United States; the editors realized this in granting it such focus in the first issue of the *Journal of American History*. Champion's article also celebrated the successes of the Spanish-American War and emphasized economic prospects for the future of the United States. "To-day the American knight holds the commercial supremacy of the world," she wrote. Clearly making a comparison to the imperial expansion of Great Britain, she explained how, even before the Philippine Islands were "taken under our care," the sun never set on the Stars and Stripes: "the Aleutian Islands, a part of Alaska, extend so far to the westward that when it is sunset on the most westerly part, it is sunrise in Eastport, Maine."[6] Subsequent histories of the American flag written in the twentieth century would, for the most part, continue this pattern of combining historical documentation with nationalistic rhetoric, connecting the evolution of the flag (most often emphasizing the addition of stars) with American "progress."

Champion's article served as the main source of information for Alfred Pirtle, of Louisville, Kentucky, when he delivered a speech on the history of the American flag before a meeting of his Loyal Legion post on 7 December 1910. The Loyal Legion was a Civil war veteran's organization, for former officers, which actively supported the efforts to establish legislation against flag desecration. Although Pirtle did not take up that theme in his speech, he did provide a few useful bits of information about the status of the cult of the flag at the end of 1910.

Pirtle's history began with a recognition of various European flags before tracing the roles of Betsy Ross and John Paul Jones, as he understood them, in contributing to the creation and use of the first flag of the United States. He pointed out that "the custom of rising and standing in respectful silence" during the playing of the "Star-Spangled Banner," "at all places where there is an assemblage of people, is a growing one, and it should become national and universal."[7] So, although by 1910 the practice was required for all persons in military service, it still was not securely established among the civilian populace. In closing his speech, Pirtle reaffirmed the civil religious goal of supporters of the cult of the flag: "Let the children be brought up to place 'The Colors' [the national flag] next to the Cross, in their feeling of veneration."[8]

Also in 1910, the Daughters of the American Revolution appointed Mrs. Jacob M. Dickinson of Nashville, Tennessee, chairman of their national committee dedicated to preventing desecration of the flag. Dickinson used in part the influential fact that her husband was Secretary of War to secure an opportunity to speak before the House Committee on the Judiciary on 11 February 1913. She continued the longstanding effort of the hereditary societies to seek federal legislation against flag desecration. Although the committeemen only gave her ten minutes to testify and had no apparent intention of acting upon her wishes, her speech reflected the perseverance of this lobbying effort. She noted that many states had passed laws against flag desecration but that the practice was just beginning in the South. Federal action would, in her words, make all the states "fall in line."

An obstacle to such legislation, both here and earlier, was the inherent difficulty of drafting laws that would permit accepted, customary practice while curtailing what the hereditary societies considered "desecration." The bounds of propriety in flag use, as in other social practices, fluctuated in different regions and between different classes or subcultures; establishing a law mandating specific behavior could arouse protests of individual liberties being denied, such as those of businessmen in the cases of Ruhstrat and McPike. Dickinson indicated an awareness of such complaints, for her plea included a list of exceptions the D.A.R. would allow if it would help win over those who felt such a flag desecration bill curtailed individual liberty:

> That this act shall not apply to any newspaper, periodical, book, pamphlet, circular, certificate, diploma, warrant, commission or appointment to office, ornamental picture, badges, or stationery, for use in correspondence, on any of which shall be printed, painted, or placed any such flag, ensign, or standard, disconnected from any advertisement for the purpose of sale, barter, or trade; nor shall it apply to any act permitted by the Army or Navy regulations of the United States; nor shall it apply to any flag, standard, or ensign belonging to a Grand Army Post, a camp of the Legion of Spanish War Veterans, or which is the property or is used in the service of the United States or of any State or Territory, upon which shall be placed the names of battles or the name and number of any organization lawfully entitled to the use thereof; nor shall it apply to any patriotic demonstration or decoration.[9]

The last phrase would have allowed for broad interpretation of flag use, but this bill, as was true of all the federal bills of this period against misuse of the flag, never made it through the entire process to become law. However, in 1917 the National Conference of Commissioners on Uniform State Laws approved a "Uniform Flag Statute," virtually identical to the New York State law of 1905, which served as the model for all subsequent state legislation. The National Conference of Commissioners on Uniform States Laws was "a body of Commissioners deriving their authority by appointment of the Governor of their respective states" which had met annually since the 1890s to consider and approve such model laws. This "Uniform Flag Statute" (see Appendix) contained virtually the same provisions as Dickerson and the D.A.R. wished to see in federal legislation—but it only served as law in those states that made it a state law, and as late as 1980 that number had only increased to fifteen.[10]

The D.A.R. had, since 1895, been encouraging respect for the flag and the anthem "The Star-Spangled Banner" in chapters of their youth subsidiary, the Children of the American Revolution (C.A.R.). Since C.A.R. membership was also limited to those whose ancestors had fought in the American Revolution, and not every D.A.R. chapter developed its own C.A.R. offshoot, growth was limited, listing under one thousand members by 1900, and those almost exclusively in the states of Pennsylvania, New York, Massachusetts, and Connecticut.[11] During the second decade of the twentieth century, however, other organizations dedicated to molding the character of American youth developed that attracted far more followers. All of these groups emphasized learning proper respect for the national flag. Chief among them was the Boy Scouts of America.

Drawing on the popularity of Lord Baden-Powell's scouting movement in England, organizers, working out of YMCA offices in New York, created the Boy Scouts of America (BSA) in 1910. By the time the United States entered World War I, membership had grown to 281,044 members throughout the country.[12] A 1913 statement issued by the main office claimed the BSA's goal to be teaching the young men of the United States "honor, loyalty, obedience, and patriotism." Boy Scouts gave the flag the military salute, carried it in "preparedness" parades as war drew near, and flew it at their campsites. Although the organization emphasized the usual woodcraft and camping skills, Secretary of the Treasury William Gibbs McAdoo praised it as "one of the most potential agencies we could employ to Americanize America." Historian David I. Macleod has noted that, during and following World War I, "as 'character and citizenship' became the standard formula for Boy Scouting's goals, public figures virtually ignored the outdoor program to praise the BSA as a force for patriotism."[13]

A scan of various editions of the *Boy Scout Handbook* from the first edition in 1911 through the thirtieth edition following the First National Flag Conference in 1923 reveals that flag etiquette is mentioned in the earlier volumes, but a much more significant emphasis is placed on proper flag use following the conference. The first edition of the *Handbook* includes a chapter on "Patriotism and Citizenship" written by Waldo H. Sherman, author of *Civics— Studies in Citizenship.* Within the thirty-five-page chapter, Sherman devotes two and a half pages to a discussion of the flag. He credits Betsy Ross with making the first flag, mentions that Flag Day is a recognized holiday in several states, and includes five rules on flag etiquette taken from the New York Branch of the Sons of the Revolution, limiting flag flying to daylight hours, encouraging Scouts to adopt the military salute, and explaining how to fly the flag at half-staff. This same material reappears in each edition published through 1921, although after World War I Sherman replaces the section crediting Betsy Ross with a discussion of the Grand Union Flag of the United Colonies, also adding President Wilson's wartime Flag Day Address.

Starting with the thirtieth edition, published in 1924, the Boy Scouts of America included at the very back of the handbook the entire Flag Code, well-illustrated to clarify hanging and carrying procedures.[14] Although the Boy Scouts of America was the most prominent youth organization to teach respect for the flag to its members during the 1910s and 20s, girls responding to nationalism provoked throughout the society by the war in Europe could express their patriotism by participating in the Camp Fire Girls or the Girl Scouts movements. These groups, too, taught respect for the flag, but the emphasis of the Boy Scouts on military drilling in army-styled uniforms during the war years led to further use of the flag as the young men appropriated military ritual and procedure, practicing for the day when they might serve as soldiers.

Boy Scouts were not the only Americans increasingly caught up in flag display and flag ceremonies when Woodrow Wilson finally brought the United States into World War I. Flag flying had increased in both the private and the public sector. In response to this, and as a demonstration of civic pride, a few businesses produced and distributed pamphlets and small handbooks celebrating the flag. John Wanamaker, owner of a prominent department store in Philadelphia, had already issued such a work, entitled *My Flag*, a few years earlier when the war first began in Europe. Following Wilson's declaration of war against Germany on 4 April 1917, Marshall Field & Company of Chicago commissioned Professor Bernard J. Cigrand of the University of Illinois, an authority on heraldry in America, to prepare a guidebook summarizing accepted uses and customs associated with the flag.

Cigrand drew on military and naval custom in preparing this guide. In sixteen pages, he quickly summarized how to hang, carry, and drape the flag of the United States. He advised that nothing should be placed above the flag, that it should not be flown at night or in a storm, and that, when old or torn, it should be disposed of with respect. He also listed, according to "accepted custom," the six days when the flag was most generally flown: Lincoln's Birthday, Washington's Birthday, Mother's Day, Memorial Day, Flag Day, and Independence Day. In his introduction he stated: "In presenting to the public this booklet for distribution it is with the hope that it may prove of service in making readily available such information as will tend to increase the evidences of public respect for our national emblem."[15]

The National Geographic Society devoted a special issue of its well-circulated magazine to flags of the world in October 1917. Although this "Flag Number" included illustrations and descriptions of flags from all over the world, it gave special emphasis to the flags of the United States. Referring to the American servicemen then risking their lives for democracy, editor Gilbert Grosvenor wrote: "History can bestow upon such soldiers no higher enconium than that of Defenders of the Flag." [16] Patriotic Americans could read in this issue such articles as "The Story of the American Flag," "Flags of Our Army, Navy, and Government Departments," "Our State Flags," "Famous Flags of American History," "The Insignia of Our Uniformed Forces," and "The Correct Display of the Stars and Stripes." The Navy's leading expert on the United States flag, Lieutenant Commander Byron McCandless, put this issue together for Grosvenor, and in return the editor donated five thousand free copies of the issue to both the Army and the Navy, for distribution among enlisted men.

The articles evidence McCandless's naval background. In "The Story of the American Flag," he reviews naval uses of first the Grand Union Flag and then the Stars and Stripes. Betsy Ross's contribution is deemed "a picturesque legend"; because the Marine Committee submitted the Flag Resolution to Congress on 14 June 1777, McCandless maintains that the Navy gave the nation its flag. In explaining "The Correct Display of the Stars and Stripes," McCandless summarizes naval ceremonies of raising and lowering the colors, naval flag salutes, and appropriate flag display when a fleet sails forth to battle. He does lament two "unfortunately quite common" examples of flag use among the general public that he deemed improper: draping a flag over a speaker's dais "like a tablecloth," and tying small United States flags to the bottom of a

stage curtain.[17] Three years later, Gridley Adams, a Chicago cartoonist and collector of political anecdotes, argued that the common practice of placing a bust or picture of George Washington
upon the flag of the United States was an insult to both. In an
article entitled "Not law-compelled 'etiquette' but—real love and
reverence for the Flag," Adams avowed "the Flag is never sub-
jected to the insult of being used as a decoration. Its position is
never subjugated."[18] In 1923, Adams would be an influential
force in establishing a law-compelled code of etiquette to protect
the flag he revered.

World War I, however, still preceded such a code, and citizens
used flags as decorations for a variety of patriotic events. Because
of the increased flag display in response to the war, more and
more flags were needed to meet the demand, causing the price of
flags to more than double. The Federal Trade Commission (FTC)
reported to the U.S. Senate on 26 July 1917, that in the United
States five million dollars a year was spent on flags of normal
price, but that retailers had raised public prices 100 to 300 percent from April 1916 to May 1917. Retailers pointed out that
leading manufacturers had raised their wholesale prices 100 to
150 percent in the same period, and many smaller firms just
entering the industry had "secured prices 100 to 500 percent
higher by May 1917."[19] What this meant to the consumer was that
a simple five- by eight-foot wool bunting American flag that had
cost $2.75 in May 1916 could easily go for as high as ten dollars in
May 1917.

The FTC's study revealed that "for some years" flagmakers who
controlled the bulk of American flag production had, prior to
1915, agreed together to fix prices at a level they considered
comfortable but not unreasonable. However, the "unprecedented
demand and runaway market" created by the war brought new,
smaller competitors into the field who could charge more and
succeed, which induced the original association to put aside its
agreement. The government representatives noted that, in July
1917, the major flag manufacturers, looking ahead to beyond the
war, were attempting "to fix a new standard basis list at 100 per
cent above the old price list as a means of preventing prices from
declining when the supply again overtakes the demand."[20] When
the world should be made safe for democracy, the American flag
would cost twice as much for those who wanted to wave it in
celebration.

One reason that more flags were needed was an increased
demand for them on the part of communities and schools that, to

Entry into World War I increased the demand for flags. These seamstresses employed at the Brooklyn Navy Yard Flag Shop in July 1918 worked to help meet that demand. (Photo courtesy of the Library of Congress.)

keep spirits running high on the homefront during the war, were staging patriotic pageants. In 1917, Homer A. Rodeheaver produced a "patriotic exercise for juniors" entitled *Building of the Flag, or Liberty Triumphant.* This production, designed for a group of schoolchildren to present before an auditorium or other large gathering, weaves together the cult of the flag with more traditional Christian demonstrations, illustrating how some enthusiasts wished the young to venerate cross and flag together during the First World War.

Rodeheaver's pageant featured the Christian flag—a white flag with a red cross upon it—suspended from the ceiling above the stage. During the course of the ceremony, schoolchildren brought paper stripes and pasteboard stars onto the stage, "building" an American flag directly below the Christian one. The children wore red, white, and blue outfits, some represented Columbia and the original thirteen states. The participants all carried flags (as well as created the larger flag) and the procession was led by a banner inscribed "Righteousness Exalteth a Nation" and closed by one reading "Blessed is that Nation whose God is the Lord."

The pageant included the songs "Columbia, the Gem of the Ocean" and "America," as well as readings from the Declaration of

Independence and Drake's "The American Flag," with a group recitation of the Pledge of Allegiance once the larger flag had been "built." The underlying message throughout seems to be that the United States will prosper as long as she remembers she is a Christian nation. Twelve girls performed a flag drill, six with the flag of the United States and six with the Christian flag. "They march, counter march, etc., with flags just above the shoulder. When crossing flags at the close the Christian flag should be held a trifle higher than the U.S. flag."[21] The "Flag Drill Song" itself weaves together Christian references and homage to the American flag. The first verse praises the Stars and Stripes, the second, the flag of Christ, and the third verse resolves that both flags are Christian: "Lift them higher, Christian flags so true, Red and white and blue, Both so dear to you! Liberty to all mankind proclaim Thro' the dear Redeemer's name."[22] At the end of this number, the pageant closes with a group singing of "The Star-Spangled Banner."

H. Augustine Smith, a professor at Boston University, wrote *A Pageant of the Stars and Stripes* the following year, as "a patriotic service for Churches, Church Schools, Public Schools, Boy and Girl Scouts, Civic Celebrations."[23] Professor Smith's pageant drew heavily on Secretary of the Interior Franklin K. Lane's Flag Day Address of 1914, mentioned at the outset of this study. Although Christian commitment had a place in this pageant's ceremonies as well, and it was published and distributed through the American Institute of Religious Education, no Christian flag was introduced to detract from the emphatic focus on the flag of the United States.

Smith divided his pageant into two parts. After the opening hymn of "America" and a prologue, "The Spirit of Patriotism," the first part of the pageant summarizes the historical evolution of the flag, through music and three tableaux. The first tableau displays the Grand Union and Pine Tree flags of the Revolution, the second Betsy Ross creating her flag before Washington and other distinguished members of the Flag Committee who visited Ross in her Philadelphia home. The third tableau, building to a climactic finish, honors America at war. To the music of "Rally Round the Flag, Boys," G.A.R. veterans bring battle flags from the Civil War on stage, then members of the homeguard—or civilians dressed as soldiers in khaki—bring flags from 1917–18 onstage to the music of "Stars and Stripes Forever." Next, to the strains of "America," Boy Scouts or Girl Scouts enter, bearing "Service Flags of Church, School, and Community," and take their place in front of the men in khaki. Finally, representatives of Church and Church School, dressed in their religious vestments and carrying "the Church Flag and the Conquest Flag," enter and take their position in front of the G.A.R. veterans, all joining in a rousing chorus of "Onward Christian Soldiers."[24]

The second part of Smith's pageant, entitled "Making the Flag," replicates the structure of Rodeheaver's, using Lane's Flag Day address as a litany. Twenty-eight grammar school girls, dressed all in white, come on stage two at a time, reciting lines from the address and bearing stripes to fill in an eight- by four and a third-foot wooden frame raised on the stage. Two attendants fasten the stripes onto the frame, and when this job is completed, the stars are announced and positioned on a carefully placed blue field. As in the other pageant, all recite The Youth's Companion Pledge of Allegiance, and "The Star Spangled Banner" serves as the finale to an exercise in flag veneration.

Secretary Lane reacted warmly to Smith's adoption of his speech to this pageant. In a letter to Smith dated 8 May 1918, Lane wrote, "I think it will be a good idea if you can let me know the first time it is to be produced. If possible, I would attend. At any rate, I would ask the committee on Public Information to have a moving picture film of it."[25] Lane was aware of the potential of that relatively new medium, and sought to use it to spread this practice of glorifying the flag of the United States through song and ceremony. Years later, when television was established, it would become standard procedure to end each day's broadcast with a tribute to the flag and a rendition of the national anthem, but Lane's use of the Committee on Public Information is one of the earliest examples of reinforcing or spreading the cult of the flag through the use of film.[26]

Occasionally seeing images of the flag when one went to the moving picture shows in the 1910s and 20s would have been a new way for many Americans to be reminded of the significance of the national banner during these years. The same was true for hearing the national anthem played at sporting events. Today, athletic events—amateur, Olympic, professional—have become an area of life in which the practices of reciting the Pledge of Allegiance or standing for "The Star-Spangled Banner" are so well established that few consider their historical origins at such events. The first sports event that began with the national anthem is the sport Albert Goodwill Spalding, the millionaire sporting goods manufacturer, so determinedly aligned with nationalism in his 1911 book America's National Game: baseball. There is evidence of flags

flying in some ball parks in the 1890s. Due to the aroused nationalism of the Spanish-American War, musicians first performed "The Star-Spangled Banner" at a baseball game as part of
the special events for opening day of the 1898 season at New York
City's Polo Grounds.[27] Subsequent uses for opening days become
sporadic.

Durng World War I, a more organized introduction of flag
veneration into pregame activities began in professional baseball.
In 1916, Woodrow Wilson, who was indirectly responsible for this
practice, approved an order designating "The Star-Spangled Banner" the official military anthem. When war came a year later,
major league baseball clubs hired bands to play this song at the
beginning of games, in support of the military. After the war,
although bands were no longer hired regularly, home clubs host-
ing games falling on patriotic holidays continued the practice of
hiring bands to play "The Star-Spangled Banner," as did those in
charge of organizing the World Series, a particularly American
event. Years later, during the heightened nationalism of World
War II, the present custom of playing and singing the anthem
before each game took hold[28] and soon spread to other professional sports.

Although World War I quite logically aroused patriotic pride,
which led to the introductions of the flag into new social arenas
for more constant recognition as a venerated, national symbol, it
also created a situation in which those who did not choose to
venerate it could be censured (to a degree that might seem extreme by modern standards). Fear of acts of treachery by enemy
supporters at home drove many Americans to demonstrate their
patriotism by reporting supposed traitors. In the summer of
1918, each editorial page of the *Helena Independent,* a Montana
newspaper, displayed the following quote from General Pershing:
"I will smash the German line in France if you will smash that
damnable Hun propaganda at home." In this political climate, it is
not surprising that on 31 July 1918, Tony Diedtman, a naturalized
citizen of German extraction, was sentenced to not less than ten
years of hard labor for making a remark sympathetic to Germans
suffering because of the war. The defendant accepted his sentence in silence; the judge admonished him, reminding him that if
he had been convicted of such an offense in Germany, he would
have been killed.[29]

Diedtman's offense was sedition. According to section three of
the Uniform State Flag Law (see appendix), subversive elements
could be arrested not only for supporting the enemy but also for

casting contempt upon the flag of the United States by word or deed. During the war a pair of cases that appealed to higher courts on both the state and federal level ended with the same decision, upholding *Halter v. Nebraska* from 1907: states had the right to pass laws on usage of the American flag and could enforce those laws as they saw fit.

In 1915 Kansas passed a flag law that contained the following lines: "Any person who . . . shall publicly mutilate, deface, defile, or defy, trample upon, or cast contempt, either by words or act, upon any such flag, standard, color, or ensign [of the United States] shall be deemed guilty of a misdemeanor."[30] Under this law Frederick Shumaker, Jr., was tried and convicted for suggesting to someone in a blacksmith shop in Wetmore, Kansas, on 12 February 1918 (Lincoln's Birthday) a "very vulgar and indecent use of the flag," the exact details of which were considered too rude, on the part of the court, to be permitted in the written record.

Found guilty in a lower court, Shumaker appealed to the Supreme Court of Kansas, which heard his case 9 November 1918. The court refused any allowance for coarse humor: "Such language will not, cannot, be used by any man in any place concerning our flag, if he has any proper respect for it. The man who uses such language concerning it, either in jest or in argument, does not have that respect for it that should be found in the breast of every citizen of the United States."[31]

Allowing support for the case against Shumaker, the court permitted evidence from a year earlier. A witness claimed that in February 1917, on the day of the funeral of a General Funston, the town of Wetmore flew some United States flags at half-staff. Shumaker, coming into town and unaware of the general's death, asked someone. "What in hell is going on? I see you got the rags on the poles." The presiding judge instructed the justices that such language was in violation of the law, and that if they believed Shumaker had made these statements, to find him guilty. All the justices concurred; his conviction was upheld.[32]

The Shumaker case demonstrated that in states with a flag law, irreverential reference to the flag in public could lead to a fine. The modern notion of "symbolic speech," the claim that the right to deface or defile the American flag is protected by the First Amendment, had not been developed. And for a man from Montana, E. V. Starr, the price he would pay for such an offense went beyond a fine to years of hard labor in the state penitentiary.

From the records it is not clear what Starr's political opinions were, but a vigilante mob of some sort cornered him in March 1918, and tried to force him to kiss the American flag in their presence. His deviance does not seem to be pro-German, for others turned upon by mobs for treasonous speech or behavior during World War I received detailed description of their political allegiance in the court records and newspaper accounts. Most probably he was a labor sympathizer of some sort; for in 1918, the i.w.w., better known as "the Wobblies," had enough of a following to alarm many less radical citizens. Whatever his beliefs, Starr refused to kiss the flag as a matter of principle. He also made the mistake of saying, "What is this thing anyway? Nothing but a piece of cotton with a little paint on it and some other marks in the corner there. I will not kiss that thing. It might be covered with microbes."[33]

Starr was a realist. In another context, four years earlier, Secretary of the Interior Franklin K. Lane received praise for his realistic insight, speaking for the flag, "I am what you make of me, nothing more." On a factual level Starr was correct in his assertions, even in his concern for the presence of microbes. The crowd, however, did not appreciate his analysis. In August 1918, Starr was tried and convicted of sedition for this statement and sentenced to not less than ten years nor more than twenty years at hard labor in the state penitentiary, along with a five hundred dollar fine and responsibility for all court costs.

He appealed to the Federal District Court of Montana for a writ of habeas corpus, claiming that he was being imprisoned unfairly since the law was "repugnant to the federal Constitution." That court heard his case 31 January 1920. In offering his decision, District Judge Bourquin spoke eloquently on the irony of Starr's arrest, decrying the behavior of the mob: "Its unlawful and disorderly conduct, not his just resistance, nor the trivial and innocuous retort into which they goaded him, was calculated to degrade the sacred banner and to bring it into contempt. Its members, not he, should have been punished."

Bourquin then turned to the subject of patriotism. "Patriotism is the cement that binds the foundation and the superstructure of the state. The safety of the latter depends upon the integrity of the former. Like religion, patriotism is a virtue so indispensable and exalted, its excesses pass with little censure." He lamented when patriotism turned to "fanaticism," and quoted Irish playwright George Bernard Shaw as having said "that during the war the courts in France, bleeding under German guns, were very severe; the courts in England, hearing but the echoes of those guns, were grossly unjust; but the courts of the United States, knowing naught save censored news of those guns, were stark, staring, raving mad."[34]

Despite this poignant siding with Starr in the matter, the issue was habeas corpus, and Bourquin terminated his discussion by upholding the state law, pointing out the federal court could not relieve the petitioner in this case, and denying the writ. Although he found the situation distressing, he was judging the constitutionality of the law, not how it had been interpreted in this instance. By then Starr had been serving his sentence for quite some time already, for he was convicted in August 1918 and Bourquin did not hand down this decision until 31 January 1920. Research has not uncovered any more information about what happened to E. V. Starr after he went to prison.

In 1919, a new type of flag-salute law was passed in the state of Washington. Earlier flag-salute laws, in New York, Rhode Island, Arizona, Kansas, and Maryland, had assigned the State Superintendent of Education the responsibility of preparing flag salute ceremonies for use in the state schools. Under the new Washington law, however, "Every board of directors . . . shall cause appropriate flag exercises to be held in every school at least once in each week at which exercises the pupils shall recite the following salute to the flag: [the *Youth's Companion* Pledge then follows]."[35] David R. Manwaring, a legal historian, believes this law was passed in response to i.w.w. disorders in Centralia, Washington, as a means of maintaining social control. Failure for school boards to comply could lead to the dismissal of their members and conviction as a misdemeanor.[36] Just as earlier the state laws concerning the presence of flags in schools had shifted from laws urging the practice to laws mandating compliance, so too did the Washington law trigger similar legislation during the "red scares" of the 1920s and 30s, in Delaware, New Jersey, and Massachusetts. Prior to World War II, the question of if a school child must recite the Pledge of Allegiance led to outbreaks of violence as patriotic elements clashed with Jehovah's Witnesses who claimed exemption due to freedom of religion. As in the case of Starr, the banner, hailed as a symbol of freedom and liberty, could be used as a weapon in legal disputes in which freedoms were ironically denied to substantiate the cult that celebrated the flag as that symbol of freedom.

That cult found some outlets for expression in the ritual and practice of several secret societies. Both the Freemasons and their auxiliary organization, the Eastern Star, saw special connections between their groups and the American flag. John W. Barry, an Iowa member of the Masons, wrote a Masonic version of the history of the flag of the United States, entitled *Masonry and the Flag,* which the Masonic Service Association published in 1924. Barry's main purpose, however, was to verify the belief that the United States had "a government conceived by Masons, fostered, furthered, fought, bled, and died for, by Masons."[37] Wherever possible, he documents the participation of Masons in the organization and establishment of the new government for the United Colonies, and in the position of officers waging battles against the British forces. Barry suggests that the colors and design of the American flag were rooted in Masonic symbology, and that George Washington, himself a Mason, designed the flag he asked Betsy Ross to sew based on his appreciation of the traditions of the brotherhood of Masons. Barry interpreted the lack of data available concerning the work of the original Flag Committee not as a sign of the relative unimportance of the matter to the Continental Congressmen of 1777, but rather as an indication of Masonic participation, for the secrecy of the Masonic masterminding of the formation of the new government had to remain strictly confidential. Why Barry could reveal this connection in 1924 is not made clear; obviously, the book served a function of inspiring Masons to appreciate the historic contributions of members during the American Revolution while demonstrating that Masons, too, supported the cult of the flag.

The Eastern Star took the symbolism of the flag one step further. In *Mystic Americanism,* Grace Kincaid Morey explains, in twenty lessons, the true significance of the flag and the great seal of the United States. In this secret society for Protestant women, Aryan racial pride, Old Testament theology and history, numerology, and the American flag were woven together to create a mythology that celebrated the white Protestant pioneers who forged the nation. According to Morey's interpretation, approved by society leaders and published by the Eastern Star Publishing Company, the thirteen stars come from Solomon's Seal. The United States is predicted in the Old Testament in the form of Manasseh, the son of Joseph, who represents Great Britain. Establishing an inextricable connection between the cult of the flag and the Christian religion, Morey teaches that "the symbology of the Flag dates from Mount Sinai and Moses." Israel is "a royal race descended from the Gods" now "at rest in America, a light to all nations." She concludes her book with an esoteric description of "the Flag stretched across the Republic" before predicting "the

Second Coming."[38] In celebrating the United States as a reborn Israel, the Eastern Star continued a tradition dating from the first voyage of the *Arbella* into Massachusetts Bay in 1630 and thriving in the theology of groups such as the Mormons; the concept has served as a reoccurring theme in civil religious references of the nineteenth and twentieth centuries.[39] To amplify the analogy, Morey reads into Old Testament accounts symbolic references and predictions associated with the flag of the United States.

William Norman Guthrie reached the zenith of such mingling of secular and nonsecular religion to sanctify the American flag in his 1918 call for *The Religion of Old Glory.* To Guthrie, in a land which allowed freedom of religion, the cult of the flag offered "the only unifying religious expression." Since Guthrie defined ritual as "the charter of creative feeling and thought,"[40] he fashioned a ritual of flag worship in which all citizens could participate. Guthrie prepared his text during the year that the United States entered the war in Europe. In his introduction, he explained that even an act of Congress could not alter the esteem in which Americans held their flag, "because the affections of the people in song, picture, and story have fixed an association, so that only some awful calamity, like the revolution which broke the continuity of French national life, would permit of any conscious radical change."[41]

Guthrie advocated emphasizing the association Americans had with the flag. At the core of his ideology is acceptance of the flag as a living symbol, as the one symbol that all Americans together must worship to help build a powerful state, eventually spreading that symbol throughout the world so all may have the opportunity to worship it. His theology is a combination of pagan and Old Testament references, secondary to the devotion emphasized in the service to the flag. Although patriotism is a sentiment akin to religious reverence, Guthrie's attempt to fashion a new religion combining the two curiously illustrates an extreme nationalism aroused by war. For Guthrie, the American flag is the flag of God, and service to it continues after death:

> . . . raise it solemnly again,
> Salute it reverently as never before,
> Live for it, die for it!
> And even after death,
> Send your spirit back to live for it—
> Beyond these limitations of time and tide,—
> And demand, now as then, with utmost power of your immortal being:—

That Old Glory float and live in the very wind of God's breath
As the symbol of the "faith to which we are born,"
And all mankind, thank God, along with us![42]

The Bishop of New York of the Protestant Episcopal Church authorized the performance of Guthrie's ritual "expressing the religion of Old Glory" on the Sunday afternoon after Thanksgiving—an important civil religious occasion—in 1918. St. Mark's-in-the-Bouwerie was the parish site designated.[43] Mystical rituals drawing on polytheism, idolatry, or paganism were part of Masonic, Eastern Star, and other secret societies' cultures, but to advocate such behavior in consecrated churches throughout the United States, as Guthrie did, was quite another thing. Perhaps the bishop highly valued Guthrie's ceremonies as expressions of patriotism during wartime; nevertheless, the toleration of such behavior in any Christian church, especially over sixty years ago, is a bit surprising.

A summary of the ritual might illustrate how the ceremony exemplified an extreme demonstration of the cult of the flag. Following the opening hymn to America, the Chief Officiant welcomed his "fellow Americans (and fellow Christians) . . . to express in word and action the religious meaning of our national emblem, Old Glory." He led them in an elaborate Psalm of the Flagpole, which is likened to a totem pole of old, followed by a similar Psalm of the Eagle, as both Flagpole and Eagle are displayed in the church proper. While the congregation sang "A Battle Cry of Freedom" (to the tune of "Dixie"), a Ritual Father and Ritual Mother, representing Adam and Eve, mankind, and America, helped set thirteen mystical pillars to form a base at the Flagpole. The flag of the United States, through elaborate ceremony, was displayed at the altar, as the Chief Officiant said: "Behold with reverence and grateful pride the emblem of this Elect Nation—The nation chosen of God for a mighty purpose."[44] Sections of the "Star-Spangled Banner" were sung and after a closing verse the "Preliminary Office of Old Glory" ended.

Then "The Ceremony of Worship Unto Old Glory" began. This included genuflections and prayers *to the Flag*, now upon the Flagpole, and exclamations, in unison, in Latin. During the course of this part of the service, flowers were placed on the altar, one red, one white, one blue, and one for the stars. They were then fashioned into a wreath at the base of the Flagpole—and a nest was made for the Eagle upon the altar. The Chief Officiant then kindled a fire on the altar, using incense and aromatic herbs, and wafted the smoke in the direction of the nearby flag. The service climaxed in this fashion:

> The Chief Officiant, admonished by the Second Assistant, takes the national flower, The GOLDENROD, at the hand of the first assistant, and waves it solemnly thirteen times before the flag, touches the altar with it and sets it upright above the wreath as a sceptre of power—at the bottom of the flagstaff.
> He then blows up the fire with his breath, and throws the incense on it plentifully, so that volumes of aromatic smoke arise, and almost conceal the Officiant from view.
> He beckons the Father and Mother to step out of the cloud toward the flagstaff beyond the altar and the last stanza of THE STAR SPANGLED BANNER is played and sung, during which he stands at salute to the Eagle.
> Father and Mother indicate, with the hand nearest to him, that they give him utterly up, the other hand lifted to the flag.
> When the last strain is over, the Chief Officiant in gesture embraces the flag and gathers the folds of it about the altar, and himself, and the two assistants.
> Chief Officiant stands then with the Father and Mother on either side, each earnestly placing the right hand with an attitude of command on his right and left shoulders respectively, and he throws a devout and passionate kiss to the flag.[45]

Following "The Battle Hymn of the Republic," the service concluded with a summary singing of "the doctrine of this office," a poem Guthrie wrote entitled "Our Fealty to Old Glory," which calls for one people united worshiping the American flag.[46]

Guthrie obviously had a fondness for climactic ceremony. Although an effective staging of this ritual would require quite a bit of coordination between participants, it would also entertain those who enjoy religious services rich in symbolic gestures. Guthrie included such gestures, foreign phrases, and the use of incense to heighten the congregation's sensory experience during the ceremony. He was certainly aware of the High Church Movement in Episcopal theology, which advocated the extensive use of such rituals to remind parishioners symbolically of their commitment to Christ and the historicity of the Church. The bishop might have seen Guthrie's worship of Old Glory as an appropriation of the same technique to civil religion, and permitted it for the sake of patriotism during wartime.

Guthrie's ritual never caught on, but it was undoubtedly the zenith of American civil religious attempts to celebrate the cult of the flag. Guthrie believed that making the flag a fetish would help unify a nation at war and guide it to an exalted future. Many others agreed with his patriotic views, but few were ready to push reverence for the flag that far. Following the end of World War I, a new veterans organization emerged that took the lead in the activity of spreading a more traditional respect for the flag throughout the nation. Through its Committee on Americanism, established in 1919, the same year it was founded, the American Legion committed itself to "combatting all 'anti-American tendencies,' educating immigrants in American principles, inculcating the ideals of Americanism and the principles of American government in the minds of all citizens, and fostering the teaching of Americanism in the schools." Its members also reflected the influence of Wilson's wartime declaration of "The Star-Spangled Banner" as the official anthem of the Army and the Navy by voting at the outset to recognize only this song as the national anthem.[47]

In 1922, Garland W. Powell became the American Legion's National Director of Americanism, a position he would hold through 1925. An experienced aviator, this former state senator from Maryland held a special place in his heart for the American flag, and wrote a guidebook for those interested in teaching and spreading patriotic participation in the cult of the flag, suggesting techniques to increase media coverage of flag events and heighten interest in flag etiquette in impressionable schoolchildren.[48] He also had a knack for getting representatives of various organizations to work together. Through his initiative, the American Legion sent out a call to several organizations that Powell considered patriotically inclined to participate in a conference to establish a code of flag etiquette for all American citizens. The Army and the Navy had prescribed codes of behavior associated with the flag, but civilians did not, and the use of the flag had spread into many areas of everyday life not associated with the military.

Representatives of sixty-eight civic, fraternal, business, veterans, hereditary, educational, religious and labor organizations responded to the American Legion's invitation, and the First National Flag Conference met in D.A.R. Memorial Continental Hall in Washington, D.C., on Flag Day, 1923. Presided over by Powell, the conference was attended by representatives of the Army and Navy, recognized experts in flag usage in their branches of the service. The Flag Code they worked out drew heavily on a flag code issued a few months earlier by the United States War Department[49]; however, the conference gave that code a seal of approval

New immigrants, passing through the inspection room at Ellis Island 1910–20, could hardly miss the large flags, examples of a symbol that would take on special significance in the process of Americanization. (Photo courtesy of the Library of Congress.)

that would ensure its dissemination throughout the larger society, for over five million Americans belonged to the various participating organizations.

President Harding came over from the White House to address the group in its opening ceremonies. During his forty-minute speech he said, "I hope you will succeed in forming a code that will be welcomed by all Americans and that every patriotic and educational society in the republic will commit itself to the endorsement and observance and purposes of that code." He also made a plea for introducing "The Star-Spangled Banner" more regularly into patriotic instruction, since it glorified the flag. "Don't you think we ought to insist upon America being able to sing 'The Star Spangled Banner'? I have noted audiences singing our national anthem—that is not the way to put it—I have noted them trying to sing the national anthem, but all except two percent were mumbling the words, pretending to sing."[50]

The Assistant Secretary of the Navy, the Assistant Secretary of the Army, the U.S. Commissioner of Education, and Samuel Gompers all then gave speeches praising the work of the conference. The code was worked out by a select committee. Its chairman, Gridley Adams, the Chicago cartoonist concerned about flag desecration, later became the founder and self-designated director-general of the New York-based United States Flag Foundation, dedicated to disseminating the cult of the flag. A review of those serving on the committee with him reveals which organizations were most influential in the cult of the flag at this time: John L. Riley, American Legion; Mrs. Anthony Wayne Cook, D.A.R.; O. C. Luxford, S.A.R.; Capt. George M. Chandler, U.S. Army; Lt. Col. H. S. Kerrick, American Legion; E. S. Martin, Boy Scouts of America; Henry Osgood Hoalland, National Congress of Mothers; Mrs. Livingston Rowe Schuyler, United Daughters of the Confederacy; and Capt. Chester Wells, U.S. Navy.[51]

Some basic points the conference made included recognition, from heraldry, that the right side is the side of honor, and the flag, considered a living symbol of a living nation, should take the right side position (not according to the observer, but, as the flag is considered "alive," to the flag itself). The union of stars on the canton similarly goes on the flag's right, which would usually be the observer's left. The Code, unanimously approved by the delegates at the conclusion of the 1923 conference, also specified the proper way to hang and display the flag in normal and special circumstances, how to avoid any sign of disrespect for the flag, how to pledge allegiance to it, and how to use bunting.[52]

At one point in the proceedings, the conference delegates passed a resolution showing their "deep honor and regard" for the behavior of sixteen-year-old Max Davis of Jersey City, New Jersey. Less than a month earlier, he had noticed an American flag, initially strung high across the street on a rope, then dipping perilously close to the road over which it hung. An approaching automobile threatened to run over the flag and Max, to save it from being desecrated, dove at the rope and attempted to haul the flag to safety. Unfortunately, three fingers were ripped from his right hand—but the delegates praised his motivation.[53]

All major American newspapers published the Flag Code in the weeks following the conference or made it a special feature for the week of the Fourth of July, and the American Legion distributed over three hundred thousand copies of it throughout the nation in a booklet entitled *Respect The Flag*. Fifty-one additional national organizations joined the movement, and Powell was made permanent chairman of a permanent organization that would annually convene on the subject of flag etiquette.

Nevertheless, only one subsequent national conference was held. It quickly settled the few questions remaining after the efficient work of the first. The conference met in Washington in May 1924, to permit the revised code to go into effect the following Flag Day. The only significant change from the 1923 Code was the wording in the Pledge of Allegiance: "I pledge allegiance to my flag" had been changed in 1923 to "I pledge allegance to the flag of the United States" to clarify which flag the children were saluting should any immigrant children find the phrasing ambiguous. To further clarify the point, the Second Flag Conference approved adding "of America" after the "the United States."[54]

By 1924 Powell estimated that the American Legion had distributed more than six million pamphlets on flag etiquette to schools, churches, and public officials. More than fourteen million had been distributed nationwide if one counted the efforts of other patriotic organizations, and school journals and national magazines also published illustrated versions of the Flag Code. Although the Flag Code would not be made federal law until the outbreak of World War II, when Congress took such action through joint resolution, the participation of so many diverse organizations in the project quickened its widespread acceptance. Moreover, by 1924, twenty-eight states had adopted the code for school instruction.[55]

While the American Legion sought to spread the flag code throughout society, not every group that saluted the flag had the same definition of "Americanism." For the American Legion during the Roaring Twenties, Americanism often meant a jingoistic attitude, a harsh stand on immigration and radical labor movements. The American Legion generally kept its political stance in these areas separate from its dissemination of the cult of the flag through the distribution of flag code pamphlets or copies of an American Legion-sponsored film of Hale's short story from 1863, "A Man Without a Country."[56] Another group that championed Americanism, going beyond jingoism in its celebration of the flag as a symbol of a racially and ethnically pure America and incorporating the flag into its ceremonies and rituals, was the Ku Klux Klan.

The reborn Klan was organized by Colonel William Joseph Simmons in 1915, in Atlanta, Georgia, "to keep eternally ablaze the sacred fire of a fervent devotion to a pure Americanism." It

spread throughout the South and into the North and West, peak-
ing at about four million followers at its high point in 1924, with
most of its support based in villages and small towns.[57]
    In the tradition of the Know-Nothings, the Klan dealt with
social and industrial change by advocating a vision of an earlier,
better America that a pure stock of white Americans controlled.
As part of the celebration of their America, the Klan officially
endorsed the Flag Code, and instructed the adolescent members
of its Junior Order in flag etiquette. Membership required an
oath of allegiance to the flag and the Constitution.[58]
    The reverence the Klan accorded the flag is illustrated in Klan
paraphernalia. A bronze Ku Klux Klan belt buckle of the period,
for instance, depicts a hooded Klansman standing before a fiery
cross on a hillside, clutching the Holy Bible to his heart while he
holds aloft a large American flag, the dominant element in the
design.[59] Each Klansman supported the cult of the flag, but his
interpretation of it would vary widely from that of Jacob Riis. In
1925, the year following the Second Flag Conference, the Klan,
hooded and carrying hundreds of American flags, marched down
Pennsylvania Avenue in Washington, D.C., over forty thousand
strong. At the front of the parade, in accordance with the Flag
Code, the Stars and Stripes led the way.[60] Such an image could,
with good reason, disturb a modern-day patriot; it does, however,
demonstrate how nativist groups often incorporate the national
banner into their symbology, interpreting it as an affirmation of
their particular ideological beliefs.
    Inspired by the National Flag Conferences and opposed to any
"public movement inspired by intolerance" such as the Ku Klux
Klan, Colonel James A. Moss, retired, of the U.S. Army, founded
on 10 April 1924 the United States Flag Association (U.S.F.A.).
Moss had long been interested in the history and etiquette of the
flag of the United States, and during the first World War he
coauthored with M. B. Stewart an inspirational booklet entitled
Our Flag and Its Message. The Association was mostly a one-man
effort that Moss ran as director-general "to foster reverence for
the flag of the United States and to combat all influences, conditions and forces hostile to the ideals, traditions, principles and
institutions for which that flag stands."[61]
    The U.S.F.A. listed luminaries from business, political, church,
labor, and women's organizations on its board of founders, granting Elihu Root the title of president, Otto Kahn that of treasurer,
and Calvin Coolidge that of honorary president. Financial support came mostly from Washington politicians whose aid Moss

procured. The Association's main activity was the production and distribution of pamphlets and books that Moss wrote on proper flag etiquette. The standard format he developed, which would vary only slightly in later books, came from his *The Flag of the United States: How to Display It, How to Respect It, and the Story of "The Star Spangled Banner"*, distributed under the auspices of the National American War Mothers in 1923. As the title indicates, the text began with the Flag Code and continued into a celebration of the official anthem of the Army and Navy. Moss concluded the book with a "Catechism of the Flag of the United States and 'The Star Spangled Banner.'"

The catechism consisted of ninety-six questions on flag etiquette and thirty-six questions on the history and etiquette associated with "The Star-Spangled Banner." Moss's instructions reveal how he intended the catechism to be used:

> If you can answer correctly the questions below, you will know all about YOUR Flag and YOUR National Anthem. Every American should be able to answer every one of them. Children should be taught this catechism by their parents and their school teachers. It is suggested that Flag and "Star Spangled Banner" Catechism matches, corresponding to the old-time "spelling bees," and followed by the reading of the story of "The Star Spangled Banner," and the singing of "The Star Spangled Banner," be held in all schools, Boy Scout troops, Girl Scout troops, and Camp Fire Girl Camps.[62]

The questions covered every single point of the Flag Code in detail, and were phrased so that if a child memorized the Code verbatim, he could answer the questions in order by reciting the Code in its entirety. Moss used the same strategy to prepare the list of questions on the national anthem; if a child memorized the discussion in the text, he could answer each of the questions in turn.

Moss organized a complicated system for spreading the cult of the flag and raising money for the U.S.F.A. Although it never seems to have succeeded, his plan for Living Flags deserves mention. Each Living Flag consisted of sixty-three members; any "Flag Founder" who contributed twenty-five dollars received membership certificates for sixty-three members that included his or her name as the founder of that particular Living Flag. If an individual founded twenty-five Living Flags within five years, he or she received a "Patriotic Service Medal" and the title of "Son of the Flag" or "Daughter of the Flag." Founding one hundred Living Flags within five years—which brought the U.S.F.A.

$2,500—qualified one for an "American Cross of Honor" and the title of "Knight of the Flag" or "Lady of the Flag."[63]

Moss's success in spreading the cult of the flag did not come from these Living Flags but from his military and political connections and his many books and pamphlets on flag etiquette, which the u.s.f.a. published in the 1920s and 30s. He pioneered the structure of a small but organized media operation focused on flag etiquette, supported through donations from businesses and individuals, aimed at spreading the cult of the flag to American youth and any interested adults. He originated the idea of Flag Week from 8 to 14 June every day, to emphasize the dissemination of the cult of the flag throughout American society. Moss's dedication to the cult and his success with businessmen, conservative politicians, and the media created a structure for later propagandists of the American flag to emulate.

Moss's mantle has been passed down through the years to other organizations. Colonel Noel Gaines of Frankfort, Kentucky, ran the American Flag Movement of the 1930s. Gridley Adams created a New York-based United States Flag Foundation, which was later taken over by Lawrence Tower. This organization actively worked to promote flag desecration laws and keep alive the cult of the flag.[64] Today, under the name of the National Flag Foundation, it thrives in its headquarters at the Flag Plaza in Pittsburgh, Pennsylvania, controlled by George F. Cahill. Each of these successors has continued to publish pamphlets and handbooks glorifying the flag and prescribing its proper usage, and each has survived through the support of endowments and grants from big business, individual contributions, and backing from right-wing politicians. Thus, the cult of the flag, codified by a national conferences in 1923 and 1924, continues as a significant component in the patriotic art, music, rhetoric, ritual, and ceremony of American culture.

Some Concluding Thoughts

What does one learn from an examination of cultural shifts in uses of the American flag from creation to codification? Primarily an identification marker for military and naval property in the early years, the flag entered the constellation of symbols and images invoked to celebrate national achievement and advancement. Although limited by today's standards, and of secondary importance to the anthropomorphic image of George Washington, the flag's presence and use disseminated throughout American society in the antebellum period, to a greater degree than some recent scholarship would indicate. With the firing on Fort Sumter, those loyal to the Union interpreted the union of stars in the canton of the flag with a new and invigorated appreciation, and the image of the flag rose to prominence as the most important national symbol.

During the Civil War, a cult grew up focusing on the flag, honoring it with art, music, literature, public display, and ceremony. Following the war, the commemoration of the centennial reminded patriotic citizens of their heritage, and the flag received increased attention as a subject of historical interest. Following a precedent set by George Balch, the staff of *The Youth's Companion* created the Pledge of Allegiance, which the journal distributed nationwide for the Columbus Day celebration of 1892. Veterans led the drive to place flags in all public schools, women's organizations dominated the movement to spread the practice of regular flag rituals among schoolchildren, and men's hereditary societies actively lobbied to outlaw indiscriminate use of the flag in commercial advertising. After World War I, the newly formed American Legion organized a conference of interested patriotic societies to establish a civilian code of flag etiquette, drawing heavily on military models. The acceptance of a recognized code of etiquette insured the continued existence of flag conscious groups such as Moss's United States Flag Association, organizations dedicated to promoting the cult of the flag and allying it with conservative forces in the established socioeconomic order.

One learns that various individuals, groups, and institutions have promoted the flag to satisfy particular agendas. Since the Kensington Riots of 1844, an undercurrent of nativism has appropriated the American flag as a symbol of an ethnically pure, idealized society. Balch developed his pledge to help Americanize the "scum" of Europe immigrating to the United States in great numbers. Many advertisers, promoting their wares with pictures of the American flag on their products, lost this option when status-anxious descendants of colonial settlers successfully achieved legislation on the state level to stop flag desecration, and courts upheld this right.

One learns that extreme social upheavals engender new uses for the flag, that often persist after society has reestablished a modicum of equilibrium. The flag cult emerged during the Civil War and peaked in extremism with Guthrie's *Religion of Old Glory* during World War I. Fear of immigrants disrupting the dominant culture motivated many to stress the use of the flag in Americanization programs of the late nineteenth century. By 1918, concern for a fifth column of German saboteurs or the spread of socialism among America's proletariat persuaded some state legislatures to pass tough flag laws that were strictly enforced by the courts.

One learns how legends, such as the story of Betsy Ross and the flag, are developed, promulgated, and disseminated. One learns of patriotism, and how love of the flag can lead to courageous efforts, whether by a soldier at Gettysburg or a schoolboy in New Jersey. One learns that the story of the flag should include not only moments of triumph to be reworked in Independence Day speeches, but also moments of shame, such as the sentencing of a man to at least ten years of hard labor in a state penitentiary for refusing to kiss an emblem supposedly representing individual freedom.

Emerson once said, "The use of history is to give value to the present hour and its duty." Although a better understanding of the complex shifts in American cultural use of the flag of the United States from 1777 to 1924 will not solve the pressing issues of contemporary society, it can lead to a greater appreciation of our current uses of the flag. As Robert Ellis Thompson pointed out at the turn of the century, our relationship with our national banner is unparalleled in other societies.[1]

The present study could well serve as background for another volume tracing the cultural uses of the flag from 1925 to the present. Such an analysis, continuing the search for changing uses of the flag in American society, could expect to find stricter observance and appreciation of the cult of the flag during wartime—and indeed, the Supreme Court's decision in the *Gobitis* case in 1940 and the prosecution of Abbie Hoffman under the revised Flag Law of 1968 both show this theory at work. The iconographic impact of the Flag Raising at Mount Suribachi on Iwo Jima, the power of television as a medium to spread the symbol and uses of the flag of the United States, and the rise of the "new patriotism" under Ronald Reagan all would deserve careful attention in such a study.

Although some contemporary cultural critics might consider the cult of the flag a thing of the past, an analysis of public events of national significance, such as the celebration of a victory in the Olympic games or the mourning of astronauts killed in a technological accident, would demonstrate how significant the flag continues to be in our national ritual and ceremony. A study of new customs associated with the American flag in the last fifty years supports the assertion that the cult of the flag persists.[2] To understand how that cult endures and transforms to meet changing sociohistorical needs of various components of American culture is to understand a distinctive attribute of nationalism and patriotism in the United States.

This could also pave the way for cross-cultural analyses of cults of the flag. Perhaps similarities and differences in the way other nations incorporate flag use and ritual into their patriotic ceremony and statutes can point to a deeper appreciation of national identity and international perceptions of foreigners. A study of uses of the national flag in the Third World, especially in nations born in the twentieth century, could reveal how flag customs, traditions, and rituals are modified and transformed when transplanted from one culture to another.

On Flag Day, 1914, in speaking to citizens of the United States on the significance of the American flag, Lane was correct in his assertion: the flag *is* what we make it. Because its use is culturally determined, and if we truly want to understand the complex meanings and associations related to the flag today, we need to be aware of the cultural shifts in flag usage from 1777 to 1924. Discovering the details surrounding the establishment of new uses of the flag, why these changes occurred, and what repercussions, if any, occurred can tell us something about changing perceptions of proper patriotic behavior, and the rising and falling tides of nationalism. And wherever we see the flag of the United States, whether on a giant pole in front of a used car dealer, as a patch on someone's backpack in Europe, or flying in the breeze atop the U.S. Capitol, we can recall that this symbol we have been socialized to respect, honor, and love has a rich and complex history of its own, a history that reveals how the significance of the flag can vary in different sociohistorical situations.

Appendix

Contents

The American Flag

JOSEPH RODMAN DRAKE (1819)

I.

When Freedom from her mountain height
    Unfurled her standard to the air,
  She tore the azure robe of night,
    And set the stars of glory there.
  She mingled with its gorgeous dyes
  The milky baldric of the skies
And striped its pure, celestial white
With streakings of the morning light;

    Then from his mansion in the sun
    She called her eagle-bearer down,
    And gave into his mighty hand
    The symbol of her chosen land.

II.

Majestic monarch of the cloud!
    Who rear'st aloft thy eagle form
  To hear the tempest trumpings loud,
  And see the lightning lances driven,
    When stride the warriors of the storm,
    And rolls the thunder-drum of heaven!
Child of the Sun! to thee 'tis given
  To guard the banner of the free!
To hover in the sulphur smoke,
To ward away the battle stroke,
And bid its blendings shine afar,
Like rainbows on the cloud of war,
  The harbingers of victory.

III.

Flag of the brave! thy folds shall fly,
  The sign of hope and triumph high;
When speaks the trumpet's signal tone,
  And the long line comes gleaming on,
Ere yet the life-blood, warm and wet,

Has dimmed the glistening bayonet,
Each soldier's eye shall brightly turn
    To where the sky-born glories burn;
And, as his springy steps advance,
Catch war and vengeance from the glance;
    And when the cannon-mouthings loud
    Heave in wild wreaths the battle shroud,
And gory sabres rise and fall,
Like shoots of flame on midnight's pall,—
    Then shall thy meteor-glances glow,
And cowering foes shall sink beneath
    Each gallant arm that strikes below
That lovely messenger of death!

IV.

Flag of the seas! on Ocean's wave
    Thy stars shall glitter o'er the brave;
When death, careening on the gale,
    Sweeps darkly round the bellied sail,
And frightened waves rush wildly back
    Before the broadsides reeling rack,
Each dying wanderer of the sea
    Shall look at once to heaven and thee,
And smile to see thy splendors fly
In triumph o'er his closing eye.

V.

Flag of the free heart's hope and home!
    By angels' hand to valor given;
Thy stars have lit the welkin dome,
    And all thy hues were born in heaven.
Forever float that standard sheet;
    Where breathes the foe but fails before us,
With Freedom's soil beneath our feet
    And Freedom's banner streaming o'er us.

Flag-Song of the Michigan Volunteers

D. BETHUNE DUFFIELD

(Adapted to the Anvil Chorus from Trovatore)

I.

Trumpet, and ensign, and drum-beat are calling,
    From hill-side and valley, from mountain and river,
  "Forward the flag!" e'en though heroes are falling,
    Our God will his [*sic*] own chosen standard deliver

Chorus

Star-Spangled Banner! our hopes to thee are clinging.
  Lead us to victory, or wrap us in death—
  To thee staunch are we, while yet a breath
  Remains to sing thee:
  Of arms to fling thee,
  O'er this fair land, wide and free.

II.

"Union and Freedom!" our war-cry is rolling,
    Now over the prairie, now wide o'er the billow,
Harks, 'tis the battle, and soon will be tolling
    The knell of the soldier, who rests 'neath the willow.

Chorus

III.

Banner triumphant! though grand is thy story,
    We'll stamp on thy folds, in this struggle today,
  Deeds of our armies, transcending in glory
    The bravest yet chanted in Poesy's lay.

Chorus

IV.

Wise were our fathers, and brave in the battle,
    But treason uprises their union to sever,
  Rouse for the fight! shout aloud 'mid War's rattle,
    The Union must triumph, must triumph for ever!

Chorus

V.

Trumpet, and ensign, and drum-beat are calling,
From hill-side and valley, from mountain and river,
"Forward the flag!" e'en though heroes are falling,
Our God will his [*sic*] own chosen standard deliver.

Chorus

Star-Spangled Banner! our hopes to thee are clinging,
Lead us to victory, or wrap us in death.

Detroit, 29 April 1861

The Flag O'er Our School-House Is Floating

J. C. O. REDINGTON

O'er our school-house the "Old Flag" in beauty is floating.
Its stars are as white as the purest of snow;
While the blue field they cover, a true peace denoting,
And valor-lit stripes with a radiance glow.

For that flag means a sacrifice—martyred ones dying
And suff'ring to rescue our "Home of the Free"—
For the war years were fearful that kept the flag flying,
And won the prosperity all of us see.

In the rooms of our school-house, when wearied eyes raising,
The grand flag before us doth mightily cheer;
How it rests aching heads, at its symmetry gazing,
To think of the deeds that have made it so dear.

In our hearts, too, we carry the bright flag of glory,
Its battle-tried grandeur to cherish through life;
Ever true to our country, we'll cherish the story,
How heroes have saved it from war's bitter strife.

Our Country's Flag on God's Sacred Altar

J. W. TEMPLE

Where altars to our Maker rise,
There let His standards greet the skies;
And to heaven's welcoming breezes fling
The banners of Our Lord, the King!

Where Freedom's armies guard the land,
Let her proud standard-bearers stand
O'er hill and plain, from shore to shore,
Float her blest symbols ever more!

God of the Saints! land of the free!
Let thy fair banners blended be!
And o'er heaven's sacred altars wave
The flag that guards the free and brave!

Thus blended shall to us be given
The love of home, of God, and heaven!
Thus, in our grateful hearts shall rise,
Hopes of a home beyond the skies!

Thus shall religion's sacred fire
The patriot's heart with zeal inspire;
Thus shall the patriot's gifts, in turn,
On blest religion's altars burn!

And love of God walk hand in hand
With love of man and native land!
Christ's kingdom then the earth will span,
With "peace on earth—good will to man!"

The Patriotic Influence of the American Flag when Raised above a Public School

LOUIS V. FOX, GRAMMAR SCHOOL NO. 63, NORTH THIRD AVE. AND 173RD ST., NEW YORK CITY, NEW YORK.

It shall be my object in writing on this subject, not to prove that this influence should be exerted over the older people so much, but over the boys—for two reasons: first, because being a boy, I am able to judge more accurately of the feelings of a boy; and secondly, because those who are boys now, will, in future time, be the great men of our nation—the presidents, the statesmen, the soldiers, editors, the clergymen, etc.

On coming to school and seeing the "Stars and Stripes" floating in the breeze over the school-house, what boy would not pause in admiration and think of the glorious battles in which this same beautiful banner had so triumphantly waved—at Stony Point, Saratoga, at the mastheads of Paul Jones' gallant ships, at Fort McHenry, from which the idea of our beautiful song, "The Star Spangled Banner," was taken—all through the Mexican War, and later still in the bloody battles of the "Rebellion," at Murfreesboro, Gettysburg, and on the victorious "Monitor."

And it must be a mean-spirited and unpatriotic boy indeed, who would not be willing to fight under a flag for which so many brave men have fought and died.

And then he would think what that flag represented—a country, not like Russia or Turkey, where the people are compelled to bow to the will of one man, who has but to say the word and one's head is severed from his body, or the individual is compelled to conform to some particular creed in which the despot believes—but a country where everybody is free! free to worship God as he please, free to elect the men who govern him; a country which protects him where he is now—which protects the schools and floats its flag over them as a sign of such protection, the school where some of the happiest, and, maybe, some of the bitterest hours of his life have been spent.

A country where men have equal chances to win in the struggle of life; and, as he thinks of all these glorious privileges, do you suppose for a minute that he would stand by and calmly see that emblem of freedom torn down?

No!!! the very thought rouses his ire! And as he enters school he remembers the words of the poet—

> "Forever float that standard sheet!
>   Where breathes the foe but falls before us?
> With Freedom's soil beneath our feet,
>   And Freedom's banner streaming o'er us."

And as he thinks of these words, he vows, with one all-concentrating and all-hallowing vow, that, Almighty God helping him, he will never, never, NEVER see the flag dishonored.

And every one of us from the utmost depths of his soul, echoes— "AMEN!"

Louis V. Fox

Grammar School No. 63

April 1st, 1890

"Raising the School House Flag"

HEZEKIAH BUTTERWORTH

To-day the birthright of her hopes the younger nation sings,
As on the pinions of the light the banner lifts its wings,
To-day the future on us smiles, and studious labors cease,
To set the flag above the school,
    our fortress wall of peace!
War bugles old, storm-beating drums,
    and veterans scarred and true
And children marching of the States,
    'mid roses wined with dew,
Behind ye thrice a hundred years, before a thousand grand,
What says the past to you to-day, O children of the land?
What are thy legends, O thou flag
    that gladdenest land and sea?
What is thy meaning in the air amid the jubilee?
Flag of the sun that glows for all,
Flag of the breeze that blows for all,
Flag of the sea that flows for all,
Flag of the school that stands for all,
Flag of the people, one and all—
The peaceful bugles blow and blow across the silver sea;
What is thy meaning in the air? O banner, answer me!

No azure pavon old art thou, borne on the Palmer's spear;
No oriflamme of Red Cross Knight or coiffured cavalier;
No gold pomegranates of the sun burn on thy silken cloud,
Nor Shamrock green, nor Thistle red, nor Rampant Lion proud;
No burning bees on taffeta in gold and crimson wrought,
Nor eagle poising in the sky above the ocelot.
No gaping dragons haunt thy folds
    as in the white sun's spray,
When westering Vikings turned their prows
    from noonless Norroway;
No double crowns beneath the cross are on thy hues unfurled,
Such as the Prophet Pilot led toward the sunset world;
No artist's vision, circle-crowned,
    such as with knightly pride
Old Balboa threw upon the air o'er the Pacific tide.
Not e'en St. George's Cross is there
    that led the Mayflower on,
Nor old St. Andrew's Cross of faith—
    the Double Cross is gone.
The peaceful bugles blow and blow across the silver sea;
What is they meaning, O thou flag, this day of jubilee?

Flag of the sun that shines for all,
Flag of the breeze that blows for all,
Flag of the sea that flows for all,
Flag of the school that stands for all,
Flag of the people, one and all—
What is thy meaning in the air? O banner, answer me!

O children of the States, yon flag more happy lustres deck
Than oriflammes of old Navarre or Cressy or Rosebeq.
The Covenanter's field of blue,
    caught from the clear sky, see,
And Lyra's burning stars of peace and endless unity.
The morning beams across it stream in roses red and white,
As though 'twere outward rolled from heaven
      by angels of the light.
All hail to thee, celestial flag, on this prophetic day!
That minglest with the light of heaven
    the morn's eternal ray.
The peaceful bugles blow and blow across the silver sea,
And speakest thou to every soul the great world's jubilee!

Flag of the battle-fields, with pride
    beneath thy folds I stand,
While gyveless Freedom lifts to thee
    her choral trumpets grand—
Thou stand'st for Monmouth's march of tire,
      for Trenton's lines of flame,
For rippling Eutaw's field of blood,
    for Yorktown's endless fame;
For Cape de Gatt, and fierce Algiers,
    and Perry's blood-red deck,
For Vera Cruz, and Monterey, and white Chapultepec;
Thou stand'st for Sumter's broken wall, as high above Tybee
The shouting forts uplift again the stars of unity;
Thou stand'st that all the rights of men
    may every people bless,
And God's own kingdom walk the world
    in peace and righteousness!
The silver bugles blow and blow across the silver sea,
And so thou speak'st to every soul this day of jubilee.

O my America, whose flag we throne amid the sky,
Beneath whose folds 'tis life to live
    and noblest death to die,
I hear the peaceful bugles blow across the silver sea,
And bless my God my palace stands a cottage home in thee!
So speak the voices of the Past, ye children of the land,

Behind us thrice an hundred years, before a thousand grand,
Such are the legends of yon flag that gladdens land and sea,
Such is the Hand that scrolls the air this day of jubilee.
Flag of the sun that shines for all,
Flag of the breeze that blows for all,
Flag of the sea that flows for all,
Flag of the SCHOOL that stands for all,
Flag of the people, one and all—
Hail! flag of Liberty! all hail!
Hail, glorious years to come!

National School Celebration of Columbus Day: The Official Programme

(PREPARED BY EXECUTIVE COMMITTEE, FRANCIS BELLAMY, CHAIRMAN)

The schools should assemble at 9 A.M. in their various rooms. At 9:30 the detail of Veterans is expected to arrive. It is to be met at the entrance of the yard by the Color-Guard of pupils, escorted with dignity to the building, and presented to the Principal. The Principal then gives the signal, and the several teachers conduct their students to the yard, to beat of drum or other music, and arrange them in a hollow square about the flag, the Veterans and Color-Guard taking places by the flag itself. The Master of Ceremonies then gives the command "Attention!" and begins the exercises by reading the Proclamation.

1. READING OF THE PRESIDENT'S PROCLAMATION—by the Master of Ceremonies

At the close of the reading he announces, "In accordance with this recommendation by the President of the United States, and as a sign of our devotion to our country, let the Flag of the Nation be unfurled above this School."

2. RAISING OF THE FLAG—by the Veterans

As the Flag reaches the top of the staff, the Veterans will lead the assemblage in "Three Cheers for 'Old Glory.'"

3. SALUTE TO THE FLAG—by the Pupils

At a signal from the Principal the pupils, in ordered ranks, hands to the side, face the Flag. Another signal is given; every pupil gives the flag the military salute—right hand lifted, palm downward, to a line with the forehead and close to it. Standing thus, all repeat together, slowly, "I

"ETERNAL VIGILANCE
IS THE PRICE
OF LIBERTY"
JEFFERSON.

THE GUARD OF THE COLORS

H·LANCAS
MERTINE

The Guard of the Colors: This posed shot, taken on 31 May 1922, emphasizes the enduring honor and respect for the flag by military veterans, especially poignant on Memorial Day. (Photo courtesy of the Library of Congress.)

pledge allegiance to my Flag and the Republic for which it stands; one
Nation indivisible, with Liberty and Justice for all." At the words, "to my
Flag," the right hand is extended gracefully, palm upward, toward the
Flag, and remains in this gesture till the end of the affirmation; where-
upon all hands immediately drop to the side. Then, still standing, as the
instruments strike a chord, all will sing AMERICA—"My Country, 'tis of
Thee."

4. ACKNOWLEDGMENT OF GOD—Prayer or Scripture

5. SONG OF COLUMBUS DAY—by Pupils and Audience

Contributed by The Youth's Companion Air: Lyons

> Columbia, my land! All hail the glad day
> When first to thy strand Hope pointed the way.
> Hail him who thro' darkness first followed the Flame
> That led where the Mayflower of Liberty came.
>
> Dear Country, the star of the valiant and free!
> Thy exiles afar are dreaming of thee.
> No fields of the Earth so enchantingly shine,
> No air breathes such incense, such music as thine.
>
> Humanity's home! Thy sheltering breast
> Give welcome and room to strangers oppress'd.
> Pale children of Hunger and Hatred and Wrong
> Find life in thy freedom and joy in thy song.
>
> Thy fairest estate the lowly may hold,
> Thy poor may grow great, thy feeble grow bold
> For worth is the watchword to noble degree,
> And manhood is mighty where manhood is free.
>
> O Union of States, and union of souls!
> Thy promise awaits, thy future unfolds,
> And earth from her twilight is hailing the sun,
> That rises where people and rulers are one.
>   —Theron Brown

6. THE ADDRESS

"The Meaning of the Four Centuries" A Declamation of the Special
Address prepared for the occasion by The Youth's Companion.

7. THE ODE

"Columbia's Banner," A Reading of the Poem written for the Occasion by Edna Dean Proctor [see following].

Here should follow whatever additional Exercises, Patriotic Recitations, Historic Representations, or Chorals may be desired.

8. ADDRESSES BY CITIZENS, and National Songs.

(N.B. for full reproduction of "The Meaning of Four Centuries" as well as Directions for "How to Observe Columbus Day" which includes detailed instructions for parade, press coverage, and community involvement techniques, see *The Youth's Companion* 65 [1892]: 446–47).

Columbia's Banner

EDNA DEAN PROCTOR

"God helping me," cried Columbus, "though fair or foul the breeze,
I will sail and sail till I find the land beyond the western seas!"—
So an eagle might leave its eyrie, bent, though the blue should bar,
To fold its wings on the loftiest peak of an undiscovered star!
And into the vast and void abyss he followed the setting sun;
Nor gulfs nor gales could fright his sails
            till the wondrous quest was done.
But O the weary vigils, the murmuring, torturing days,
Till the Pinta's gun, and the shout of "Land!"
            set the black night ablaze!
Till the shore lay fair as Paradise in morning's balm and gold,
And a world was won from the conquered deep,
            and the tale of the ages told!

Uplift the starry Banner! The best age is begun!
We are the heirs of the mariners whose voyage that morn was done.
Measureless lands Columbus gave and rivers through zones that roll,
But his rarest, noblest bounty was a New World for the Soul!
For he sailed from the Past with its stifling walls,
            to the Future's open sky,
And the ghosts of gloom and fear were laid
            as the breath of heaven went by;
And the pedant's pride and the lordling's scorn were lost,
            in that vital air,
As fogs are lost when sun and wind sweep ocean blue and bare;
And Freedom and larger Knowledge dawned clear,
            the sky to span,
The birthright, not of priest or king,
            but of every child of man!

Uplift the New World's Banner to greet the exultant sun!
Let its rosy gleams still follow his beams
   as swift to west they run,
Till the wide air rings with shout and hymn
   to welcome it shining high,
And our eagle from lone Katahdin to Shasta's snow can fly
In the light of its stars as fold on fold
   is flung to the autumn sky!
Uplift it, Youths and Maidens, with songs and loving cheers;
Through triumphs, raptures, it has waved,
   through agonies and tears.
Columbia looks from sea to sea and thrills with joy to know
Her myriad sons, as one, would leap to shield it from a foe!
And you who soon will be the State,
   and shape each great decree,
Oh, vow to live and die for it, if glorious death must be!
In dungeon dim, on gory fields, its light and peace were bought;
And you who front the future—whose days our dreams fulfil—
On Liberty's immortal height, Oh, plant it firmer still!
For it floats for broadest learning;
   for the soul's supreme release;
For law disdaining license,
   for righteousness and peace;
For valor born of justice; and its simplest scope and plan
Makes a queen of every woman, a king of every man!
While forever, like Columbia, o'er Truth's unfathomed main
It pilots to the hidden isles, a grander realm to gain.

Ah! what a mighty trust is ours, the noblest ever sung,
To keep this Banner spotless its kindred stars among!
Our fleets may throng the oceans—
   our forts the headlands crown—
Our mines their treasures lavish for mint and mart and town—
Rich fields and flocks and busy looms
   bring plenty, far and wide—
And statelier temples deck the land
   than Rome's or Athens' pride—
And science dare the mysteries of earth and wave and sky—
Till none with us in splendor and strength and skill can vie;
Yet, should we reckon Liberty and Manhood less than these,
And slight the right of the humblest
   between our circling seas,—
Should we be false to our sacred past,
   our fathers' God forgetting,
This Banner would lose its lustre, our sun be nigh his setting!

But the dawn will sooner forget the east,
        the tides their ebb and flow,
Than you forget our radiant Flag,
        and its matchless gifts forego!
Nay! you will keep it high advanced
        with ever-brightening sway—
The Banner whose light betokens the Lord's diviner day—
Leading the nations gloriously in Freedom's holy way!
No cloud on the field of azure—no stain on the rosy bars—
God bless you, Youths and Maidens,
        as you guard the Stripes and Stars!

Salute Old Glory

KATE BROWNLEE SHERWOOD

(sung to the tune of "Dixie")

Hail, fairest flag on land or ocean,
Setting all the world in motion!
        Awake! awake!
        Salute the flag!
Its stars so bright, its stripes so fair;
        Awake! awake!
No other can with it compare,
That sails the sea, that rules the air:
        Awake! awake!
        Awake! salute Old Glory!

Our flag has felt the tempest's rattle,
Blown by all the winds of battle.
        Awake! awake!
        Salute the flag!
For you its beauteous folds were torn;
        Awake! awake!
But now by loyal legions borne,
It views the splendors of the morn;
        Awake! awake!
        Awake! salute Old Glory!

O, come, ye patriots, to the rally!
Come from every hill and valley!
        Awake! awake!
        Salute the flag!

The Stars and Stripes for freedom stand;
  Awake! awake!
O, come, and for your country band,
And pledge your head and heart and hand,
  Awake! awake!
  Awake!, salute Old Glory!

The Uniform Flag Statute

(approved in 1917 by the National Conference of Commissioners on
Uniform State Laws)

1. Definition.—The word flag, standard, color, ensign or shield, as used in this act, shall include any flag, standard, color, ensign or shield, or copy, picture or representation thereof, made of any substance or represented or produced thereon, and of any size, evidently purporting to be such flag, standard, color, ensign or shield of the United States or of this state, or a copy, picture of representation thereof.

2. Desecration.—No person shall, in any manner, for exhibiton of display:
(a) place or cause to be placed any word, figure, mark, picture, design, drawing or advertisement of any nature upon any flag, standard, color, ensign or shield of the United States or of this state, or authorized by any law of the United States or this state; or
(b) expose to public view any such flag, standard, color, ensign or shield upon which shall have been printed, painted, or otherwise produced, or to which shall have been attached, appended, affixed or annexed any such word, figure, mark, picture, design, drawing or advertisement; or
(c) expose to public view for sale, manufacture, or otherwise, or to sell, give or have in possession for sale, for gift or for use for any purpose, any substance, being an article of merchandise, or receptacle, or thing for holding or carrying merchandise, upon or to which shall have been produced or attached any such flag, standard, color, ensign or shield, in order to advertise, call attention to, decorate, mark or distinguish such article or substance.

3. Mutilation.—No person shall publicly mutilate, deface, defile, defy, trample upon, or by word or act cast contempt upon any such flag, standard, color, ensign or shield.

4. Exceptions.—This statute shall not apply to any act permitted by the statutes of the United States (or of this state), or by the United States Army and Navy regulations, nor shall it apply to any printed or written document or production, stationery, ornament, picture or jewelry

whereon shall be depicted said flag, standard, color, ensign or shield with no design or words thereon and disconnected with any advertisement.

5. Penalty.—Any violation of Section Two of this act shall be a misdemeanor and punishable by a fine of not more than   dollars. Any violation of Section Three of this act shall be punishable by a fine of not more than   dollars, or by imprisonment for not more than   days, or by both fine and imprisonment, in the discretion of the Court.

6. Inconsistent Acts Repealed.—All laws and parts of laws in conflict herewith are hereby repealed.

7. Interpretation.—This act shall be so construed as to effectuate its general purpose and to make uniform the laws of the states which enact it.

8. Name of Act.—This act may be cited as the Uniform Flag Law.

9. Time of Taking Effect.—This act shall take effect   days after

(Source: The Uniform Flag Statute, 9B MCKINNEY'S
UNIFORM LAWS ANN. 48)

Flag Drill Song

CHARLES H. GABRIEL

(copyright 1917, by Homer A. Rodeheaver)

Flag of country waving o'er our heads,
Red and white and blue, Brave and pure and true;
Emblem of our free and happy land,
We are loyal still to you;
Flag of freedom, waving o'er our land,
Now a happy band Bravely will we stand
For our country's welfare and its right,
Shedding forth its glorious light.

Higher still we wave the Christian flag,
With its blood-stained cross Saving all from loss;
Banner of our Lord who saved from sin,
Making all the world akin;
Raise it higher, higher, higher still,

And with glad acclaim, Praise His holy name,
Who in answer to His Father's will
Came His mission to fulfill.

Blend we then our country's colors bright
With the pure white light Of our hearts delight [*sic*];
Marching forth to battle for the right,
Singing "Peace, goodwill to men."
Lift them higher, Christian flags so true,
Red and white and blue, Both so dear to you!
Liberty to all mankind proclaim
Thro' the dear Redeemer's name.

Our Fealty to Old Glory

WILLIAM NORMAN GUTHRIE (1918)

O glorious banner, we hail thy thirteen Stripes
As blood and fire, bright crimson—the holy seven
Enfolding the snow-white, cloud-white six,—fair types
Of our strife for a purer world: how they mount to heaven
Twain stairways for all to ascend with courageous endeavour
Who share in the pride of thy elect, thy consecrate people!
We worship thee flying from flagstaff, mast and steeple
With thy cruel challenge—upward and onward forever.

Chorus

Hail, great in song and story,
Dear flag of the brave and free—
O Stars and Stripes, Old Glory,
We offer our all to thee.

II

O glorious banner, we hail thy mystical Square
Of midnight blue, that only uniteth us truly
In devotion to lofty ideals all men may share—
Millions of else rebellious, fearless, unruly:
Lo, the Square of our heavenly house, it hath many mansions
For different souls of the folk that blend in one people
Who worship thee flying from flagstaff, mast and steeple:
Their emblem of generous inclusions and gracious expansions!

III

O glorious banner, we hail thy Stars that proclaim
With their five white rays the hand of the maker and worker,
The splendour of man who standeth erect, without shame,
Head high, arms wide, feet braced, no trembler or shirker!
In battle array they shine our Stars in a New Constellation,
That adds to the zone of the heaven the hope of thy people,
We worship thee flying from flagstaff, mast and steeple,
Uplifting in symbol the destinies high of our Nation.

Chorus

IV

O glorious banner, we hail the Eagle above,
Whitehooded, for that he pierced to the radiant zenith
In quest of the will of the Father of Light and of Love,
Though like angels, of billowy cirrus a veil interveneth,
Thence droppeth he laughing, assured of the triumph of virtue,
In his talons the olive-bough, yea, arrows to fight for his people.
Who worship thee flying from flagstaff, mast and steeple,
How shall victory, and joy, and valorous praise desert you?

Chorus

V

O glorious banner, we swear thee loyalty all—
Great voice of America's soul, compelling, creative,—
We shall equal our forebears, and answer together thy call,
We thy children who came overseas, both adopted, and native,
Our faces all turned to the future, alike determined
To fashion of manifold genius with marvellous temper, one people,
That shall worship thee flying from flagstaff, mast and steeple,
Their sovereignty fire-robed, in fulminant sheen enermined.

Chorus

Hail, great in song and story,
Dear flag of the brave and free—
O Stars and Stripes, Old Glory,
We offer our all to thee.

N.B. This hymn may, if preferred, be sung or read, each of its five stanzas after its respective part of the service.

END

The Flag Code

Adopted at the National Flag Conference, Washington, D.C., 14–15 June 1923

The National Flag Conference, convened at the call of the American Legion in Memorial Continental Hall, Washington, D.C., on Flag Day, June 14, 1923, composed of delegates from the principal National patriotic, fraternal, educational and civic organizations, adopts the following Code and urges that every citizen be governed by this Code in the use and care of the Flag of the United States.

The flag of the United States symbolizes that freedom, equality, justice and humanity for which our forefathers sacrificed their lives and personal fortunes. Today, this Flag represents a Nation of over one hundred million free people, its Constitution and institutions, its achievements and aspirations.

Description of the Flag. The Flag of the United States has 13 horizontal stripes—7 red and 6 white—the red and white stripes alternating, and a union which consists of white stars of five points on a blue field placed in the upper quarter next to the staff and extending to the lower edge of the fourth red stripe from the top. The number of stars is the same as the number of states in the Union. The canton or union now contains 48 stars arranged in six horizontal and eight vertical rows, each star with one point upward. On the admission of a state into the Union a star will be added to the union of the Flag, and such admission will take effect on the 4th day of July next succeeding such admission. The proportions of the flag prescribed by Executive Order of President Taft, October 29, 1912, are as follows:

Hoist (width) of flag	1
Fly (length) of flag	1.9
Hoist (width) of union	7–13
Fly (length) of union	0.76
Width of each stripe	1–13
Diameter of star	.0616

Proper Manner of Displaying the Flag. There are certain fundamental rules of heraldry which, if understood generally, would indicate the proper method of displaying the Flag. The matter becomes a very simple one if it is kept in mind that the National Flag represents the living country and is itself considered as a living thing. The union of the flag is the honor point; the right arm is the sword arm and therefore the point of danger and hence the place of honor.

1. The Flag should be displayed only from sunrise to sunset, or between such hours as may be designated by proper authority. It should be displayed on National and State holidays and on historic and special occasions. The flag should always be hoisted briskly and lowered slowly and ceremoniously.

2. **When carried in a procession with another flag,** or flags, the Flag of the United States should be either on the marching right, i.e., the Flag's own right, or when there is a line of other flags, the Flag of the United States may be in front of the center of that line.

3. **When displayed with another flag, against a wall from crossed staffs,** the Flag of the United States should be on the right, the Flag's own right, and its staff should be in front of the staff of the other flag.

4. **When a number of flags are grouped** and displayed from staffs, the Flag of the United States should be in the center or at the highest point of the group.

5. **When the flags of States or cities or pennants of societies are flown on the same halyard** with the Flag of the United States, the National Flag should always be at the peak. When flown from adjacent staffs the Flag of the United States should be hoisted first. No flag or pennant should be placed above or to the right of the Flag of the United States.

6. **When flags of two or more Nations are displayed** they should be flown from separate staffs of the same height and the flags should be of approximately equal size. (International usage forbids the display of the flag of one nation above that of another nation in time of peace.)

7. **When the Flag is displayed from a staff projecting horizontally or at an angle from the window sill, balcony or front of building,** the union of the Flag should go clear to the head of the staff unless the Flag is at half staff.

8. **When the Flag of the United States is displayed in a manner other than by being flown from a staff,** it should be displayed flat, whether indoors or out. When displayed either horizontally or vertically against a wall, the union should be uppermost and to the Flag's own right, i.e., to

the observer's left. When displayed in a window it should be displayed the same way, that is, with the union or blue field to the left of the observer in the street. When festoons, rosettes, or drapings of blue, white and red are desired, bunting should be used, but never the Flag.

9. **When displayed over the middle of the street,** as between buildings, the Flag of the United States should be suspended vertically with the union to the north in an east and west street or to the east in a north and south street.

10. **When used on a speaker's platform,** the Flag should be displayed above and behind the speaker. It should never be used to cover the speaker's desk nor to drape over the front of the platform. If flown from a staff it should be on the speaker's right.

11. **When used in unveiling a statue or monument,** the Flag should not be allowed to fall on the ground but should be carried aloft to wave out, forming a distinctive feature during the remainder of the ceremony.

12. **When flown at half-staff,** the Flag is first hoisted to the peak and then lowered to the half-staff position, but before lowering the Flag for the day it is raised again to the peak. On Memorial Day, May 30th, the Flag is displayed at half-staff from sunrise until noon and at full staff from noon until sunset for the Nation lives and the Flag is the symbol of the Living Nation.

13. **When used to cover a casket,** the Flag should be placed so that the union is at the head and over the left shoulder. The Flag should not be lowered into the grave nor allowed to touch the ground. The casket should be carried foot first.

14. **When the Flag is displayed in church,** it should be from a staff placed on the congregation's right as they face the clergyman. The service flag, the State flag or other flag should be at the left of the congregation. If in the chancel, the Flag of the United States should be placed on the clergyman's right as he faces the congregation and other flags on his left.

15. When the Flag is in such a condition that it is no longer a fitting emblem for display, it should not be cast aside or used in any way that might be viewed as disrespectful to the National Colors, but it should be destroyed as a whole, privately, perferably by burning or by some other method in harmony with the reverence and respect we owe to the emblem representing our Country.

Cautions.

1. Do not permit disrespect to be shown to the Flag of the United States.

2. Do not dip the Flag of the United States to any person or anything. The regimental color, State Flag, organizational or institutional Flag will render this honor.

3. Do not display the Flag of the United States with the union down except as a signal of distress.

4. Do not place any other flag or pennant above or to the right of the Flag of the United States.

5. Do not let the Flag of the United States touch the ground, or trail in the water.

6. Do not place any object or emblem of any kind on or above the Flag of the United States.

7. Do not use the Flag as drapery in any form whatever. Use bunting of blue, white and red.

8. Do not fasten the Flag in such manner as will permit it to be easily torn.

9. Do not drape the Flag over the hood, top, sides or back of a vehicle, or of a railroad train or boat. When the Flag is displayed on a motor car, the staff should be affixed firmly to the chassis, or clamped to the radiator cap.

10. Do not display the Flag on a float in a parade except from a staff.

11. Do not use the Flag as a covering for a ceiling.

12. Do not use the Flag as a portion of a costume or of an athletic uniform. Do not embroider it upon cushions or handkerchiefs or print it on paper napkins or boxes.

13. Do not put lettering of any kind upon the Flag.

14. Do not use the Flag in any form of advertising nor fasten an advertising sign to a pole from which the Flag of the United States is flying.

15. Do not display, use or store the Flag in such a manner as will permit it to be easily soiled or damaged.

Proper Use of Bunting. Bunting of the National Colors should be used for covering a speaker's desk, draping over the front of a platform and for decoration in general. Bunting should be arranged with the blue above, the white in the middle and the red below.

Salute to the Flag. During the ceremony of hoisting or lowering the Flag or when the Flag is passing in a parade or in a review, all persons present should face the Flag, stand at attention and salute. Those present in uniform should render the right hand salute. When not in uniform, men should remove the headdress with the right hand and hold it at the left shoulder. Women should salute by placing the right hand over the heart. The salute to the Flag in the moving column is rendered at the moment the Flag passes.

When the National Anthem is played those present in uniform should salute at the first note of the Anthem retaining this position until the last note of the Anthem. When not in uniform, men should remove the headdress and hold it as in the salute to the Flag. Women should render the salute as to the Flag. When there is no flag display, all should face toward the music.

Pledge to the Flag.

"I pledge allegiance to the Flag of the United
    States and to the Republic for which it stands,
One Nation indivisible, with liberty and justice
    for all."

The Shield of the United States. The shield of the United States has 13 vertical stripes, 7 white and 6 red with a blue chief without stars.

National Anthem. "The Star Spangled Banner" is recommended for universal recognition as the National Anthem.

There is but one Federal statute which protects the Flag throughout the country from desecration. This law provides that a trade-mark cannot be registered which consists of or comprises, among other things, "the flag, coat of arms, or other insignia of the United States or any simulation thereof" (33 Stat. L. p. 725, Feb. 20, 1905).

Congress has also enacted legislation providing certain penalties for the desecration, mutilation or improper use of the Flag within the District of Columbia. (Feb. 8, 1917, 39. Stat. L. Page 900).

Suggestions for State Legislation Regarding the Flag. Based upon opinion of the Supreme Court of the United States rendered by Justice

John Marshall Harlan, every State should enact adequate laws for the protection of the National Flag. State Flag laws should include the following:

1. That June 14th, Flag Day, be set apart by proclamation of the Governor recommending that Flag Day be observed by people generally by the display of the Flag of the United States and in such other ways as will be in harmony with the general character of the day.

2. That the Flag of the United States be displayed on the main administration building of every public institution.

3. That the Flag of the United States with staff or flag pole be provided for every school house and that the Flag be displayed during school days either from a flag pole or in inclement weather within the school buildings.

4. That the Flag of the United States be displayed in every polling place.

5. That the use of the Flag of the United States as a receptacle for receiving, holding, carrying or delivering anything be prohibited.

6. That the use of the Flag for advertising purposes in any manner be prohibited.

7. That Penalty (fine and imprisonment) be provided for public mutilation, abuse or desecration of the Flag.

Notes

Chapter 1. Assessing the Symbol

1. Franklin K. Lane, *The American Spirit: Addresses in War-Time* (New York: Frederick A. Stokes, 1918), 130–31.

2. Milo Milton Quaife, *The Flag of the United States* (New York: Grosset & Dunlap, 1942), xiv.

3. A brief example might illustrate this point: In an Introduction to American Studies class at the University of Maryland, when asked why the flag was so important to our society, one student replied: "Well, for one thing, it was used in all those Revolutionary battles." When asked how many agreed with this, every student raised his or her hand. When told that this was in fact not the case, the students maintained that it was true, "because we've seen it in lots of pictures." A few students said the truth was not an issue here; more importantly, they felt the teacher should not make suggestions about the flag that went against their earlier learnings, as this seemed "unpatriotic."

4. George Henry Preble, *History of the Flag of the United States of America, and of the Naval and Yacht-Club Signals, Seals, and Arms, and Principal National Songs of the United States, with a Chronicle of the Symbols, Standards, Banners, and Flags of Ancient and Modern Nations*, 2d ed., rev. (Boston: A. Williams and Co., 1880), xii.

5. Quaife, *Flag of the United States*, 190.

6. Boleslaw Mastai and Marie-Louise D'Otrange Mastai, *The Stars and the Stripes: The American Flag as Art and as History from the Birth of the Republic to the Present* (New York: Knopf, 1973), 231.

7. Ibid., 9.

8. William Rea Furlong and Byron McCandless, with editorial assistance from Harold D. Langley, *So Proudly We Hail: The History of the United States Flag* (Washington, D.C.: Smithsonian Institution Press, 1981), 9. Langley inherited more than one thousand pages of text from Furlong and McCandless, which he edited down to one fifth of that size. For an insightful look at the problems of an editor and a historian in such a situation, see Harold D. Langley, "Some Problems of Flag Research: A Look at the Origins and Evolution of the Furlong-McCandless History of the United States Flag," *Flag Bulletin* 19 (1980): 184–97.

9. The most seminal contribution in the field of sociology has been Sasha R. Weitman's "National Flags: A Sociological Overview," *Semiotica* 8 (1973): 328–67. Weitman does a content analysis of a variety of national flags, discussing symbolic uses of color and emblem. Of theoretical use to the present study is Weitman's distinction between the "program" of those who construct such images and the "review" (response) of those addressed (p. 366)—this reminds one to beware the danger of thinking that a "meaning" is inherent in a symbol; rather, interpretation is affected by the reviewer's sociohistorical context. In psychology, studies have focused on flag preferences among children in contemporary American society, or cross-culturally. The specialist in this field is Edwin D. Lawson. See his

"Development of Patriotism in Children: A Second Look," *Journal of Psychology* 55 (1963): 279–86; "Flag Preferences of Canadians: Before the Maple Leaf," *Psychological Report* 17 (1965): 553–54; "Flag Preference as an Indicator of Patriotism in Israeli Children," *Journal of Cross-Cultural Psychology* 6 (1975): 490–97. See also David Statt, "Flag Choices of Elite American and Canadian Children," *Psychological Report* 32 (1973): 85–86, and Leonard William Doob, *Patriotism and Nationalism: Their Psychological Foundations* (New Haven: Yale University Press, 1964).

10. Dan Sperber, *Rethinking Symbolism*, trans. Alice A. Moulton (New York: Cambridge University Press, 1975), 113.

11. Ibid., 119.

12. Ibid., 148.

13. Ibid., 136.

14. Keith B. Richburg, "America Already Has a Civil Religion," *Washington Post*, 8 September 1985, C1, C4.

15. For critical evaluations of the concept that see it as an attempt at the instillation of a revitalization movement see Michael W. Hughey, *Civil Religion and Moral Order: Theoretical and Historical Dimensions* (Westport, Conn.: Greenwood Press, 1983); John F. Wilson, *Public Religion in American Culture* (Philadelphia: Temple University Press, 1979).

16. Robert N. Bellah, "Civil Religion in America," *Daedalus* 96 (1967): 1–21.

17. Ibid. For an interesting analysis of the influence this statement had on President Carter's ideology, see Hughey, *Civil Religion and Moral Order*, 195n.

18. Phillip E. Hammond's "Commentary" on "Civil Religion in America" in *The Religious Situation: 1968*, ed. Donald R. Cutler (Boston: Beacon Press, 1968), 382.

19. Ellis M. West, "A Proposed Neutral Definition of Civil Religion," *Journal of Church and State* 22 (Winter, 1980): 39.

20. Hughey, *Civil Religion and Moral Order*, 172.

21. *Encyclopedia of Associations*, 18th ed., 1984, vol. 1, part 1, 720.

22. Whitney Smith, "Fundamental Theses in Vexillology," *Flag Bulletin* 21 (1982): 33–34.

23. Whitney Smith, *The Flag Book of the United States*, rev. ed. (New York: William Morrow & Co., 1975), 4.

24. Whitney Smith, "The Future of Vexillology," *Flag Bulletin* 21 (1982): 4–15.

25. Smith, *Flag Book*, v.

26. William G. Crampton, "Political Symbolism: Some Oblique Contributions," an unpublished essay in the possession of the author, 1.

27. See David Lister, "Some Aspects of the Law and Usage of Flags in Britain," *Flag Bulletin* 17 (1978): 14–23; Georges Pasch, "French Attitudes Toward the Symbols of France," *Flag Bulletin* 20 (1981): 119–40.

Chapter 2. The Uses of a New Constellation

1. For a discussion of this development, see Whitney Smith's explanation of proto-vexilloids in "Prolegomena to the Study of Political Symbolism," Ph.D. diss. Boston University, 1968, 96.

2. George Henry Preble, *History of the Flag*, 25–28, 48–61; Whitney Smith, *Flag Book*, (New York: William Morrow, 1975), 8.

3. Mark Mayo Boatner III, *Military Customs and Traditions* (New York: David McKay, 1956), 33.

4. Smith, *Flag Book*, 36–38; Kai T. Erikson, *Wayward Puritans: A Study in the Sociology of Deviance* (New York: John Wiley & Sons, 1966), 113.

5. Smith, *Flag Book*, 33.

6. Many of the traditional flag histories have discussed the variety of such regimental flags at length. A good place to begin in pursuit of more details in this area would be Furlong and McCandless, *So Proudly We Hail*, 33–44.

7. William Bell Clark, ed., *Naval Documents of the American Revolution* (Washington: GPO 1966–80) vol. 1, 538; Quaife, *Flag of the United States*, 51; Preble, *History of the Flag*, 140–42.

8. Clark, *Naval Documents*, 565.

9. Quaife, *Flag of the United States*, 36; Milo Milton Quaife, Melvin J. Weig and Roy Applebaum, *The History of the United States Flag, from the Revolution to the Present, Including a Guide to Its Use and Display* (New York: Harper, 1961), 26–27.

10. Quaife, *Flag of the United States*, 60–61.

11. The naval use of the Continental Colors might have presented some confusion, as an identical representation had already been in use for some time by the East India Company. However, some historians believe it highly unlikely that the East India flag in question ever flew in the New World, in which case the similarity would pose a problem not for the colonists, but still perhaps for British soldiers trying to discern symbolic meaning. See Smith, *Flag Book*, 60.

12. Preble, *History of the Flag*, 212.

13. Smith, *Flag Book*, 55.

14. The Flint Institute of Arts, *The American Indian: The American Flag* (Flint, Mich.: The Institute, 1975), 5–6.

15. Flint Institute, *American Indian*, 5; Smith, *Flag Book*, 55.

16. *Who Was Who in American History—The Military* (Chicago: Marquis Who's Who, 1975): 466. As historian of the Pennsylvania Navy, John W. Jackson has explained, "Committees or Councils of Safety were the bridge between the crude but necessary revolutionary committees of colonies prior to 1775 and the organization of permanent state legislatures following the Declaration of Independence." Pennsylvania had "the most capable leadership in the state," and Ben Franklin chaired the group as president. See John W. Jackson, *The Pennsylvania Navy 1775–1781; The Defense of the Delaware* (New Brunswick, N.J.: Rutgers University Press, 1974), vii, 8–9, 26–27.

17. Quaife, *Flag of the United States*, 107; Smith, *Flag Book*, 58; Mastai and Mastai, *Stars and the Stripes*, 44.

18. Arnold Rabbow, "A New Constellation: What Did the First Stars and Stripes Look Like?" *Flag Bulletin* 19 (1980): 50; Richard S. Patterson and Richard Dougall, *The Eagle and the Shield: A History of the Great Seal of the United States* (Washington: Office of the Historian, Bureau of Public Affairs, Department of State, 1976), 40–43. Rabbow's argument is a bit complicated to summarize quickly: first, he points out that Trumbull and Peale would use a flag they were familiar with (this variant) in painting, even if that flag was not actually carried in the particular battle that they were painting. He also refers to the variant's use in a Society of Cincinnati diploma ca. 1783. His most convincing data is reference to this variant as "the Ensign of U.S. proper" in William Barton's proposals for the Third Great Seal Committee of Congress in May 1782.

19. Kenneth Silverman, *A Cultural History of the American Revolution* (New York: Thomas Y. Crowell, 1976), 58–59, 687; Patterson and Dougall, *The Eagle and the Shield*, 34.

20. Patterson and Dougall, *The Eagle and the Shield*, 43; Smith, *Flag Book*, 68.

21. Rabbow, *passim;* Patterson and Dougall, *The Eagle and the Shield,* 63.

22. Robert Morris, *The Truth about the American Flag* (Levittown, Pa.: Bucks County Printing House, 1976), 40.

23. Mastai and Mastai, *Stars and the Stripes,* 29.

24. Morris, *The Truth about the American Flag,* 60.

25. Mastai and Mastai, *Stars and the Stripes,* 59.

26. See, for example, Furlong and McCandless, *So Proudly We Hail,* 147, for illustrations of the flag variants listed on the Mondhare flag sheet of 1781 and the Lotter flag sheet of 1783, and 163 for the Scotti flag sheet of 1776. For an excellent introduction to the variations in star patterns, see Grace Rogers Cooper, *Thirteen-star Flags: Keys to Identification* (Washington, D.C.: Smithsonian Institution Press, 1973), passim.

27. Morris, *The Truth about the American Flag,* 62.

28. Ratcliffe M. Hills, *The Naval Origin of the United States Flag* (Hartford, Conn.: Hill, 1947), 18.

29. Hills, *Naval Origin,* 19.

30. Boatner, *Military Customs,* 34. Quaife gives earlier dates for the adoption of the Stars and Stripes as the "national colors" in different segments of the Army, but he also points out that practice lingered far behind official proclamations for change in flag use. According to Quaife, the Stars and Stripes was introduced as the national colors of the artillery in 1834, the infantry in 1841, and the cavalry in 1887, all still much later than many would surmise. See Quaife, Weigs, and Applebaum, *History of the United States Flag,* 87–93.

31. Whitney Smith, "Face to Face with Betsy Ross," *Flag Bulletin* 14 (1975): 20–21.

32. Smith, "Face to Face with Betsy Ross," 20–21.

33. Morris, *The Truth about the American Flag,* 32–34. This "square frame" formation appears to have been a more popular variant in this period than the Betsy Ross "wreath" later celebrated in paintings from the second half of the nineteenth century. The "square frame" formation was still used at sea as late as the 1850s.

34. Cooper, *Thirteen-star Flags,* 9.

35. Mastai and Mastai, *Stars and the Stripes,* 45, 65, 89.

36. Furlong and McCandless, *So Proudly We Hail,* 147–49; *The American Flag in the Art of Our Country* (Allentown, Pa.: Allentown Art Museum, 1976), 6.

37. Marian Klamkin, *American Patriotic and Political China* (New York: Charles Scribner's Sons, 1973), 2–17.

38. Klamkin, *American Patriotic and Political China,* 10–11.

39. Ibid., 17.

40. Index of American Design, *Emblems of Unity and Freedom* (New York: Metropolitan Museum of Art, 1943?). The illustrations in this booklet are reproductions of drawings from the Index of American Design compiled by States Arts Project of the Work Projects Administration.

41. Patterson and Dougall explain why the pattern of seven red stripes and six white stripes on the flag is reversed on the coat of arms, shield, and seal of the United States: "in heraldry a color such as red *(gules)* is placed upon a metal such as silver *(argent)* but never vice versa. The field or background of the seal is therefore *argent* (silver or white) with six red stripes on it, but with the tincture of the field showing at the sides. Theoretically the field is solid white or silver, but the six red stripes on it make it look instead like seven white or silver stripes." *The Eagle and the Shield,* 81.

42. Wilbur Zelinsky, "O Say Can You See? Nationalistic Emblems in the Landscape," *Winterthur Portfolio* 19 (Winter 1984): 280.

43. Herbert Ridgeway Collins, *Threads of History: Americana Recorded on Cloth 1775 to the Present* (Washington, D.C.: Smithsonian Institution Press, 1979), 48–65.

44. Milton W. Brown *et al., American Art* (New York: Harry N. Abrams, 1979), 138.

45. Preble, *History of the Flag,* 724.

46. Smith, *Flag Book,* 71.

47. Oscar George Theodore Sonneck, *The Star Spangled Banner* (Washington, D.C.: GPO, 1914), 65.

48. Sonneck, *Star Spangled Banner,* 83.

49. Joseph Muller, *The Star Spangled Banner Words and Music Issued Between 1814–1864* (New York: G. A. Baker & Co., 1935), 28–29.

50. Sonneck, *Star Spangled Banner,* 83.

51. Ibid., 62.

52. Ibid., 62–63.

53. Muller, *Star Spangled Banner,* 34–35.

54. Mabel R. Bennett, *So Gallantly Streaming* (New York: Drake, 1974), 70.

Chapter 3. Flag Culture in the Antebellum Period

1. Edward S. Delaplaine, *Francis Scott Key, Life and Times* (New York: Biography Press, 1937), 477.

2. Boatner, *Military Customs,* 48.

3. Smith, *Flag Book,* 74–75; Henry Baldwin, A. Floyd Delafield, and Alexander Hamilton, *Report on Desecration of the American Flag* (Connecticut Society of the Sons of the Revolution, Privately printed, 1896), 8.

4. *History of Congress,* 1458–59.

5. Ibid., 1459.

6. Ibid., 1460.

7. Ibid., 463.

8. Robert Spiller *et al., Literary History of the United States,* 4th ed. (New York: Macmillan, 1974), 176.

9. Ibid., 277. The poem is "On the Death of Joseph Rodman Drake," published in 1820. It contains the often quoted couplet: "None knew thee but to love thee, Nor named thee but to praise."

10. A brief biographical note on Drake along with a copy of the poem may be found in Preble, *History of the Flag,* 734–36. The complete text of "The American Flag," which was first published in the *New York Evening Post* on 29 May 1819, may be found in the appendix.

11. Preble, *History of the Flag,* 351, 353.

12. Ibid., 353n.

13. Mastai and Mastai, *Stars and the Stripes,* 190.

14. For a fine introduction to the persona of George Washington as preeminent symbol in American civil religion as presented in antebellum schoolbooks, see Ruth Miller Elson, *Guardians of Tradition: American Schoolbooks of the Nineteenth Century* (Lincoln: University of Nebraska Press, 1964), 196–205. In a survey study of American education, Lawrence A. Cremin has also touched on the role of civil religion in the antebellum classroom. Discussing the McGuffey readers,

he notes "the heroes of American history were portrayed as exemplars of industriousness, honesty, and intelligence and assigned the stature of Biblical heroes: George Washington, for example, was often compared to Moses. The events of American history were portrayed as developments in a holy design . . . And the significance of American history was equated with 'the divine scheme for moral government.'" Lawrence A. Cremin, *American Education: The National Experience 1783–1876* (New York: Harper and Row, 1980), 73.

15. Mastai and Mastai, *Stars and the Stripes,* 190.

16. The historical analysis of the culture of children is still a relatively unexplored field. Several useful studies have laid the groundwork, however. The Association for the Anthropological Study of Play has published several collections of essays through Leisure Press in West Point, New York. In American Studies, Bernard Mergen has contributed "Discovery of Chilren's Play," *American Quarterly* 27 (October 1975): 399–420. Two standard citations in the field of children's culture are Mary Goodman, *The Culture of Childhood: Child's Eye Views of Society and Culture* (New York: Teachers College Press, 1970) and Margaret Mead and Martha Wolfenstein, *Childhood in Contemporary Cultures* (Chicago: University of Chicago Press, 1955). Most significant because they adopt a historical perspective are B. G. Rosenberg and Brian Sutton-Smith, "Sixty Years of Historical Change in the Game Preferences of American Children," *Journal of American Folklore* 74 (1961): 17–46; and N. Ray Hiner and Joseph M. Hawes, eds., *Growing Up in America: Children in Historical Perspective* (Champaign: University of Illinois Press, 1985).

17. Ray Allen Billington, *Westward Expansion,* 4th ed. (New York: Macmillan, 1974), 324.

18. Collins, *Threads of History,* 87.

19. Zelinsky, "O Say Can You See?" 282.

20. Edmund B. Sullivan, *Collecting Political Americana* (New York: Crown Publishers, 1980), 27.

21. Collins, *Threads of History,* 88, 102, 109.

22. Ibid., 102–5.

23. Ibid., 88.

24. Ibid., 117–305.

25. For descriptions of these and other examples of landmark plantings and carryings of the flag in this period see Preble, *History of the Flag,* 353–76.

26. Jean H. Baker, *Ambivalent Americans: The Know-Nothing Party in Maryland* (Baltimore: Johns Hopkins University Press, 1977), 37.

27. Justin H. Smith, *The Annexation of Texas* (1911; New York: AMS Press, 1971), 310–11.

28. John Hancock Lee, *The Origin and Progress of the American Party in Politics.* (1855; Freeport, N.Y.: Books for Libraries Press, 1970), 115; Baker, *Ambivalent Americans,* 109.

29. Baker, *Ambivalent Americans,* 37.

30. *United States Gazette,* Philadelphia, 7 May 1844, p. 2.

31. Ibid., p. 2.

32. Lee, *Origin and Progress,* 54–55.

33. Ibid., 54–55.

34. *United States Gazette,* Philadelphia, 8 May 1844, p. 2. An editorial note in the paper comments: "We are not sure that the words are exact."

35. *Gazette,* 8 May 1844, p. 2.

36. Lee, *Origin and Progress,* 79.

37. *United States Gazette,* Philadelphia, 9 May 1844, p. 2.

38. For complete details on participants and organization of the parade, see Lee, *Origin and Progress,* 136–61.

39. The name "Supreme Order of the Star Spangled Banner" could be a result of proximity to Fort McHenry and the recent death of Francis Scott Key. Although the Supreme Order of the Star Spangled Banner was the forerunner of the Know-Nothing Party, other organizations, such as the Sons of America and the Order of United American Mechanics, also served as "feeder groups" to the Know-Nothings. See Baker, *Ambivalent Americans,* 108–13.

40. Billington, *Westward Expansion,* 514.

41. I am thinking here specifically of Zelinsky's unsubstantiated assertion, "If the ascendancy of the flag began in earnest with the Mexican conflict and perhaps also with the growing popularity of Francis Scott Key's "Star-Spangled Banner" (Zelinsky, 280). What I hope to begin to illustrate in this chapter is that, although the Civil War triggered a wide-scale display of and devotion to the national banner, the flag did not suddenly pop into the hierarchy of American civil religious symbols but had been gaining importance since its introduction in 1777, and that its rise to dominance is the result of a variety of complex influences and uses. It should also be noted that the Mexican-American War did provide enough demand for flags to stimulate the creation of the first full-time professional flag-manufacturing company, Annin & Company. Annin continues in operation today, and claims that it "directs as much effort at encouraging respect for the flag as for urging its display," presenting a "Betsy Ross Award" from time to time "for individual contributions to patriotism." See Bennett, *So Gallantly Streaming,* 77.

42. See *American Flag in the Art of Our Country.*

43. Collins, *Threads of History,* 126.

44. *American Flag in the Art of Our Country.*

45. I make this hypothesis based on the first appearance of political advertisements on flags in the campaign of 1840 and a passing comment on page fifteen of the 1896 "Report on the Desecration of the American Flag" by the Connecticut Sons of the Revolution. I reason that the gentlemen in 1896 refer to the postwar period as "in late years" then refer back to this occurrence as "years ago." Also, perhaps a bit cynical, I am inclined to believe that if politicians saw the advantage of writing their names on the white stripes, people renting hotel rooms to politicians could not have been far behind. I do submit that my opinion remains insufficiently supported and that more research is required for conclusive evidence.

46. Mastai and Mastai, *Stars and the Stripes,* 184–85.

47. These and all later references in this chapter to the use of the American flag in fine art, unless otherwise noted, are taken from the unpaginated yet one definitive catalog of an exhibit on the subject, *The American Flag in the Art of Our Country.*

48. *Britannica Encyclopedia of American Art* (Chicago: Encyclopedia Brittanica Corporation, 1973), 325–26.

49. Ibid. See also Nicholas B. Wainwright, compiler, *Paintings and Miniatures of the Historical Society of Pennsylvania* (Philadelphia: Historical Society of Pennsylvania, 1974), 136–37.

50. Collins, *Threads of History,* 110.

51. Brown *et al., American Art,* 228.

52. Charles Peterson, "The Truth About Washington Crossing the Delaware," *Parade* 23 May 1976, on file at Flag Research Center, Winchester, Mass.

53. Robert M. MacPherson, "George Washington Will Cross the Delaware,"

New York Times 14 December 1965.

54. Smith, "Face to Face with Betsy Ross," 20–21.

55. Chris Flannigan, during class discussion in the author's Introduction to American Studies class at the University of Maryland, Spring, 1985. Such an attitude exists also in academia, by those who see themselves as defenders of tradition against the onslaught of iconoclasts. For an example of this attitude, see Morris, *Truth about the American Flag*, 28. In the field of vexillology, at the 1985 convention of the North American Vexillological Association, George F. Cahill, director of the National Flag Foundation, recognized usage of the term "patriotic articulators" to describe those vexillologists, including himself, who valued faith more than historical data.

56. A scan of mid-February newspaper and magazine advertisements will show the tenacity of this image, which can also be understood as an "icon" of American civil religion. For the Sak's advertisement, see *New York Times* 17 Feb. 1975.

57. Anonymous painting found reproduced on greeting cards—a sample can be found at the Flag Research Center. Katz's painting is illustrated in *New Jersey Historical Commission Newsletter* for October 1975.

58. Preble, *History of the Flag*, 353–54.

59. Ibid., 355.

60. Ibid., 356.

61. Nicholas Smith, *Our Nation's Flag in History and Incident* (Milwaukee: The Young Churchman Co., 1903), 96; Smith, *Flag Book*, 147.

62. See, for example, Mastai and Mastai, *Stars and the Stripes*, 126 or Preble, *History of the Flag*, 394.

Chapter 4. Symbol of the Union: Flag Use during the Civil War

1. Bruce Catton, *The Coming Fury* (Garden City, N.Y.: Doubleday & Co., 1961), 156–57.

2. Ibid., 171.

3. Ibid., 175.

4. Ibid., 181.

5. Ibid., 307.

6. Ibid., 311, 322.

7. James Ferrigan III, "Flags in the Land of AHS," North American Vexillological Association Conference, Kansas City, Mo., 13 October 1985. See also Mastai and Mastai, *Stars and the Stripes*, 125.

8. Preble, *History of the Flag*, 449–452. It is one of the amazing ironies of history that the date of this restoration ceremony designated by Abraham Lincoln was the date of his own fatal shooting at the hands of John Wilkes Booth.

9. Preble, *History of the Flag*, 445, 453.

10. Mary A. Livermore, *My Story of the War* (1889 New York: Arno Press, 1972), 90.

11. Livermore, *My Story of the War*, 91–92.

12. "The Resurrection of Patriotism," *New York Times* 16 April 1861, p. 4, col. 2.

13. Ibid., p. 8, col. 3.

14. *New York Times* 17 April 1861, page 1, col. 5.
15. *New York Times* 16 April 1861, page 3, col. 4.
16. *New York Times* 17 April 1861, page 1, col. 5.
17. *Chicago Tribune* 20 April 1861, p. 1.
18. Preble, *History of the Flag*, 456.
19. Ibid., 459–61.
20. Ibid., 459.
21. George T. Balch, *Methods of Teaching Patriotism in the Public Schools* (New York: D. Van Nostrand, 1890), 61–62.
22. The Architect of the Capitol's Art and Reference Library in the U.S. Capitol in Washington, D. C., holds a variety of photocopied samples of such patriotic envelopes from the private collection of Dr. Francis Lord of Bethesda, Maryland. See also Mastai and Mastai, *Stars and the Stripes*, 150–51, 141.
23. Preble, *History of the Flag*, 455–65. For a complete version of all eight verses of "The Star-Gemmed Banner," see page 455.
24. Ibid., 463.
25. *Harper's Weekly* 5 (6 July 1861): 427.
26. [George Palmer Putnam] *Soldiers' and Sailors' Patriotic Songs* (New York: Loyal Publication Society, 1864), 8–11, 15. For the complete text of the "Flag-Song of the Michigan Volunteers" see the appendix.
27. Nicholas Smith, *Our Nation's Flag in History and Incident* (Milwaukee: The Young Churchman Co., 1903) 101.
28. The Nicholas Smith text lists some good examples, but perhaps the best, most contemporary treatment of the subject is Livermore's *My Story of the War*.
29. Nicholas Smith, *Our Nation's Flag*, 100.
30. Ibid., 95.
31. Amos Stevens Billingsley, *From the Flag to the Cross* (Philadelphia: New York Publishing, 1872), 25.
32. Ibid., 39–40.
33. Ibid., 158–60; Smith, *Our Nation's Flag*, 102–3.
34. Livermore, *My Story of the War*, 117. My interpretation of the female war allegory in French sculpture 1870–1918 is based on June Hargrove's presentation "War Memorials in France" given before the Department of Art, University of Maryland-College Park, on 16 November 1983. For German use of the female war allegory in this same period, see Siegmar Holsten, *Allegorische Darstellungen des Krieges 1870–1918* (Munchen: Pestel, 1976), Chapter 1.
35. For the definitive analysis of the development of the "woman's sphere" in New England, see Nancy F. Cott, *The Bonds of Womanhood* (New Haven: Yale University Press, 1977). Ann Douglas, *The Feminization of American Culture* (New York: Avon, 1977) provides a thorough background for nineteenth-century women's participation in the development of modern mass culture. Sherbrooke Rogers offers the best biography to date on the influential editress of *Godey's: Sarah Josepha Hale* (Grantham, N.H.: Tompson & Rutter, 1985).
36. Preble, *History of the Flag*, 456.
37. Ibid., 460.
38. (Smethport, Pennsylvania) *M'Kean Miner*, 1, no. 36 (18 June 1861): 2. The author is indebted to Alberta Curry of Wellesley, Massachusetts, for making this particular reference available, since it demonstrates how the study of history can tell more about one's particular heritage. Miss Otto is the author's great-great-great-aunt and Captain Cory is the author's great-great-great-uncle.
39. Mastai and Mastai, *Stars and the Stripes*, 127.

40. *Dictionary of American Biography* iv (1960): 99–100.

41. Hale, Edward Everett. "The Man Without a Country," *The Atlantic Monthly* 12 (1863): 667.

42. Hale, "Man Without a Country," 675, 677–78.

43. "Editor's Table," *Harper's* (1861): 266.

44. "Editor's Drawer," *Harper's* (1863): 283.

45. "Editor's Drawer," *Harper's* (1864): 272.

46. "Our Flag!" and "The Flag and the Army," *Harper's Weekly* 16 July 1874, p. 450.

47. "Our Flag," *Harper's Weekly* 16 July 1864: 456–57.

48. Preble, *History of the Flag*, 458–59.

49. Smith, *Our Nation's Flag*, 92–93; Preble, *History of the Flag*, 457–58.

50. Smith, *Our Nation's Flag*, 93.

51. Preble, *History of the Flag*, 457.

52. James W. Silver, *Confederate Morale and Church Propaganda* (Tuscaloosa, Ala.: Confederate Publishing Co., 1957), 101, 78.

53. Silver, *Confederate Morale*, 88. Silver cites William W. Sweet, *The Methodist Episcopal Church and the Civil War* (Cincinnati: 1912), 56–57 for this rather violent summation by the Christian leader: "I trust our troops will rally and wipe out the disgrace of Manassas, though it cost the life of every rebel under arms. Let Davis and Beauregard be captured, to meet the fate of Haman. Hang them up on Mason's and Dixon's line, that traitors may be warned. Let them hang until vultures shall eat their rotten flesh from their bones; let them hang until the crows shall build their filthy nests in their skeletons; let them hang until the rope rots, and let their dismembered bones fall so deep into the earth that God Almighty can't find them in the day of resurrection."

54. Although I have looked extensively in all three fields I can find no handling of this topic. Talks with clergymen, historians, and vexillologists have led me to believe that the need to identify one's group as "American" has greatly influenced the introduction of the flag into the house of worship, as has the outbreak of war or crisis. Further work on the first point could look at use of the American flag in the house of worship by Roman Catholics, Jews, or, more recently, the Nicheren Shoshu of America, a sect of Buddhists who incorporate not only massive flag displays but baton twirlers and cowboys into their patriotic/religious extravaganzas (see their *Seikyo Times*, published monthly, and their *World Tribune*, published weekly, for examples of such patriotic activities combined with the propagation of religious views). Even in such highly structured churches as the Roman Catholic, use of the flag varies widely even within a diocese; the Protestant Episcopal Church customarily maintains the presence of both the church's banner and the national banner within the church proper, but this is a tradition that has evolved rather than the result of any canonical ruling. A fascinating tangent, delving into this particular aspect of the career of the American flag could be the basis of a later study designed to elucidate the historical dynamics of this symbolic church-state interaction.

Chapter 5. The Cult of the Flag Develops

1. Paul H. Buck, *The Road to Reunion 1865–1900* (Boston: Little, Brown & Co., 1937), chapter 4.

2. Matthew Josephson, *The Politicos 1865–1896* (New York: Harcourt, Brace & Co., 1938), 139–40.

3. Josephson, *Politicos*, 36–37.

4. Ibid., 224. See also "Ingersoll, Robert G." in *Dictionary of American Biography*, 1961 ed., 5:469–70.

5. Preble, *History of the Flag*, 453.

6. *Revised Statutes of the United States*, 2d ed. 1878, Title XX Flag and Seal, sec. 1748.

7. Cooper, *Thirteen-star Flags*, 17.

8. Ibid., 22.

9. Ibid., 22–24.

10. Joseph Neumann presented the first known American flag made of American silk to the United States Senate on 12 July 1870, which later conveyed it to the Smithsonian for safekeeping in 1884. By 1880, the United States had become the second most important silk manufacturing country in the world. In 1885, representatives of the Women's Silk-Culture Association of the United States, in celebration of their industrious growth, presented the Senate with another flag. *Congressional Record*, 25 April 1884: 3380; *Congressional Record* 23 January 1885: 942–43.

11. See the contemporary picture of a mother smiling approvingly as her son marches about with a flag in Mastai and Mastai, *Stars and the Stripes*, 202.

12. Ibid., 202.

13. Ibid., 183.

14. Doris Huffman, *Oregon's Flamboyant Fourth 1876* (Portland, Oreg.: privately printed, 1976), 6, 10–11.

15. An analysis of how preparation for the centennial introduced increased representation of the American flag in *St. Nicholas*, a popular juvenile magazine of the period, is included in "Sanctification of a Banner: Children's Periodicals and the Rise of the Cult of the American Flag," the author's Master's Thesis, University of Maryland, 1981, 10–11. For illustrations of flags, flag souvenirs, and flag paraphernalia of the centennial, see Mastai and Mastai, *Stars and the Stripes*, 159, 165–71.

16. James W. Campbell, *America in the Centennial Year 1876* (Washington, D.C.: University Press of America, 1980), ix–x.

17. William Pierce Randel, *Centennial: American Life in 1876* (Philadelphia: Chilton, 1969), 296.

18. J. C. Julius Langbein, *The American Flag: Its Origin and History* (New York: Union Printing and Publishing, 1876), 15.

19. For complete details of the arrangement and distribution of flags at the Philadelphia Centennial Exhibition, see Preble, *History of the Flag*, 599. For photographs of the textile products described, see Collins, *Threads of History*, 198, 205, 211.

20. Collins, *Threads of History*, 206–7; Mastai and Mastai, *Stars and the Stripes*, 169.

21. Collins, *Threads of History*, 208; Mastai and Mastai, *Stars and the Stripes*, 156–59. This fascinating banner is preserved today in the extensive private collection of Boleslaw and Marie-Louise Mastai.

22. Campbell, *America in the Centennial Year*, 9; Huffman, *Oregon's Flamboyant Youth*, 39–200, 115–17.

23. Randel, *Centennial*, 300.

24. Alert historians rescued the manuscript from obscurity and printed limited facsimiles in 1977. See Des Moines Public Schools, Third Ward, no. 10, Des Moines, Iowa. *1876: A Centennial Offering: Original Stories, Essays and Poems by the Third Ward Pupils. Des Moines, Iowa, 1876* (Ames: Iowa State University Press, 1977). Dedication is discussed in preface. This is an unpaginated text, but all subsequent references are taken from the essay "Stars and Stripes" by Nellie C. Saylor.

25. Morris, *The Truth about the American Flag,* 56; Elizabeth McKinnon, "The Spirit of '76," unpublished report from Selectman's Office, Marblehead, Massachusetts, 11 August 1970.

26. Anne Scott MacLeod, *A Moral Tale: Children's Fiction and American Culture, 1820–1860* (Hamden, Conn.: Archon, 1975), 60.

27. Preble, *History of the Flag,* 600.

28. Carmack, "Famous Firsts in History," *Roll Call* 14 June 1956.

29. Benjamin Foltz, *The Banner We Love and The Old Flag Insulted* (Rockford, Ill.: privately printed, 1879).

30. Mastai and Mastai, *Stars and the Stripes,* 164.

31. Ibid.

32. R. Gordon Kelly, *Mother Was a Lady: Self and Society in Selected American Children's Periodicals, 1865–1890* (Westport, Conn.: Greenwood Press, 1974), 23; Frank Luther Mott, *A History of American Magazines, 1865–1885* (Cambridge: Harvard University Press, 1938), 500–503.

33. Edward W. Tuffley, "Origin of the Stars and Stripes," *St. Nicholas* 11 (1882): 66. For a more thorough discussion of the presentation of the character of George Washington in *St. Nicholas,* 1873–1898, see Scot M. Guenter, "Sanctification of a Banner: Children's Periodicals and the Rise of the Cult of the American Flag," Masters Thesis, University of Maryland, 1981, 10–16.

34. Mastai and Mastai, *Stars and the Stripes,* 164; Preble, *History of the Flag,* 283.

35. Preble, *History of the Flag,* 280–83; Quaife, Weig, and Applebaum, *History of the United States Flag,* 99–101.

36. "First Stars and Stripes," addendum to Preble's History of the Flag. Duplicate of *Washington Post* article from 1880s (undated).

37. Telephone interview with Harold D. Langley, Associate Curator, Division of Naval History, National Museum of American History, Smithsonian Institution, 17 January 1986. Langley noted that this board convened before textile analysis had been developed, and that it was one of the first examples of noted historians participating in the evaluation of material culture.

38. For a bibliography on the growth of the Betsy Ross flag tradition and a summary of historical accuracy, see Theodore D. Gottlieb's *The Origin and Evolution of the Betsy Ross Flag Legend or Tradition* (Newark: privately printed, 1938); see also Smith, *Flag Book,* 66–68 and Smith, "Face to Face with Betsy Ross," 3–28.

39. Many readers may be familiar with learning the Betsy Ross legend during their own grammar-school days. A review of the patriotic offerings listed in *The Education Index* in the 1930s, for instance, reveals the Betsy Ross legend presented in poems, plays, and pageants for young children. Many pedagogical journals encouraged elementary and junior high school teachers to use these materials in the classroom, among them *Normal Instructor, Grade Teacher,* and *Sierra Educational News.*

40. Jane Mayer, *Betsy Ross and the Flag* (New York: Random House, 1952), Introduction.

41. Louise Lawrence Devine, *The Story of Our Flag* (Chicago: Rand McNally, 1960), inside front cover.

42. Smith, *Flag Book*, 66; Furlong and McCandless, *So Proudly We Hail*, 115–17.

43. Charles F. Jenkins, "The Five-Pointed Star," *St. Nicholas* 19 (1892): 713; Henry Russell Wray, "The Stars and Stripes," *St. Nicholas* 20 (1893): 864–68.

44. Morris, *The Truth About the American Flag*, 56; Furlong and McCandless, 116–17.

45. Wallace Evan Davies, *Patriotism on Parade: The Story of Veterans' and Hereditary Organizations in America 1783–1900* (Cambridge: Harvard University Press, 1955), 218–19.

46. Davies, *Patriotism on Parade* 24–27.

47. Ibid., 22–35, 75.

48. Mary R. Dearing, *Veterans in Politics: The Story of the G.A.R.* (Baton Rouge: Louisiana State University Press, 1952), 80–96.

49. *Lafayette Post and the Flag*, Lafayette Post, no. 140, Department of New York, Grand Army of the Republic (New York: privately printed, 1899), 105–6; *Presentation of a National Flag to the College of the City of New York on Friday Evening, June 8th, 1888 in the Academy of Music by Lafayette Post, no. 140, Department of New York, Grand Army of the Republic* (New York: J. J. Little and Co., 1888), 8, 18.

50. *Presentation of National Flags to the Public Schools of the City of Rochester on Washington's Birthday, 1889, in the City Hall by George H. Thomas Post, no. 4, Department of New York, Grand Army of the Republic* (Rochester, N.Y.: Democrat and Chronicle Print, 1889), 5–6.

51. Davies, *Patriotism on Parade*, 219.

52. Dearing, *Veterans in Politics*, 405–6; "Will Raise a Flag." *Chicago Daily Tribune*, 23 July 1892, p. 1, col. 5; "They Raised a Flag. School Directors Forestall the Visiting Veterans," *Chicago Daily Tribune*, 3 August 1892, p. 1, col. 5.

53. George W. Gue, *Our Country's Flag* (Davenport, Iowa: Egbert, Fidlar, and Chambers, 1890), 95–96.

54. Gue, *Our Country's Flag*, 92–93, 97. See Appendix for complete text of these two poems.

55. Davies, *Patriotism on Parade*, 50–53.

56. Ibid., 215–16, 222–26.

57. "Celebrations and Proceedings," *American Historical Register* 2 (May 1895): 902.

58. Mrs. James B. Clark, "The Influence of Patriotic Societies," *American Monthly Magazine* 7 (December 1895): 524–25.

59. Janet E. Hosmer Richards, "The National Hymn," *American Monthly Magazine* 7 (December 1895): 539–40.

60. This rare old book is held at the Flag Research Center, Winchester, Massachusetts. *The Old Flag* (Philadelphia: American Sunday School Union, 1864).

61. The following summary of the shifting applications of the American flag in *St. Nicholas* is based on chapter 1 of Guenter, "Sanctification of a Banner," where a more thorough treatment of the subject may be found.

62. Kate Foote, "Our Flag," *St. Nicholas* 3 (1876): 566.

63. Huldah Morgan, "Ringing in the Fourth," *St. Nicholas* 15 (1888): 666; Willis J. Abbot, "A Pig That Really Caused a War," *St. Nicholas* 15 (1888): 686; Edmund Alton, "The Routine of the Republic," *St. Nicholas* 16 (1889): 55; Mrs. C.

Emma Cheny, "For Their Country's Sake," *St. Nicholas* 15 (1888): 700; Edmund Alton, "Among the Law-Makers," *St. Nicholas* 12 (1885): 707.

64. J. William Fosdick, "The Studlefunk's Bonfire," *St. Nicholas* 21 (1894): 829; Victor Mapes, "A Story of the Flag," *St. Nicholas* 19 (1892): 646.

65. Alice Balch Abbot, "Dee and Jay," *St. Nicholas* 20 (1893): 835.

66. Pauline Wesley, "Toby Hinkle, Patriot," *St. Nicholas* 23 (1896): 732.

67. Helen Gray Cone, "The Ship's Colors," *St. Nicholas* 20 (1893): 643; Harriet Prescott Spofford, "On the Fourth of July," *St. Nicholas* 19 (1892): 708.

68. W. J. Henderson, "Honors to the Flag," *St. Nicholas* 9 (1891): 140–41; Charles Sydney Clark, "Honors to the Flag in Camp and Armory," *St. Nicholas* 24 (1897): 760–62.

69. Clark, "Honors to the Flag" 762.

Chapter 6. Flag Ritual Comes to the Public Schools: Development and Dissemination of the Pledge of Allegiance

1. George T. Balch, *Methods of Teaching Patriotism in the Public Schools* (New York: D. Van Nostrand, 1890), ix–xii, xxvi–vii.

2. Balch, *Methods of Teaching Patriotism*, xxxvii, i. Contemporary historians of education have neglected this movement. Two recent scholarly texts on the history of education in America do not mention Balch at all, although they do touch on the concept of "Americanization": John D. Pulliam, *History of Education in America*, 3d ed. (Columbus: Charles E. Merrill, 1982); H. Warren Button and Eugene F. Provenzo, Jr., *History of Education and Culture in America* (Englewood Cliffs, N.J.: Prentice-Hall, 1983).

3. Balch, *Methods of Teaching Patriotism*, 1.

4. Ibid., 27, 12.

5. George T. Balch, *A Patriotic Primer for the Little Citizen* (Indianapolis: William B. Burford, 1895), 11–12.

6. Balch, *Methods of Teaching Patriotism*, 84, 43–44; Balch, *Patriotic Primer*, 16. The practice of imprinting information on American flags had not yet fallen into disfavor by 1890, and Balch urged embroidering the name of the school, in silk, upon the middle red stripe of the school flag, even suggesting the use of different colors to designate primary, middle, or advanced grades. Here, too, Balch encouraged the socialization into what he, along with other "cultural custodians," considered appropriate behavior: "As embroidery is an art particularly adapted to the ability and aesthetic taste of young girls, and in which many are quite skillful, I would suggest that in every school in which there are girls, the work of executing the embroidery of the name be placed in the hands of a committee of the most competent pupils. In boys' grammar schools, a committee of boys might be appointed to wait upon the Principal of the nearest girls' grammar school to solicit the aid of the girls in the matter of thus lettering their flag; the boys rendering the girls some equivalent favor" (Balch, *Methods of Teaching Patriotism*, 44–45).

7. Balch, *Patriotic Primer*, 16. The salute is slightly altered in an 1898 example: "We offer our Heads and our Hearts to our God and Country! One Country! One Language! One Flag!" This version of "The American Patriotic Salute to the Flag" captions a rare photograph of six grammar school children, dressed in white, who pose with their arms outstretched toward a huge Amer-

ican flag, the staff of which is held by a woman who appears to be their teacher. The flag's size necessitates its draping down onto the floor, and ironically one pig-tailed girl steps on its edge. See the back cover of the third edition, revised and enlarged, of Balch, *Patriotic Primer for Little Citizens* (Indianapolis: Levey Bros., 1898).

8. Margaret S. Miller, *I Pledge Allegiance* (Boston: Christopher Publishing, 1946), 151–52.

9. Davies, *Patriotism on Parade*, 240–43.

10. Davies, *Patriotism on Parade*, 361.

11. Wallace Foster, "Introduction," in Balch's *Patriotic Primer*, first edition.

12. Davies, *Patriotism on Parade*, 244.

13. Balch, *Patriotic Primer* (1895), 29. The Patriotic League was open to any student who owned the primer. By accepting principles and a pledge of good citizenship that stated in general terms Balch's philosophy of proper moral and patriotic behavior, each new member subscribed by signing his name on the last page, after reading through the entire primer.

14. Balch, *Patriotic Primer* (1895), 50.

15. Ibid., 53.

16. Guenter, "Sanctification of a Banner," 50.

17. Gue, *Our Country's Flag*, 17; Balch, *Patriotic Primer* (1895), 48.

18. Mott, *History of American Magazines 1865–1885* vol. iii, 7 and vol. iv, 16.

19. Marjorie Richardson, "George Washington II," *The Youth's Companion* 64 (1891): 371; Marian L. Cummings, "His Day for the Flag," *The Youth's Companion* 65 (1892): 310. For an example of a child wearing such a sash in a Civil War drawing of a celebration in Frederick, Maryland, on 21 September 1862, see Mastai and Mastai, *Stars and the Stripes*, 200. The discussion of *The Youth's Companion's* promotion of flag ritual here and following is adapted from chapter 2 of Guenter, "Sanctification of a Banner."

20. "Teaching Patriotism," *The Youth's Companion* 62 (1889): 429.

21. Miller, *I Pledge Allegiance*, 51. It is interesting to note that James B. Upham was a first cousin to Edward Bellamy, author of the bestselling and influential novel of this period, *Looking Backward*.

22. "The Flag and the Public Schools," *The Youth's Companion* 63 (1890): 31.

23. Hezekiah Butterworth, "Raising the School House Flag," *The Youth's Companion* 63 (1890): 359. Complete text of this poem is included in the appendix.

24. "The Flag and the School," *The Youth's Companion* 63 (1890): 370. For a rare example of one of the winning essays (by Louis V. Fox, Grammar School No. 63 in the 24th Ward of New York City) see, in the appendix, Fox's "The Patriotic Influence of the American Flag when Raised above a Public School," taken from Balch, *Methods of Teaching Patriotism*, 78–80.

25. "Discouraged Patriots," *The Youth's Companion* 64 (1891): 36.

26. Wisconsin, *Journal of the Senate* 20 February 1889: 239; Louis Harris, *The Flag over the Schoolhouse* (Providence, R.I.: C. A. Stephens Collection, Brown University, 1971), 161; Balch, *Methods of Teaching Patriotism*, 65–67. By 1940 nearly every state had "statutory provisions calling for the inculcation of patriotism by the public schools." For a thorough treatment of state legislation in the U.S. related to voluntary or compulsory exercises in the public schools, see David Roger Manwaring, *Render Unto Caesar: The Flag-Salute Controversy* (Chicago: University of Chicago Press, 1962), 1–16.

27. Miller, *I Pledge Allegiance*, 84–85. This text is slightly romanticized and therefore suspect as to its historical accuracy.

28. Harris gives Upham credit for the idea in *Flag over the Schoolhouse*, 16. She has a chip on her shoulder about the credit Bellamy has been given for writing the Pledge, and spends much of this book, and all of another—*Old Glory—Long May She Wave!* (Providence, R.I.: C. A. Stephens Collection, Brown University, 1981)—struggling to prove that James B. Upham deserves credit for writing it. Relatives of Upham and Bellamy had been arguing for years when the United States Flag Association called a board of scholars to decide the matter in 1930. Charles C. Tansill, Professor of American History at Fordham University, chaired that board (he had also decided on the authenticity of the Stafford flag for the Smithsonian—see note 37, chapter 5) of three scholars, which also included historian Bernard Mayo and political scientist W. Reed West. The board decided unanimously in favor of Bellamy. Harris claims that *The Youth's Companion* itself should have been included as historical evidence. Some of her arguments are convincing; unfortunately, speculations and nostalgia are mixed in with her authoritative research. Based on all the evidence from all sides, it seems most likely that the Pledge went through several drafts, with Upham probably contributing one version and Bellamy, as Chairman of the Committee, deciding on the final approved copy for the "Official Programme." The Pledge was published anonymously and credit was originally intended for the staff as a group; unfortunately, as its recitation became integral to public school patriotic ritual, authorship became an issue of prestige for the Bellamy and Upham families. Rather than join the fray in the determination of "authorship," which itself can have a variety of meanings, this study hopes to give some sociohistorical credit in the introduction of flag salutes to Balch, whose contributions to the development of flag culture in public schools have gone largely unemphasized or unnoticed for many years.

29. *The Youth's Companion* 64 (1891): 61.

30. Ibid., 297.

31. "The Schoolhouse Flag," *The Youth's Companion* 64 (1891): 376.

32. References to the Grand Army of the Republic appear from time to time in both magazines during these years, often in the context of stories or articles devoted to patriotic holidays. In *St. Nicholas* 7 (1880): 574–76, for example, "Sally's Soldier" by Christine Chaplin Brush dealt with a girl learning the significance of Decoration Day from a patriotic veteran, while in *The Youth's Companion*, in commemoration of Memorial Day 1891, James Parton contributed an informative article on the good works and aspirations of the G.A.R. (see James Parton, "The Grand Army of the Republic," *The Youth's Companion* 64 [1891]: 307).

33. Miller, *I Pledge Allegiance*, 88–89; Harris, *Flag over the Schoolhouse*, 43–44.

34. *Education* 13 (May 1892): 568.

35. "Message to the Public Schools of America," *The Youth's Companion* 65 (1892): 162.

36. "A Patriotic Education," *The Youth's Companion* 65 (1892): 85.

37. "Message to the Public Schools of America," 162.

38. Miller, *I Pledge Allegiance*, 98–110.

39. *The Youth's Companion* 65 (1892): 457.

40. Ibid.

41. Francis Bellamy, "The Official Programme of the National School Celebration of Columbus Day, 21 October 1892," *The Youth's Companion* 65 (1892): 446.

42. See, for example, Mrs. Daniel Lothrop, the Massachusetts-based author of the "Five Little Peppers" series of books, in "The National Society of the Children of the American Revolution," *American Monthly Magazine* 7 (December 1895): 531–33. Although "The Star-Spangled Banner"'s popularity grew with each war

and patriotic exhibition or exposition from the War of 1812 down through the rest of the nineteenth century, different regions had different favorite patriotic tunes. Since a dominant portion of the publishing industry in this period remained centered in the Northeast, and New England sent hundreds of teachers to spread public education throughout the Midwest and the West, these forces proved influential in ensuring "America'"s inclusion in songbooks, primers, and patriotic literature distributed and used in schools throughout much of the United States. For information on Dr. Samuel F. Smith, see Harry Dichter and Elliott Shapiro, *Early American Sheet Music: Its Lure and Its Lore, 1768–1889* (New York: R. R. Bowker, 1941), 46; Preble, *History of the Flag,* 739–43.

43. "How to Observe Columbus Day," *The Youth's Companion* 65 (1892): 446–47.

44. Although outside the perimeters of this study, the most historically significant rejection of the pledge, and the reactionary backlashes that resulted, would be the controversy stirred up by members of the Jehovah's Witnesses sect who refused, on religious grounds, to participate in the ritual. This led to two monumental Supreme Court decisions: in 1940, as World War II grew in fury in Europe, in the *Gobitis* decision the Court upheld the right to demand compulsory flag salutes in public schools. This position was reversed, coincidentally, on Flag Day, 1943, when the Court ruled with the *Barnette* decision that compulsory flag salute laws were unenforceable. This landmark decision set a precedent for First Amendment arguments that were cited during the counterculture's adoption of the national banner for various political and artistic statements from 1968 to 1972, a time when three fourths of all flag abuse litigation since the inception of flag desecration statutes would fill the courts. For more on this final point, see Albert M. Rosenblatt, "Flag Desecration Statutes: History and Analysis," *Washington University Law Quarterly,* 1972: 193–237. For the sociohistorical and legal situation of the Jehovah Witnesses' case, see Manwaring, *Render Unto Caesar.* A less scholarly book but still useful is Leonard A. Stevens, *Salute! The Case of The Bible vs. The Flag* (New York: Coward, McGann & Geoghegan, Inc., 1973).

45. *New York Senate Journal,* 28 March 1898: 1207; *Albany Evening Journal,* 26 April 1898: 5, col. 3; Manwaring, *Render Unto Caesar,* 3–4.

Chapter 7. The Emergence of Legislation against Flag Desecration

1. Mastai and Mastai, *Stars and the Stripes,* 211–12; Henry Papale, *Banners, Buttons and Songs: A Pictorial Review and Capsule Almanac of America's Presidential Campaigns,* rev. ed. (New York: St. Martin's Press, 1984), 39.

2. Dearing, *Veterans in Politics,* 460–62; Davies, *Patriotism on Parade,* 218–19.

3. Collins, *Threads of History,* 20.

4. Charles Kingsbury Miller, *"Desecration of the American Flag and Prohibitive Legislation,"* an address delivered at a banquet given by the Illinois Society, Sons of the American Revolution at the Athletic Club, Chicago, November second, eighteen hundred and ninety-eight (privately printed, 1898), 3.

5. Collins, *Threads of History,* 177–79, 184.

6. Society of Colonial Wars, Illinois, *The Misuse of the National Flag of the United States of America,* proceedings of the National Flag Committee of the Society of Colonial Wars in the State of Illinois, an Appeal to the Fifty-fourth Congress of the United States (Chicago, 1895), 28–29.

7. Mastai and Mastai, *Stars and the Stripes*, 208.

8. Collins, *Threads of History, passim.* For quick analysis of the evolution of partisan banners throughout these different presidential campaigns, refer to pages 38, 215, 223–24, 229–31, 234, 236–39, 262, 264, 269, 273–75, 297–98, 305, 334.

9. Collins, *Threads of History*, 25, see plates 56–58.

10. Mastai and Mastai, *Stars and the Stripes*, 183.

11. *Harper's Weekly* 42 (1898): 623, 651.

12. Much valuable work has been done recently examining the complex inter-relationships between this period's emerging American cultural system geared to—to use Veblen's classic phrase—"conspicuous consumption," its rising managerial class, and the development of nationwide marketing and advertising. Especially useful for an introductory reading in this area are T. J. Jackson Lears's "From Salvation to Self-Realization: Advertising and the Therapeutic Roots of the Consumer Culture, 1880–1930" and Christopher P. Wilson's "The Rhetoric of Consumption: Mass-Market Magazines and the Demise of the Gentle Reader, 1880–1920," both of which can be found in Richard Wightman Fox and T. J. Jackson Lears, eds., *The Culture of Consumption: Critical Essays in American History, 1880–1980* (New York: Pantheon, 1983).

13. Baldwin, Delafield, and Hamilton, *Report on Desecration of American Flag*, 4; Charles K. Miller, "Desecration of the American Flag," 12.

14. *Browne Trade-Marks*, 2d ed., sec. 265 as quoted in Rosenblatt, "Flag Desecration Statutes," 201.

15. Charles K. Miller, "Desecration of the American Flag," 3–4.

16. This theme of a white Anglo-Saxon class (whose members had been in the United States for at least a few generations) experiencing status-anxiety in fin de siècle America runs through many historical analyses of this period. See, for example, Richard Hofstadter, *The Age of Reform: From Bryan to F.D.R.* (New York: Vintage Books, 1955), especially chapter 4; Stow Persons, *The Decline of American Gentility* (New York: Columbia University Press, 1973); Gerald W. McFarland, *Mugwumps, Morals & Politics* (Amherst: University of Massachusetts Press, 1975); and T. J. Jackson Lears, *No Place of Grace: Anti-Modernism and the Transformation of American Culture, 1880–1920* (New York: Pantheon Books, 1981).

17. Charles K. Miller, "Desecration of the American Flag," 11–12.

18. Preble, *History of the Flag*, 603; *Congressional Record* 7 January 1880: 221.

19. Charles K. Miller, "Desecration of the American Flag," 4; Gue, *Our Country's Flag*, 19, 127.

20. Although this pamphlet does not list the offending companies, organizations, and individuals, it does include a meticulous list of misuses of the flag in the Chicago area compiled by committee members in 1895. This list demonstrates the widespread and varied uses of the flag of the United States on: "Auction Stores, Awning Makers, Bicycles, Belts, Breech-clouts, Boat-houses, Bock Beer Advertisements, Barrooms, Barberpoles, Barber Shops, Banner Decorations, Baseball Grounds, Breweries, Beer Gardens, Beer Saloons, Bottling Companies, Blotting pads, Burlesque shows, Billboards, Clowns, Cigar Makers, Carriage Cushions, Chewing Gum, Casks, Charity Balls, Chimney Sweeps, Christian Endeavor Badges, Cuff Buttons, Coat Racks, Confectionary Boxes, Covers for Street Venders Stands [sic], Cotton Mills Trademark, Decorations in Department Store, Dime Museum, Dental Association, Door Mat, Dress for Ballet Dancer, Drug Store, Drapery, Dry Goods, Exchange Saloon, Festival Hall, Fire Works Store, Fancy Photographs, Furriers, Fish Houses, Figure-heads for Vessels, Furniture Vans, Grocery Stores, Hat Booths, Hardware Store, Hotel Attrac-

tions, Ice Companies, Japanese Auction Store, Japanese Goods, Labels on Cigar Boxes, Lapel Buttons, Laundry Wagons, Lemon Wrappers, Liquor Stores, Lemonade Stands, "Living Pictures," Music Covers, Mineral Water Labels, "Old Glory" Saloon, "Old Glory" Laundry, "Old Glory" Lunch Room, Piano Makers, Picnic Grounds, Patent Medicines, Personal Adornments, Political Clubs, Partition in Rooms, Polo Games, Pool Rooms, Pails, Pocket Handkerchiefs, Pillow Covers, Panoramas, Paper Napkins, Portieres, Pyrotechnic Advertisements, Prize Fighters, Refrigerator Cars, Restaurants, Roof Gardens, Real Estate Booths, Regalia Companies, Railroad Advertisements, Salvation Army Meetings, Street "Fakirs," Sashes, Shoe Stores, Sampler Rooms, Sign Painters, Soap Makers, Scenic Decorations, Storage Warehouses, Saloons, Soda Water Fountains, Society Pins, "Shooting the Chutes," Shooting Galleries, Stage Displays, Steamboat Companies, Tar Soap, Table Napkins, Tailoring Establishments, Tent Makers, Theatres, Theatrical Plays, Toy Manufacturers, Tobacco Dealers, Transom Screens, Trade Mark's Domestic Fabric's, Variety Halls, Vaudeville Shows, Warehouse Advertisements, War Decorating, War Dramas, War Museums, Water Carnivals, Window Shades, Whisky Barrels, Whisky Bottles." This fascinating pamphlet is available on microfilm at the Library of Congress. See Society of Colonial Wars, Illinois, *Misuse of the National Flag,* p. 6.

21. Davies, *Patriotism on Parade,* 221; Charles K. Miller, "Desecration of the American Flag," 8–9.

22. Society of Colonial Wars, Illinois, *Misuse of the National Flag,* 10–11.

23. Davies, *Patriotism on Parade,* 220–21; Charles K. Miller, "Desecration of the American Flag," 8.

24. Charles K. Miller, "Desecration of the American Flag," 5, 3.

25. Davies, *Patriotism on Parade,* 221, Charles K. Miller, "Desecration of the American Flag," *passim;* Baldwin, Delafield, and Hamilton, *Report on Desecration of American Flag,* 4.

26. Charles K. Miller, "Desecration of the American Flag," 6.

27. Ibid., 11, 4.

28. It is a bit ironic that Theodore Roosevelt signed into law the state enactment against flag desecration that would serve as the model for all subsequent legislation in this area, for this statute prohibited political candidates from advertising their names or portraits on American flags, making illegal the tradition of partisan banners. This is ironic because the Union League Club of New York, the following year, illegally flew an American flag inscribed "THE UNION LEAGUE/MCKINLEY AND ROOSEVELT/1900." Roosevelt was a member of the club and dined there sometimes when in New York City. It is not known if he ever saw the banner, but no one arrested officials of the Union League for this infraction. For a thorough biography of Roosevelt from his birth up until his nomination for the vice-presidency, see Edmund Morris, *The Rise of Theodore Roosevelt* (New York: Coward, McCann and Geoghegan, 1979).

29. "Flag Law to be Tested," *New York Times* 5 August 1899, p. 1, col. 2.

30. Rosenblatt, *Flag Desecration Statutes,* 198–99.

31. Ibid., 199.

32. Ibid., 200–201.

33. Ibid., 200–203.

34. Walter LaFeber, *The New Empire: An Interpretation of American Expansion, 1860–1898* (Ithaca, N.Y.: Cornell University Press, 1963), 408.

35. Mastai and Mastai, *Stars and the Stripes,* 226. Portraits of Dewey, the military hero of the hour, graced the covers of popular magazines, his image surrounded by flags. A child's toy drum of the period survives, the sides of which alternate

thirteen-star flags with Dewey's portrait emblazoned on a red, white, and blue shield. This, and flag reproductions serving as souvenir pillow cases and sachets (to mark a 1909 "goodwill" around the world cruise of twenty-eight warships of the U.S. Navy) are examples of commercial products employing flag motifs, perhaps escaping censure as they celebrate nationalistic successes. See Mastai and Mastai, *Stars and the Stripes*, 203, 220–21.

36. Dearing, *Veterans in Politics*, 492–93.

37. Mastai and Mastai, *Stars and the Stripes*, 226; "The Birthday of Old Glory: Washington School Children," undated photo from Times Wide World Photos, Washington Bureau, held in category of "Flag—Newspapers" in the Art and Reference Library Archives, Office of the Architect of the Capitol, U.S. Capitol, Washington, D.C. New waves of nationalism have periodically resulted in the resurgence of the notion of "living flags." For photographs of such displays during World War I, see *National Geographic Magazine* 32 (October 1917): 408, 410. The latter picture is fascinating in that the participants, filling the street as far as the viewer can see, also have their arms raised in extended salute to the flag, in a pose not unlike many German propaganda shots of Nuremberg in the years of Nazi power. For a more recent example of a "living" flag of the United States, see Megan Rosenfeld, "The Human Flag! 3,500 Students Line Up as the Red, White & Blue," *Washington Post* 14 June 1985, C1, C11. The validity of the Mastais' account of the New Orleans incident is questionable, since a careful reading of two prominent New Orleans papers for the coverage of the McKinley visit reveals recognition of one thousand school children singing "Hail to the Chief" but makes no mention of any "living flag," a demonstration that would probably receive notice. If it did occur but was disregarded by both newspapers, an evaluation of the significance of such a custom would have to assess this trivialization. See (New Orleans) *Daily Picayune*, 3 May 1901, p. 1; (New Orleans) *Times-Democrat*, 3 May 1901, pp. 1, 3.

38. Paul E. Bierley, *John Philip Sousa: American Phenomenon* (Englewood Cliffs, N.J.: Prentice-Hall, 1973), 3, 19, 43, 47–48, 55, 143.

39. Mastai and Mastai, *Stars and the Stripes*, 186, 198. For an excellent example of the "Artemis" version of Columbia, logically used to represent the newly arrived world power at war, see the frontispiece of *Harper's Pictorial History of the War with Spain* (New York: Harper & Bros., 1899).

40. Charles Sydney Clark, "Honors to the Flag in Camp and Armory," *St. Nicholas* 24 (1897): 760.

41. Dearing, *Veterans in Politics*, 473.

42. P. Williams Filby and Edward G. Howard, compilers, *Star-Spangled Books* (Baltimore: Maryland Historical Society, 1972), 168; Edward S. Delaplaine, *Francis Scott Key and the National Anthem* (Washington, D.C.: Wilson-Epes Press, 1947), 9; Charles Francis Stein, Jr., *Our National Anthem The Star-Spangled Banner: Its History and Significance* (Baltimore: Wyman Park Federal Savings & Loan Association, 1964), 28.

43. Jacob A. Riis, *The Making of an American* (1901; London: Collier-Macmillian, Ltd., 1970), 283. The biographical data on Riis is taken from the *Dictionary of American Biography* (1963), vol. viii, 606–8.

Chapter 8. A Civilian Code of Flag Etiquette

1. John McCabe, *George M. Cohan: The Man Who Owned Broadway* (Garden City, N.Y.: Doubleday & Co., 1973), 72.

2. McCabe, *George M. Cohan*, 73–74.

3. Ibid., 74–78 includes a review by James Metcalfe, drama critic for a pre-Luce *Life,* lamenting the vulgarity of American taste to grant Cohan success for blatant patriotism: "If he can bring himself to coin the American flag and national heroes into box-office receipts, it is not his blame but our shame."

4. Howard Dietz and Arthur Schwartz, composers, "That's Entertainment," *Judy Garland Concert,* Trophy Records, TR7-2145, 1974.

5. *Journal of American History,* New Haven, Conn., 1 (1907): 3.

6. Mrs. Henry Champion, "American Flag—The Ensign of Liberty: The Sun Never Sets on the Stars and Stripes," *Journal of American History* 1 (1907): 9, 16.

7. Alfred Pirtle, *Our Flag,* read before the Ohio Commandery of the Loyal Legion, 7 December 1910 (privately printed, 1910), 12.

8. Pirtle, *Our Flag,* 12.

9. U.S. Congress, House Committee on the Judiciary, *Protection of the American Flag, Statement of Mrs. Jacob M. Dickinson of Nashville, Tennessee,* 62nd Cong., 3rd sess., 11 February 1913 (Washington: GPO, 1913), 4–5. For some interesting contemporary data that indicates, despite the geographic mobility of many Americans, a comparatively persistent disinterest in the cult of the flag in Dixie, see Zelinsky, "O Say Can You See?" 283.

10. 1 U. L. A. v, xi; *Uniform Commercial Code* xvi; Furlong and McCandless, *So Proudly We Hail,* 211. The procedure for approving uniform state laws was thorough: "No draft is considered by the Conference until it has been studied in detail by the Committee having it in charge. Acts are not approved by the Conference until they have been considered section by section, by at least two annual Conferences." (1 U. L. A. v).

11. Davies, *Patriotism on Parade,* 77.

12. David I. Macleod, *Building Character in the American Boy: The Boy Scouts, YMCA, and Their Forerunners, 1870–1920* (Madison: University of Wisconsin Press, 1983), 154.

13. Macleod, *Building Character,* 182. Hubert Beckwith Groves of the Americanization Society of America published a special book on the flag for Boy Scouts in 1924. See Groves, *History and Etiquette of Our Flag* (Portland, Oreg.: Americanization Society of America, 1924). Groves dedicated the book to the Boy Scouts of America as the "father of a Boy Scout" since "Boy Scouts are national standard bearers, and are solemnly pledged to protect the national emblem" (pp. 1–5).

14. Boy Scouts of America, *The Official Handbook for Boys* (Garden City: Doubleday, Page & Co., 1911), 323–58, esp. 339–41. This is the first edition of the handbook; later editions consulted in the holdings of the Library of Congress include 14th ed. (1916), 16th ed. (1917), 22nd ed. (1920), 23rd ed. (1921), 30th ed. (1924). In the final edition cited, for comparison with the first edition, see pp. 464–88.

15. *My Flag* (Philadelphia: Keystone Type Foundry, right to reproduce sold to John Wanamaker, n.d.), *passim;* Bernard J. Cigrand, *Laws and Customs Regulating the Use of the Flag of the United States* (Chicago: Marshall Field & Co., 1917), 3. It is highly likely that this is the same B. J. Cigrand who, as a school teacher in Fredonia, Wisconsin, in 1885, had students first observe the "Flag Birthday" in

public school exercises. Nine years later, in Chicago, Cigrand organized the American Flag Day Association's handling of such activities for Chicago public schools. James A. Moss calls him "the father of Flag Day" in his work *The Flag of the United States: Its History and Symbolism* (Washington: United States Flag Association, 1930), 144.

16. Gilbert Grosvenor, "Our Flag Number," *National Geographic Magazine* 32 (October 1917): 283.

17. Grosvenor, "Our Flag Number," 284; Byron McCandless, "The Story of the American Flag" and "The Correct Display of the Stars and Stripes," *National Geographic Magazine* 32 (October 1917): 286–303, 404–13.

18. Gridley Adams, *Well-well* (Chicago: Federal Advertising Agency, 1920), 12–13.

19. U.S. Congress, Senate Report from Federal Trade Commission, *Prices of American Flags*, 65th Cong., 1st sess (Washington: GPO, 1917), 5.

20. Ibid., 6. Flag companies are less than eager to share information of their participation in such associations or to discuss their past sales and prices. Most assuredly one of the participants was Annin Flag Company of New York. The nation's oldest continuing flag company, it began in 1847 to supply needs created by the Mexican-American War, and endures today as one of the largest flag manufacturers in the country.

21. *A Patriotic Exercise for Juniors: Building of the Flag or Liberty Triumphant* (Chicago: Rodeheaver Co., 1917), 3.

22. Ibid., 13, see Appendix for the complete text of "The Flag Drill Song."

23. H. Augustine Smith, *A Pageant of the Stars and Stripes* (Boston: American Institute of Religious Education, 1918), 1.

24. Ibid., 5–7.

25. Franklin K. Lane, "To Prof. H. Augustine Smith," 8 May 1918, *A Pageant of the Stars and Stripes* 1.

26. One example of the use of film to capture demonstrations of the cult of the flag during these years were the activities of the William McKinley Post of the G.A.R. in Canton, Ohio. In the G.A.R. Grand Review in Washington, D.C., on 29 September 1915, post members carried "the largest flag in the world," measuring 120 by 53½ feet in size. This flag was the idea of A. E. Lomady of Canton. Private subscriptions paid the expenses; patriotic ladies donated their time to its sewing. On 29 September it "surmounted the great capitol [sic] dome" in D.C., and on 12 and 13 January 1916, patrons of the Canton City Auditorium could see its participation in the Grand Review "reproduced in motion pictures." See Samuel Jenne Spalding, *A Sketch of the World's Largest United States Flag Owned by the City of Canton, Ohio* (Canton: privately printed, 1916). The back cover of this souvenir pamphlet pictures the giant flag in the parade "Rounding Sherman Circle, off Pennsylvania Avenue." In this photograph, the buildings of Pennsylvania Avenue are adorned with much bunting and flags, and many of the flags are hanging backward, in a manner later prohibited by the Flag Code.

27. Clifford Kachline, Society for American Baseball Research, letter to the author, 6 May 1985; Don Burns, "America's Upstanding Song," *American Legion Magazine* 105 (July 1978): 42.

28. Delaplaine, *Francis Scott Key*, 9; David Vogel, *America Through Baseball* (Chicago: Nelson Hall, 1976), 87.

29. *Helena* (Montana) *Independent*, 1 August 1918, p. 1, col. 6.

30. *State v. Shumaker*, 103 Kan. 741 P. 979 (1918).

31. Ibid.

32. Ibid.
33. Ex parte Starr, 263 F. 145 (D. Mont. 1920).
34. Ibid., 146–47.
35. Manwaring, *Render Unto Caesar*, 3.
36. Washington Laws 1919 at 210 as quoted in Manwaring, *Render Unto Caesar*, 3.
37. John W. Barry, *Masonry and the Flag* (Washington: Masonic Service Association of the United States, 1924), *passim*.
38. Grace Kincaid Morey, *Mystic Americanism* (East Aurora, N.Y.: Eastern Star Publishing, 1924), 14–15, 109–17.
39. Many scholars have discussed this theme. See, for example, the classic essay "Civil Religion in America," found as chapter 9 in Robert N. Bellah, *Beyond Belief: Essays on Religion in a Post-Traditional World* (New York: Harper and Row, 1970). See also George Armstrong Kelly, *Politics and Religious Consciousness in America* (New Brunswick, N.J.: Transaction Books, 1984); John F. Wilson, *Public Religion in American Culture* (Philadelphia: Temple Press, 1979). Vine Deloria Jr., the Amerindian author, has summarized the attitude, perhaps bitterly: "Believing that the New England coast was a new Israel, a promised land, that the American people had a 'manifest destiny' to control and settle, exploit, and eventually destroy the interior of the continent, and the belief that God was always on the side of the American people, are all objective manifestations of the fundamental belief that the world was intended for a certain group of people who followed the commands of Genesis to populate and subdue" (*New York Times* 27 November 1975: 38).
40. William Norman Guthrie, *The Religion of Old Glory* (New York: George H. Doran, 1918), vi.
41. Ibid., 14.
42. Ibid., 17.
43. William Norman Guthrie, *A Proposed Ritual Expressing the Religion of Old Glory* (New York: George H. Doran, 1918), 1.
44. Ibid., 4–17.
45. Ibid., 22–25, 37–39.
46. Ibid., 39–43. For the complete text of "Our Fealty to Old Glory," see the Appendix.
47. Richard Seelye Jones, *A History of the American Legion* (Indianapolis: Bobbs-Merrill, 1946), 236–37, 239.
48. See Garland W. Powell, *Service: For God and Country* (Indianapolis: Cornelius Printing, 1924), 40–43. Powell's "plan of flag education" involves newspaper promotionals, a contest on knowledge of flag etiquette and history for school children, the display of prize flags in downtown business windows, ceremonies on national holidays to award the flags to the various school classes, the use of "moving pictures" to "cover" the ceremonies, or photography if cinema is not available. He aims to involve and reach the entire community, for he believes that "only through concentrated effort can the mass of our people be shown the right from the wrong [in flag use]."
49. See U.S. War Department, Adjutant General's Office, *Flag Circular* (Washington: GPO, 1923), and also take a look at U.S. War Department, Adjutant General's Office, *Flag Circular* (Washington: GPO, 1924), which mentions the adoption of the Flag Code.
50. "A New Code for Old Glory: The Work of the Washington Flag Conference," *American Legion Weekly* 6 July 1923: 12; James A. Moss, *The Flag of the*

United States: How to Display It, How to Respect It, and the Story of "The Star Spangled Banner" (Menasha, Wis.: George Banta, 1923), 1.

51. "A New Code for Old Glory," 12; American Legion, "Report of the National Americanism Committee of the American Legion," *Proceedings of the National Convention,* Fifth Annual Convention (1923): Div. II, 4.

52. For the complete text of the Code issued by the 1923 Conference, see the Appendix.

53. "A New Code for Old Glory," 12.

54. American Legion, "Report of the National Americanism Committee," Sixth Annual Convention (1924): 127–28.

55. American Legion, "Report of the National Americanism Committee," (1924): 128.

56. American Legion, Div. I, "Report of National Adjutant," *Proceedings of the National Convention,* Sixth Annual Convention (1924): 14–17. In 1924, the American Legion had forty prints of *The Man Without a Country,* which it distributed to local posts to use as a fundraiser. This was more than twice as many prints as it held of *Flashes of Action,* the closest competitor for top fundraising honors. The National Adjutant reports: "In addition to the money profits obtained by the Posts, the pictures sponsored by the Legion have gone far to place the post in a popular position in the community. *The Man Without a Country* has brought in hundreds of letters applauding the National Headquarters for sponsoring the film."

57. Manwaring, *Render Unto Caesar,* 7; Arnold S. Rice, *The Ku Klux Klan in American Politics* (New York: Haskell House, 1972), 13.

58. Manwaring, *Render Unto Caesar,* 7; Julia E. Johnson, comp. *Ku Klux Klan, The Reference Shelf,* (New York: H. Wilson, 1923) vol. 1, no. 10: 7, 35, 40.

59. Mastai and Mastai, *Stars and the Stripes,* 180.

60. David Chalmers, *Hooded Americanism: The History of the Ku Klux Klan* (New York: Franklin Watts, 1981), 281–90.

61. Norman Hapgood, ed., *Professional Patriots* (New York: Albert & Charles Boni, 1928), 165; "Moss, James Alfred," *The National Cyclopaedia of American Biography* XXX (1943): 560–61. The u.s.f.a. did not tolerate socialism, however, and helped spread the Red Scare. It encouraged small companies and banks to start "flag circles" to support "the basic aim of the United States Flag Association, to counteract and ultimately destroy the insidious forces, sinister influences, and disturbing elements, which, in these days of discord and divided counsels, are working and spreading to divide the unity of American citizenship and finally undermine the Republic. In organizing a Flag Circle the firm would be doing its bit to help counteract these growing forces and influences which carry a disregard not only for *property rights* but also for *personal liberty.*" Moss claimed that "communist" presidential candidate William Z. Foster received half a million votes in 1924 and that his party predicted they would draw four or five million votes in 1928. Actually, Foster received 33,076 votes and no Communist paper or official published such a prediction for 1928 (Hapgood, *Professional Patriots,* 80).

62. Moss, *The Flag of the United States: How to Display It,* 30.

63. Hapgood, *Professional Patriots,* 166–67.

64. Adams published his equivalent to Moss's *The Flag of the United States* Handbook in 1953: *So Proudly We Hail. . . !* (New York: United States Flag Foundation, 1953). He claims therein to have begun his organization immediately after the 1923 Flag Conference, and he also claims credit for revising the Pledge of Allegiance (p. 3). Although this book comes along thirty years after the origin of Moss's u.s.f.a., Adams also connects loving the flag with anticom-

munism. He maintains that because the Post Office created a stamp displaying the flag of the United States, the organization is infiltrated by Communists. (Cancelling the stamp violates the flag.) These Communists use "infiltration tactics toward getting American citizens to commence weakening their respect for our flag and by such gradual lessons to soon become emancipated from allegiance to our form of government" (p. 73). Adams also mentions the threat of "progressive education" (p. 80). This reactionary political view is interspersed in the text with directions for flag display and flag use, patriotic anecdotes, and quotes that emphasize the cult of the flag.

Some Concluding Thoughts

1. Robert Ellis Thompson, "The Significance of Our Flag," in Ray Brousseau, comp., *Looking Forward: Life in the Twentieth Century as Predicted in the Pages of American Magazines from 1895 to 1905* (New York: American Heritage Press, 1970), n.p.

2. For an example of such an analysis of a relatively new custom associated with the flag of the United States, see Scot M. Guenter, "This Flag Flew over the U.S. Capitol," *Flag Bulletin* 25 (1986): 147–59.

Select Bibliography

Primary Sources

Adams, Gridley. *So Proudly We Hail. . . !* New York: United States Flag Foundation, 1953.

———. *Well-well.* Chicago: Federal Advertising Agency, 1920.

American Legion. "Division I. Report of National Adjutant." *Proceedings of the National Convention.* Sixth Annual Convention (1924): 14–17.

———. "Report of the National Americanism Committee of the American Legion." *Proceedings of the National Convention.* Fifth Annual Convention (1923): Division II, 1–9.

American Legion. "Report of the National Americanism Committee of the American Legion." *Proceedings of the National Convention.* Sixth Annual Convention (1924): 127–29.

Balch, George T. *Methods of Teaching Patriotism in the Public Schools.* New York: D. Van Nostrand, 1890.

———. *A Patriotic Primer for the Little Citizen.* Indianapolis: William B. Burford, 1895.

———. *A Patriotic Primer for the Little Citizen.* 3d ed. Revised and enlarged by Wallace Foster. Indianapolis: Levey Bros., 1898.

Baldwin, Henry, A., Floyd Delafield, and Alexander Hamilton. *Report on Desecration of American Flag.* Read at annual meeting of the Connecticut Society of the Sons of the Revolution, 8 December 1896. Privately printed, 1896.

Barry, John W. *Masonry and the Flag.* Washington: Masonic Service Association of the United States, 1924.

Billingsley, Amos Stevens. *From the Flag to the Cross.* Philadelphia: New York Publishing, 1872.

Blau, Eleanor. "Educators Weigh a Civil Religion." *New York Times* 27 November 1975: 38.

Boy Scouts of America. *The Official Handbook for Boys.* Garden City: Doubleday, Page & Co., 1911; 14th ed. (1916); 16th ed. (1917); 22d ed. (1920); 23d ed. (1921); 30th ed. (1924).

Brooks, Elbridge S. *The Story of the Government: The Century Book for Young Americans.* Issued under the auspices of the Society of the Sons of the American Revolution. New York: Century Co, 1894.

"Celebrations and Proceedings." *American Historical Register* 2 (May 1895): 902.

Champion, Mrs. Henry. "American Flag—The Ensign of Liberty; The Sun Never Sets on the Stars and Stripes." *Journal of American History* 1 (1907): 9–16.

Cigrand, Bernard J. *Laws and Customs Regulating the Use of the Flag of the United States.* Chicago: Marshall Field & Co., 1917.

Clark, Mrs. James B. "The Influence of Patriotic Societies." *American Monthly Magazine* 7 (December 1895): 521–26.

Congressional Record. 7 January 1880: 221; 25 April 1884: 3380; 23 January 1885: 942–43.

Crampton, William G. Director of the Flag Institute, Chester, England. Letter to the author 3 January 1986.

Des Moines Public Schools, Third Ward, No. 10, Des Moines, Iowa. *1876: A Centennial Offering: Original Stories, Essays and Poems by the Third Ward Pupils. Des Moines, Iowa, 1876.* Ames: Iowa State University Press, 1977.

Education. Vols. 12–13 (1891–1892).

Ex parte Starr, 263 F. 145 (D. Mont. 1920).

"Flag Law to be Tested." *New York Times* 5 August 1899: 1, c. 2.

Foltz, Benjamin. *The Banner We Love and The Old Flag Insulted.* Rockford, Ill.: Privately printed, 1879.

Fuhrmann, Adam. *The Star-Spangled Banner.* St. Louis, Mo.: Privately printed, 1918.

George H. Thomas Post, No. 4. Department of New York. Grand Army of the Republic. *Presentation of National Flags to the Public Schools of the City of Rochester on Washington's Birthday, 1889, in the City Hall by George H. Thomas Post, No. 4, Department of New York, Grand Army of the Republic.* Rochester, N.Y.: Democrat and Chronicle Print, 1889.

Grosvenor, Gilbert. "Our Flag Number." *National Geographic Magazine* 32 (October 1917): 281–84.

Groves, Herbert Beckwith. *History and Etiquette of Our Flag.* Portland, Oreg.: Americanization Society of America, 1924.

Gue, George W. *Our Country's Flag.* Davenport, Iowa: Egbert, Fidlar and Chambers, 1890.

Guthrie, William Norman. *A Proposed Ritual Expressing the Religion of Old Glory.* New York: George H. Doran, 1918.

———. *The Religion of Old Glory.* New York: George H. Doran, 1918.

Hale, Edward Everett. "The Man Without a Country." *The Atlantic Monthly* 12 (1863): 665–79.

Harper's Pictorial History of the War with Spain. New York: Harper & Bros., 1899.

Harrison, Peleg. *The Stars and Stripes and other American Flags.* Boston: Little, Brown, & Co., 1906.

History of Congress.

Index of American Design. *Emblems of Unity and Freedom.* New York: Metropolitan Museum of Art, 1943?

Johnson, Julia E., comp. *Ku Klux Klan.* The Reference Shelf, vol. 1, no. 10. New York: H. Wilson, 1923.

Lafayette Post, No. 140. Department of New York. Grand Army of the Republic. *Lafayette Post and the Flag.* New York: Privately printed, 1899.

Lafayette Post, No. 140. Department of New York. Grand Army of the Republic. *Presentation of a National Flag to the College of the City of New York on Friday Evening, June 8th, 1888 in the Academy of Music by Lafayette Post, No. 140, Department of New York, Grand Army of the Republic.* New York: J. J. Little & Co., 1888.

Lane, Franklin K. "Makers of the Flag." Address delivered on Flag Day, 1914, before the employees of the Department of the Interior, Washington, D.C. Included in *The American Spirit: Addresses in War Time.* New York: Frederick A. Stokes, 1918, 128–31.

Langbein, J. C. Julius. *The American Flag: Its Origin and History.* New York: Union Printing and Publishing, 1876.

Lee, John Hancock. *The Origin and Progress of the American Party in Politics.* 1855. Freeport, N.Y.: Books for Libraries Press, 1970.

Livermore, Mary A. *My Story of the War.* 1889. New York: Arno Press, 1972.

Lothrop, Mrs. Daniel. "The National Society of the Children of the American Revolution." *American Monthly Magazine* 7 (December 1895): 531–33.

McCandless, Byron. "The Correct Display of the Stars and Stripes." *National Geographic Magazine* 32 (October 1917): 404–13.

————. "The Story of the American Flag." *National Geographic Magazine* 32 (October 1917): 286–303.

Merrefield, Joseph. "The Starry Flag Waves o'er thy Shore, Maryland, my Maryland." Piano sheet music. Baltimore: Miller & Beacham, 1862.

Miller, Charles Kingsbury. *Desecration of the American Flag and Prohibitive Legislation.* An address delivered at a banquet given by the Illinois Society, Sons of the American Revolution at the Athletic Club, Chicago, November second, eighteen hundred and ninety eight. Privately printed, 1898.

Morey, Grace Kincaid. *Mystic Americanism.* East Aurora, N.Y.: Eastern Star Publishing, 1924.

Moss, James A. *The Flag of the United States: How to Display It, How to Respect It, and the Story of "The Star Spangled Banner."* Menasha, Wisc.: George Banta, 1923.

————. *The Flag of the United States: Its History and Symbolism.* Washington, D.C.: United States Flag Association, 1930.

————. *Origin and Significance of Military Customs.* Menasha, Wisc.: George Banta, 1917.

Moss, James A. and M. B. Stewart. *Our Flag and Its Message.* Philadelphia: J. B. Lippincott, 1917.

"Mrs. Benjamin Harrison." *American Monthly Magazine* 1 (July 1982): 12–13.

My Flag. Philadelphia: Keystone Type Foundry. Right to reproduce sold to John Wanamaker, n.d. [ca. 1914–15].

"New Code for Old Glory: The Work of the Washington Flag Conference, A." *American Legion Weekly* 6 July 1923: 12.

Old Flag, The. Philadelphia: American Sunday School Union, 1864.

"Our Flag Number." Special issue of *National Geographic Magazine* 32 (October 1917).

Patriotic Exercise for Juniors, A: Building of the Flag or Liberty Triumphant. Chicago: Rodeheaver Co., 1917.

Pirtle, Alfred. *Our Flag.* Read before the Ohio Commandery of the Loyal Legion, December 7th, 1910. Privately printed, 1910.

Powell, Garland W. *Service: For God and Country.* Indianapolis: Cornelius Printing, 1924.

Preble, George Henry. *History of the Flag of the United States of America, and of the Naval and Yacht-Club Signals, Seals, and Arms, and Principal National Songs of the*

United States, with a Chronicle of the Symbols, Standards, Banners, and Flags of Ancient and Modern Nations. 2nd ed. rev. Boston: A. Williams and Co., 1880.

"Principle of Organization of the National Society of the Daughters of the American Revolution." *American Monthly Magazine* 1 (July 1892): 8–11.

Putnam, George Palmer [attributed]. *Soldiers' and Sailors' Patriotic Songs*. New York: Loyal Publication Society, 1864.

Revised Statutes of the United States. 2nd ed. 1878. Secs. 218, 428, 1554, 1555, 1748, 1791, 1792, 2764.

Richards, Janet E. Hosmer. "The National Hymn." *American Monthly Magazine* 7 (December 1895): 536–40.

Richburg, Keith B. "America Already Has a Civil Religion." *Washington Post* 8 September 1985: C1, C4.

Riis, Jacob A. *The Making of an American*. New York, 1901; London: Collier-Macmillian, Ltd., 1970.

Rosenfeld, Megan. "The Human Flag! 3,500 Students Line Up as the Red, White & Blue." *Washington Post* 14 June 1985: C1, C11.

St. Nicholas: An Illustrated Magazine for Young Folks. Vols. 1–25 (1873–98).

Smith, H. Augustine. *A Pageant of the Stars and Stripes*. Boston: American Institute of Religious Education, 1918.

Smith, Nicholas. *Our Nation's Flag in History and Incident*. Milwaukee: The Young Churchman Co., 1903.

Society of Colonial Wars. Illinois. *The Misuse of the National Flag of the United States of America*. Proceedings of the National Flag Committee of the Society of Colonial Wars in the State of Illinois. An Appeal to the Fifty-fourth Congress of the United States. Chicago, 1895.

Sonneck, Oscar George Theodore. *The Star Spangled Banner*. Washington: GPO, 1914.

Spalding, Samuel Jenne. *A Sketch of the World's Largest United States Flag Owned by the City of Canton, Ohio*. Canton: Privately printed, 1916.

Stanton, Robert Livingston. *The Church and the Rebellion*. 1864. Freeport, N.Y.: Books for Libraries, 1971.

State v. Shumaker, 103 Kan. 741 P. 979 (1918).

"They Raised a Flag." *Chicago Daily Tribune* 3 August 1892, p. 1, col. 5.

Thompson, Robert Ellis. "The Significance of Our Flag" in Ray Brousseau, comp. *Looking Forward: Life in the Twentieth Century as Predicted in the Pages of American Magazines from 1895 to 1905*. New York: American Heritage Press, 1970.

Uniform Commercial Code. Introduction.

Uniform Laws Annotated (1940). Introduction.

United States Congress House Committee on the Judiciary. *Protection of the American Flag. Statement of Mrs. Jacob M. Dickinson of Nashville, Tennessee. February 11, 1913*. 62nd Cong., 3d sess. Washington: GPO, 1913.

United States Congress Senate Report from Federal Trade Commission. *Prices of American Flags*. 65th Cong., 1st sess. Washington: GPO, 1917.

United States. Naval History Division. *Naval Documents of the American Revolution*. Washington: GPO, 1964–81.

United States. War Department. Adjutant General's Office. *Flag Circular.* Washington: GPO, 1923; 1924.

"Will Raise a Flag." *Chicago Daily Tribune* 23 July 1892, p. 1, col. 5.

Wisconsin. *Journal of the Senate.* 20 February 1889: 239.

Youth's Companion, The. Vols. 58–65 (1885–92).

Secondary Sources

Allentown Art Museum. *The American Flag in the Art of Our Country.* Allentown, Pa.: Allentown Art Museum, 1976.

Baker, Jean H. *Ambivalent Americans: The Know-Nothing Party in Maryland.* Baltimore: Johns Hopkins University Press, 1977.

Bellah, Robert N. *Beyond Belief: Essays on Religion in a Post-Traditional World.* New York: Harper & Row, 1970.

————. "Civil Religion in America." *Daedalus* 96 (1967): 1–21.

Bellah, Robert N. and Phillip E. Hammond. *Varieties of Civil Religion.* New York: Harper & Row, 1980.

Bennett, Mabel R. *So Gallantly Streaming.* New York: Drake, 1974.

Berger, Peter L., and Thomas Luckmann. *The Social Construction of Reality: A Treatise on the Sociology of Knowledge.* Garden City, N.Y.: Doubleday, 1966; Anchor Books, 1967.

Bierley, Paul E. *John Philip Sousa: American Phenomenon.* Englewood Cliffs, N.J.: Prentice-Hall, 1973.

Billington, Ray Allen. *The Protestant Crusade 1800–1860: A Study of the Origins of American Nativism.* New York: Macmillan, 1938; Chicago: Quadrangle Books, 1964.

————. *Westward Expansion.* 4th ed. New York: Macmillan, 1974.

Boatner, Mark Mayo, III. *Military Customs and Traditions.* New York: David McKay, 1956.

Brown, Milton W., et al. *American Art.* New York: Harry N. Abrams, 1979.

Buck, Paul H. *The Road to Reunion, 1865–1900.* Boston: Little, Brown & Co., 1937.

Burns, Don. "America's Upstanding Song." *American Legion Magazine* 105 (July 1978): 11, 42.

Campbell, James W. *America in the Centennial Year, 1876.* Washington: University Press of America, 1980.

Carmack. "Famous First in History." *Roll Call* 14 (June 1956).

Catton, Bruce. *The Coming Fury.* Garden City, N.Y.: Doubleday & Co., 1961.

Chalmers, David. *Hooded Americanism: The History of the Ku Klux Klan.* New York: Franklin Watts, 1981.

Collins, Herbert Ridgeway. *Threads of History: Americana Recorded on Cloth 1775 to the Present.* Washington: Smithsonian Institution Press, 1979.

Cooper, Grace Rogers. *Thirteen-star Flags: Keys to Identification.* Washington: Smithsonian Institution Press, 1973.

Cott, Nancy F. *The Bonds of Womanhood.* New Haven: Yale University Press, 1977.

Crampton, William G. "Political Symbolism: Some Oblique Contributions." Unpublished review essay.

————, ed. *Webster's Concise Encyclopedia of Flags and Coats of Arms*. New York: Crescent Books, 1985.

Cremin, Lawrence A. *American Education: The National Experience, 1783–1876*. New York: Harper and Row, 1980.

Crouthers, David D. *Flags of American History*. Maplewood, N.J.: Hammond, 1978.

Davies, Wallace Evan. *Patriotism on Parade: The Story of Veterans' and Hereditary Organizations in America 1783–1900*. Cambridge: Harvard University Press, 1955.

Dearing, Mary R. *Veterans in Politics: The Story of the G.A.R.* Baton Rouge: Louisiana State University Press, 1952.

Delaplaine, Edward S. *Francis Scott Key and the National Anthem*. Washington, D.C.: Wilson-Epes Press, 1947.

Devine, Louise Lawrence. *The Story of Our Flag*. Chicago: Rand McNally, 1960.

Dichter, Harry and Elliott Shapiro. *Early American Sheet Music: Its Lure and Its Lore, 1768–1889*. New York: R. R. Bowker, 1941.

Doob, Leonard William. *Patriotism and Nationalism: Their Psychological Foundations*. New Haven: Yale University Press, 1964.

Douglas, Ann. *The Feminization of American Culture*. New York: Avon, 1977.

Elson, Ruth Miller. *Guardians of Tradition: American Schoolbooks of the Nineteenth Century*. Lincoln: University of Nebraska Press, 1964.

Encyclopedia of Associations. 18th ed. (1984) Vol. 1, Part 1: 720.

Filby, P. William and Edward G. Howard, comp. *Star-Spangled Books*. Baltimore: Maryland Historical Society, 1972.

Firth, Raymond. *Symbols, Public and Private*. Ithaca, N.Y.: Cornell University Press, 1973.

Flint Institute of Arts. *The American Indian: The American Flag*. Flint, Mich.: The Institute, 1975.

Fox, Richard Wightman and T. J. Jackson Lears, eds. *The Culture of Consumption: Critical Essays in American History, 1880–1980*. New York: Pantheon, 1983.

Furlong, William Rea, Byron McCandless, and Harold D. Langley. *So Proudly We Hail: The History of the United States Flag*. Washington, D.C.: Smithsonian Institution Press, 1981.

Goen, C. C. *Broken Churches, Broken Nation: Denominational Schisms and the Coming of the American Civil War*. Macon, Ga.: Mercer University Press, 1985.

Gottlieb, Theodore D. *The Origin and Evolution of the Betsy Ross Flag Legend or Tradition*. Newark, N.J.: Privately published, 1938.

Guenter, Scot M. "Sanctification of a Banner: Children's Periodicals and the Rise of the Cult of the American Flag." Master's Thesis. University of Maryland, 1981.

"Hale, Edward Everett." *Dictionary of American Biography* (1960).

Hammond, Phillip E. Commentary on Civil Religion in America in Donald R. Cutler, ed. *The Religious Situation: 1968*. Boston: Beacon Press, 1968, 381–88.

Hapgood, Norman. *Professional Patriots*. New York: Albert & Charles Boni, 1928.

Harris, Louise. *The Flag over the Schoolhouse.* Providence, R.I.: C. A. Stephens Collection, Brown University, 1971.

———. *Old Glory—Long May She Wave!* Providence, R.I.: C. A. Stephens Collection, Brown University, 1981.

Heathcote, Charles William. *The Lutheran Church and the Civil War.* New York: Fleming H. Revell Co., 1919.

Higham, John. *Strangers in the Land: Patterns of American Nativism, 1860–1925.* New Brunswick, N.J.: Rutgers University Press, 1955.

Hills, Ratcliffe M. *The Naval Origin of the United States Flag.* Hartford, Conn.: Hill, 1947.

Hobsbawn, Eric, ed. *The Invention of Tradition.* New York: Cambridge University Press, 1983.

Hofstadter, Richard. *The Age of Reform: From Bryan to F.D.R.* New York: Vintage Books, 1955.

Holsten, Siegmar. *Allegorische Darstellungen des Krieges, 1870–1918.* Muenchen: Prestel, 1976.

Huffman, Doris. *Oregon's Flamboyant Fourth, 1876.* Portland, Oreg.: Privately printed, 1976.

Hughey, Michael W. *Civil Religion and Moral Order: Theoretical and Historical Dimensions.* Westport, Conn.: Greenwood Press, 1983.

"Ingersoll, Robert G." *Dictionary of American Biography* (1961).

Jackson, John W. *The Pennsylvania Navy, 1775–1781: The Defense of the Delaware.* New Brunswick, N.J.: Rutgers University Press, 1974.

Jones, Richard Seelye. *A History of the American Legion.* Indianapolis: Bobbs-Merrill, 1946.

Josephson, Matthew. *The Politicos, 1865–1896.* New York: Harcourt, Brace & Co., 1938.

Kelly, George Armstrong. *Politics and Religious Consciousness in America.* New Brunswick, N.J.: Transaction Books, 1984.

Kelly, R. Gordon. *Mother Was a Lady: Self and Society in Selected Modern Children's Periodicals, 1865–1890.* Westport, Conn.: Greenwood Press, 1974.

———. "*The Social Construction of Reality:* Implications for Future Directions in American Studies." *Prospects* 8 (1983): 49–58.

Klamkin, Marian. *American Patriotic and Political China.* New York: Charles Scribner's Sons, 1973.

"Krimmel, John Lewis." *Britannica Encyclopedia of American Art* (n.d.).

Kupferberg, Herbert. "The Cartoon That Became a Famous Patriotic Painting." *Parade* 1 July 1973.

LaFeber, Walter. *The New Empire: An Interpretation of American Expansion, 1860–1898.* Ithaca, N.Y.: Cornell University Press, 1963.

Langley, Harold D. "Some Problems of Flag Research: A Look at the Origins and Evolution of the Furlong-McCandless History of the United States Flag." *Flag Bulletin* 19 (1980): 184–97.

Lawson, Edwin D. "Development of Patriotism in Children: A Second Look." *Journal of Psychology* 55 (1963): 279–86.

———. "Flag Preference as an Indicator of Patriotism in Israeli Children." *Journal of Cross-Cultural Psychology* 6 (1975): 490–97.

————. "Flag Preferences of Canadians: Before the Maple Leaf." *Psychological Report* 17 (1965): 553–54.

Lears, T. J. Jackson. *No Place of Grace: Anti-Modernism and the Transformation of American Culture, 1880–1920.* New York: Pantheon, 1981.

Lister, David. "Some Aspects of the Law and Usage of Flags in Britain." *Flag Bulletin* 17 (1978): 14–23.

McCabe, John. *George M. Cohan: The Man Who Owned Broadway.* Garden City, N.Y.: Doubleday & Co., 1973.

McFarland, Gerald W. *Mugwumps, Morals & Politics, 1884–1920.* Amherst: University of Massachusetts Press, 1975.

McKinnon, Elizabeth. "The Spirit of '76." Unpublished report from Selectmen's Office, Marblehead, Mass., 11 August 1970.

MacLeod, Anne Scott. *A Moral Tale: Children's Fiction and American Culture, 1820–1860.* Hamden, Conn.: Archon, 1975.

Macleod, David I. *Building Character in the American Boy: The Boy Scouts, YMCA, and Their Forerunners, 1870–1920.* Madison: University of Wisconsin Press, 1983.

MacPherson, Robert M. "George Washington Will Cross the Delaware." *New York Times,* 14 December 1965.

Manwaring, David Roger. *Render Unto Caesar: The Flag-Salute Controversy.* Chicago: University of Chicago Press, 1962.

Mastai, Boleslaw and Marie-Louise D'Otrange Mastai. *The Stars and the Stripes: The American Flag as Art and as History from the Birth of the Republic to the Present.* New York: Knopf, 1973.

Matheson, J. R. *Canada's Flag: A Search for a Country.* Boston: G. K. Hall & Co., 1980.

Mayer, Jane. *Betsy Ross and the Flag.* New York: Random House, 1952.

Miller, Margaret S. *I Pledge Allegiance.* Boston: Christopher Publishing, 1946.

Moorhead, James H. *American Apocalypse: Yankee Protestants and the Civil War, 1860–1869.* New Haven: Yale Univeristy Press, 1978.

Morris, Edmund. *The Rise of Theodore Roosevelt.* New York: Coward, McCann and Geoghegan, 1979.

Morris, Robert. *The Truth about the American Flag.* Levittown, Pa.: Bucks County Printing House, 1976.

"Moss, James Alfred." *National Cyclopaedia of American Biography* (1943).

Mosse, George L. *The Nationalization of the Masses.* New York: Howard Fertig, 1975.

Mott, Frank Luther. *A History of American Magazines, 1865–1885.* 5 vols. Cambridge: Harvard University Press, 1938.

Muller, Joseph. *The Star Spangled Banner Words and Music Issued Between 1814–1864.* New York: G. A. Baker & Co., 1935.

Mussell, Kay. *"The Social Construction of Reality:* Notes Toward a Method in American Studies." *Prospects* 9 (1984): 1–6.

Norwood, John Nelson. *The Schism in the Methodist Episcopal Church 1844: A Study of Slavery and Ecclesiastical Politics.* Alfred, N.Y.: Alfred University Press, 1923.

Papale, Henry, comp. *Banners, Buttons, & Songs: A Pictorial Review and Capsule Almanac of America's Presidential Campaigns.* Revised ed. New York: St. Martin's Press, 1984.

Pasch, Georges. "French Attitudes Toward the Symbols of France." *Flag Bulletin* 20 (1981): 119–40.

Patterson, Richard S. and Richard Dougall. *The Eagle and the Shield: A History of the Great Seal of the United States.* Washington: Office of the Historian, Bureau of Public Affairs, Department of State, 1976.

Persons, Stow. *The Decline of American Gentility.* New York: Columbia University Press, 1973.

Peterson, Charles. "The Truth About Washington Crossing the Delaware." *Parade,* 23 May 1976.

Quaife, Milo Milton. *The Flag of the United States.* New York: Grosset & Dunlap, 1942.

Quaife, Milo Milton, Melvin J. Weig, and Roy Applebaum. *The History of the United States Flag, from the Revolution to the Present, Including a Guide to Its Use and Display.* 1st ed. New York: Harper, 1961.

Rabbow, Arnold. "A New Constellation: What Did the First Stars and Stripes Look Like?" *Flag Bulletin* 19 (1980): 47–64.

Randel, William Pierce. *Centennial: American Life in 1876.* Philadelphia: Chilton, 1969.

"Reed, Colonel Joseph." *Who Was Who in American History—The Military* (1975).

Rice, Arnold S. *The Ku Klux Klan in American Politics.* New York: Haskell House, 1972.

"Riis, Jacob A." *Dictionary of American Biography* (1963).

Rogers, Sherbrooke. *Sarah Josepha Hale.* Grantham, N.H.: Tompon & Rutter, 1985.

Rosenblatt, Albert M. "Flag Desecration Statutes: History and Analysis." *Washington University Law Quarterly* 1972: 193–237.

Saker, Harry. *The South African Flag Controversy, 1925–28.* Cape Town: Oxford University Press, 1980.

Sawitzky, William, *Paintings and Miniatures in the Historical Society of Pennsylvania.* Philadelphia: Historical Society of Pennsylvania, 1942.

Sexton, Jessie Ethelyn. *Congregationalism, Slavery and the Civil War.* Lansing: Michigan Civil War Centennial Observance Commission, 1966.

Silver, James W. *Confederate Morale and Church Propaganda.* Tuscaloosa, Ala.: Confederate Publishing Co., 1957.

Silverman, Kenneth. *A Cultural History of the American Revolution.* New York: Thomas Y. Crowell, 1976.

Simon, Rita J. *Public Opinion and the Immigrant: Print Media Coverage, 1880–1980.* Lexington, Mass.: D. C. Heath and Co., 1985.

Smith, Justin H. *The Annexation of Texas.* 1911. New York: AMS Press, 1971.

Smith, Whitney. "Face to Face with Betsy Ross." *Flag Bulletin* 14 (1975): 3–28.

———. *The Flag Book of the United States.* Revised ed. New York: William Morrow & Co., 1975.

———. "The Flag in Advertising." *Recueil du IV Congres International de Vexillologie* (Torino, Italy, 24–27 June 1971): 45–54.

———. "Fundamental Theses in Vexillology." *Flag Bulletin* 21 (1982): 33–34.

———. "The Future of Vexillology." *Flag Bulletin* 21 (1982): 4–15.

————. "Prolegomena to the Study of Political Symbolism." Diss., Boston University, 1968.

Sperber, Dan. *Rethinking Symbolism*. Translated by Alice A. Moulton. New York: Cambridge University Press, 1975.

Spiller, Robert, et al. *Literary History of the United States*. 4th ed. New York: Macmillan, 1974.

Spradley, James P. and David W. McCurdy. *The Cultural Experience: Ethnography in Complex Society*. Chicago: Science Research Associates, 1972.

Statt, David. "Flag Choices of Elite American and Canadian Children." *Psychological Reports* 32 (1973): 85–86.

Stein, Jr., Charles Francis. *Our National Anthem The Star-Spangled Banner: Its History and Significance*. Baltimore: Wyman Park Federal Savings & Loan Association, 1964.

Stevens, Leonard A. *Salute! The Case of The Bible vs. The Flag*. New York: Coward, McCann & Geoghegan, 1973.

Sullivan, Edmund B. *Collecting Political Americana*. New York: Crown Publishers, 1980.

Vogel, David. *America Through Baseball*. Chicago: Nelson Hall, 1976.

Wainwright, Nicholas B., comp. *Paintings and Miniatures of the Historical Society of Pennsylvania*. Philadelphia: Historical Society of Pennsylvania, 1974.

Wallace, Anthony F. C. *Culture and Personality*. 2nd ed. New York: Random House, 1970.

Watts, John T. "Robert N. Bellah's Theory of America's Eschatological Hope." *Journal of Church and State* 22 (Winter 1980): 3–22.

Weitman, Sasha R. "National Flags: A Sociological Overview." *Semiotica* 8 (1973): 328–67.

West, Ellis M. "A Proposed Neutral Definition of Civil Religion." *Journal of Church and State* 22 (Winter 1980): 23–40.

Wilson, John F. *Public Religion in American Culture*. Philadelphia: Temple University Press, 1979.

Wise, Gene. " 'Paradigm Dramas' in American Studies: A Cultural and Institutional History of the Movement." *American Quarterly* 31 (1979): 293–337.

Zelinsky, Wilbur. "O Say Can You See? Nationalistic Emblems in the Landscape." *Winterthur Portfolio* 19 (Winter 1984): 277–86.

Index